A GUIDE TO

FOSSILS

A GUIDE TO

FOSSILS

Dr Helmut Mayr

Translated by
D. Dineley & G. Windsor

Princeton University Press
Princeton, New Jersey

3 9082 05706699 8

All photographs by Franz Höck from the
Bavarian State Collection for Palaeontology and
Historical Geology, Munich

Drawings by Helmut Hoffman

Photo page 2: *Placenticeras meeki,* Upper Cretaceous,
South Dakota, USA. Diameter 24cm.

Published by Princeton University Press
41 William Street, Princeton, New Jersey 08540

Library of Congress Cataloging-in-Publication Data
Mayr, Helmut.
  [Fossilien, English]
  A guide to fossils / Helmut Mayr; translated by D. Dineley, G. Windsor
  p. cm.
  Includes bibliographical references and index.
  ISBN 0-691-08789-X
  1. Fossils. 2. Paleontology. I. Title.
QE711.2.M3913 1992
560–dc20   92-15856
                                                  CIP

Title of the original German edition
Fossilien: über 500 Versteinerungen in Farbe
© 1985 BLV Verlagsgesellschaft mbH, München
English translation © HarperCollins*Publishers* 1992

Printed and bound by Butler & Tanner Ltd., Frome, Somerset, England

10 9 8 7 6 5 4 3 2

CONTENTS

This book presents a series of photographs and short descriptions of fossils, both animal and plant. It is for the amateur fossil collector to use in the field or home but is also a gallery of remarkable photographs which should delight any natural history enthusiast.

In his foreword to the original German text Professor Mayr was exercised to draw to the reader's attention just how extraordinary is the profusion of fossils to be found in the sedimenary rocks around us. They provide abundant evidence of the evolution of life in the past. The amateur collector is almost immediately faced with the problems of identifying and categorizing his materials and of understanding something of the classification of both animals and plants. Take, for example, the mollusc group, which since the beginning of Cambrian time some 570 million years ago has revealed about 100,000 different genera. A good college text-book of palaeontology can only deal with a small fraction of this number, and a guide such as this makes do with 180 or so. These are, however, the invertebrate fossils one finds most commonly in the field. Here is offered a representative selection of all such fossil groups.

What is attempted here is brief general diagnoses of some of the more common kinds of fossils, each listing the essential characteristics of the genus depicted. The collection of specimens which forms the basis of these illustrations is in the Bavarian State Museum of Palaeontology and Historical Geology in Munich. Such fossils, or others very like them, are of course found not only in southern Germany but in many countries beyond the boundaries of Bavaria. Professor Mayr was able to reduce the descriptive text to an admirable minimum without losing its value, and we have followed his lead. There are already several pocket guides to fossils; each has its limitations. This little volume presents a unique collection of excellent photographs of uncommonly well-preserved material.

DLD, GW

PALAEONTOLOGY

Human interest in fossils is manifested from prehistoric times, in grave-gifts of the Old Stone Age. Herodotus (415 BC) interpreted the shells of bivalves found in the interior of Egypt as the remains of living creatures left behind after a flood. The concept of abiogenesis and the theory of the creative force present in the primeval mud mentioned by Aristotle (374-322 BC) were still, even as late as the 16th century, a source of confusion, in which fossils were accepted as no more than freaks of nature. Nicolaus Steno (1638-1686) realised the significance of rock strata and defended the notion that fossils had originated as the remains of earlier forms of life. The simple collecting of fossils gave way to a scientific interest in their description and classification, and with the introduction of binomial nomenclature (i.e. genus and species) by the Swedish scientist Carl Linnaeus (1707-1778), who included fossils in his descriptive system along with zoological and botanical forms, the way was prepared for palaeontology to develop as an independent branch of natural science. The work of Lamarck and Darwin, and the concept of the evolution of species, led to a shift in the focus of interest to the attempt to establish the history of the various phyla of living organisms.

BRANCHES OF PALAEONTOLOGY

Inevitably, as palaeontological knowledge has grown, specialisation in the component areas of the subject has developed. The obvious major division into **palaeozoology** and **palaeobotany** was followed by the development of areas based on various geological and biological criteria, which, though concerned with different aspects of palaeontology, still overlap to a considerable extent.

Biostratinomy is concerned with the whole range of events that occurs between the death of an animal and its final inclusion in a sediment. The fate of the fossil and the chemical changes produced by pressure and temperature are the concern of research in the field of **fossil diagenesis** or taphonomy. In **biostratigraphy** we attempt to integrate fossils of the greatest variety of zoological and botanical types into a time structure and to establish a relative chronology of successive rock formations and their index fossils. The tendency towards further specialisation is evident here too, in the effort to refine the over-generalised structure of relative geological ages by sub-dividing widely distributed forms, occurring over shorter and shorter periods, into what are called biozones. Independent studies of the vertical and horizontal distribution of a wide variety of groups of plants and animals produce more information in this area. This is closely related to **palaeoecology,** which investigates the composition of fossil faunas in terms of their mode and conditions of existence. This allows us to compare, with due caution, these conditions with those observed today, and to distinguish groupings of fossils on an ecological basis. **Palaeobiogeography,** on the other hand, is concerned with the original distribution of the fossil forms and aims at a reconstruction of the location of seas and land-masses at the appropriate periods. The concept of the drift of continental plates and the creation of new seas, as suggested by Alfred Wegener, has, to a large extent, clarified previously inexplicable palaeogeographical data and their relative significance in a large-scale view of the earth's surface. Comparative **palaeoanatomy** investigates the anatomical details of fossils and attempts to fit them into the existing systems of palaeontological classification and so in its turn has influenced some aspects of the classification of modern animals and plants. **Phylogeny** traces the development of particular groups of organisms and so contributes a palaeontological element to the understanding of evolution. The term **micropalaeontology** originally related only to the size of the objects investigated, and was limited principally to the foraminifera, which must be studied under the microscope. As a result of the use of electron microscopes and the increased study of microscopic plant and animal remains, such as pollen, algae or radiolaria, the term has been widened in its application and may now more properly be taken to describe the method of investigation employed. As smaller and smaller details become the object of

study, it is not surprising that the methods of micropalaeontology are applied to the microstructure of larger palaeontological specimens too.

FOSSILS

Fossil (from the Latin *fodere*, to dig) was originally a general term for all the objects hidden in the earth's surface (including even relics of ancient civilisations) which had to be dug out. Today the term refers only to fossilised forms of the remains of prehistoric plants and animals which have been turned to stone. By prehistory is understood the whole period up to the point when we can begin to date human history. Fossils are only found in rocks which once formed part of an earlier sea or land-mass. It is rare to

Index fossil: *Psiloceras planorbe* (ammonite); a short-lived but widely distributed zone-fossil which is characteristic of the lowest levels of marine sedimentation in Central European Black Jurassic Beds (Lias). Greek letters are used to indicate the typical arrangement of strata in the Jurassic system in the area of the Swabian and Franconian Alps. Locality: Esslingen/Württemberg/Germany.

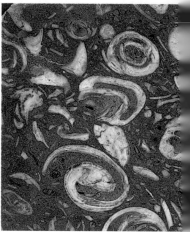

Facies fossil: *Montlivaltia* sp. (coral); corals are typical facies fossils, since their distribution is confined to a very limited habitat (the reef) in which special ecological conditions must persist, such as light penetration, depth, temperature, water movement etc. Locality: Upper (White) Jurassic system Nattheim/Württemberg.

Protective charm: *Actaeonella* sp. (snail); longitudinal and lateral sections in a fossil layer. It was the spiral lateral sections of this snail which, until the end of the last century, were held to be protective charms against the staggers in cattle and so were placed in cattle-troughs as amulets. Locality: Windischgarsten/Austria.

find only one fossil form in a particular rock stratum, usually there are numerous widely differing forms from various plant and animal groups. This may mean that remains of certain organisms are present in such quantities that they make up by far the greater part of the rock and may be said indeed to form the rock itself (see p.160). In palaeontology, particular significance is attached to the index fossils (see photo p.9). These are forms present only within a defined, geologically brief period but geographically widely distributed. Their occurrence enables us to assign different rocks from areas very remote from each other to the same geological period and to give the fossil and the rock in which it lies their appropriate place in the chronological succession of the earth's history, as exactly as the prevailing state of knowledge allows. This framework, which was originally very crude, has been further and further

refined through many decades of observation. The ability to define precisely the age of rocks by reference to the radioactive decay of certain isotopes made it possible to confirm the length of the individual geological periods in millions of years (see tables pp.26-27).

In contrast to index fossils, **facies fossils** characterise the environment prevailing in any particular area of sedimentation (see photo above). Particular sedimentary structures which, for the specialist, indicate animal activity of some kind, such as building a den or burrow or searching for food, are called **trace fossils** (see p.211). In this case, we can extremely rarely name or give a zoological classification of the creatures responsible for this activity, and only in the most fortunate special circumstances are both the animal and the resulting structure preserved. We also speak of **living fossils** when types of plants and animals which exist today also existed millions of years ago and left their remains as fossils (see p.182).

Pseudofossil is the term used for objects which look very like true fossils but which owe their appearance to chemical, physical or mechanical processes operating either during or after the formation of the rock (see p.247). Even during the last century some fossils were held as a result of their appearance to be amulets preventing certain diseases. So, for example, sections of fossil Actaeonellae (snails) were put into cattle-troughs as a protection against the staggers (see photo opposite) or twig-corals with their star-like form were ground into heart shapes and worn as amulets against slander and bewitchment.

THE FORMATION OF FOSSILS

As a general rule in the cycle of nature, organisms and their remains are reduced after death to their original component elements. Their soft tissues, shells and skeletons are chemically dissolved or mechanically ground down, or even destroyed by other living creatures. Plant cellulose is decomposed into water and gases. But special rules apply in the case of fossilisation with its stages of deposition, embedding by sedimentation, and the increase in pressure and temperature of the overlying rock. These rules are determined on the one hand by the prevailing environment, and on the other by the structure of the organism itself. Thus in comparison to sea creatures, land organisms are much less frequently preserved in the fossil state, since there are far more destructive than preservative factors in operation on land.

Organisms which possess an internal or external skeleton to provide stability or protection are far more likely to be preserved than those with only a soft body. Theoretically, even the body of a creature with only soft body-parts can be directly preserved as a fossil, as, for example, that of a spider preserved in amber. Usually, however, it is the hard parts of the body which are preserved (the elements of shell or skeleton), which consist of calcium carbonate, calcium phosphate, skeletal opal, chitin or cellulose (see photos p.12). These substances are rarely preserved in unchanged form and with the same chemistry. An exchange of substances takes place through the effect of water, which penetrates into the pores of the rock and both brings in and carries away material in solution. Equally, one or more changes of location or excessive crystal growth can render the original remains of the creature unrecognisable. An example of the exchange of mineral substances as a result of water penetration is found in pyritised ammonites, in which the original material of the shell consisting of calcite and aragonite has been replaced by pyrite or marcasite. In silicified fossils the original hard parts of the body have been replaced by silica. Under special chemical conditions, however, it is possible for silica itself to be replaced by calcium. For plant fossils the process known as carbonisation (literally, turning into coal) is the usual mode of preservation. If plant remains are buried by rock particles forming an overlying stratum, they are cut off from the supply of oxygen. Under the pressure of the overlying mass of rock a relative enrichment of carbon sets in, accompanied by the emission of methane, carbon dioxide and water, and this can transform the substance into coal, given a suitable increase in pressure and temperature.

It is often forgotten that even after an organism or its remains have been fossilised, weathering may destroy a fossil if the rock bed in which it lies is exposed. In addition, a large number of fossils is lost when the fossil-bearing beds are buried within the earth's crust during movements such as the forma-

Sponge spicules: In marine sponges the soft body-parts are stiffened by minute skeletal elements formed of calcium carbonate, silica or a horn-like substance. They can occur individually in the soft tissue or be combined into a kind of supporting scaffold and form the outer wall. Their spatial arrangement and form are significant factors in identification.
Above: Tetraxon (elements with 4 axes not lying in one plane) skeletal elements of calcareous sponges from chalk at Misburg near Hanover (×100).
Below: Skeleton of a siliceous sponge; the arrangement of the intersections in the frame work (diagonal buttressing) is characteristic of representatives of the order Lychniskida (×125).

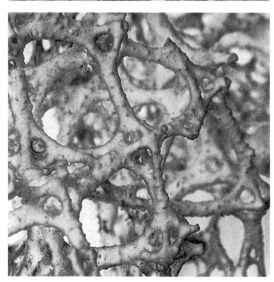

tion of mountain ranges. Then the rock itself is transformed as a result of the increase in pressure and temperature and the fossils are destroyed. If we remember that fossilisation is itself a special case of preservation, we realise that only the most abundant forms of life have had any real chance of surviving as fossils to the present day. The proportion of original organisms represented by fossil forms has been estimated as less than one per cent.

THE EMPLACEMENT OF FOSSILS (TAPHONOMY)

Here we are concerned with the relationship between an organism and its position within the surrounding sediment. It is difficult to reconstruct the sequence of events between the death of the organism and its ultimate inclusion in the rock. In the simplest case, the place of death represents the original abode or habitat of the living organism. We often find bivalves which were buried in mud while still alive and which in fossil form retain the position adopted in life. A corresponding example in plants is the preservation of tree-trunks in an upright position with the attached roots still hanging below them.

However, the burial of an organism commonly takes place after it has been transported some distance on land or in water. Obviously, transport does not help the formation or preservation of a fossil. In most cases the organisms are reduced to their component parts by collision with particles of sediment, or they may be worked on by organisms boring into them, so that when they reach the spot where they are finally embedded only fragments of skeletal elements remain. Of course, this transport may take place in several episodes, separated in time. An isolated tooth of a small mammal, preserved in the sediment, may have been subjected to a whole series of displacements. Once it formed part of the teeth and jaw of the animal, which then became the prey of some raptor and its indigestible remains were regurgitated in the bird's pellets, far from the place where the animal was killed. After the pellet has broken up and the bones have been carried still further by water flow, the individual teeth break free from the jaw and finally arrive at the place of their actual inclusion according to the degree of buoyancy they possess.

Under approximately the same water flow conditions, bodies containing a closed hollow space, such as fruits, pollen or foraminifera, will be transported much further because of their built-in buoyancy. Such factors as the buoyancy of the object and the resistance to movement offered by its shape, determine the way in which currents may arrange bodies at recurring similar angles of attitude, lines of direction or levels of deposition. Bodies tend to adopt the position of least resistance to the flow and of maximum stability. Bowl-shaped objects such as mussel shells are normally embedded with the curved surface upward. An example of regular longitudinal arrangement of conical objects is the configuration of the internal rostra in "belemnite battlefields" (see photo p.125).

In most cases we do not find just one isolated fossil included in the sedimentary rock, but a whole community of fossilised forms belonging to the widest variety of animals and plants. These "burial communities" are called taphocoenoses. The well-known crevice-infills of the Swabian Alps, which contain a huge number of widely differing vertebrate creatures, are the accumulated burial communities of the animals that populated the region.

THE PRESERVATION OF FOSSILS

Here we are dealing with the state of preservation of a fossil, as it has been handed down to us in the rock following on the processes of embedding and fossilisation. If the original soft tissue of an animal (e.g. a snail) has been destroyed and the resulting space within the hard tissues filled with rock particles, we speak of an entire fossilisation, since both the shell and its filling are preserved (see photo p.14).

If the substance of the shell has been removed so that only the filling of the original space within the hard tissue is preserved, we speak of internal cast (see photo p.14). If the shell of a now fossilised creature was built up in

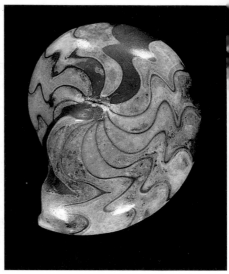

Entire fossilisation (left): *Oxycerites* sp.; the longitudinal section through this specimen of entire fossilisation of an ammonite shows the different substances deposited in individual chambers. Some of the chambers are filled with sediment, while those near the mouth are unfilled but are lined, along with the dividing walls between chambers, with a layer of crystallised calcite. Locality: Dogger Formation, east of Sengenthal/Upper Palatinate/Germany.

Internal cast (right): *Sporadoceras* sp.; this ammonite, originally preserved without its shell, was polished to expose the suture line (line of contact between outer shell and walls dividing chambers). The individual chambers are filled with sediment and calcite. Location: Devonian, Erfoud/Morocco.

layers and so had considerable thickness or if the exterior is heavily sculpted with whirls or spikes, the range of difference in quality of preservation may be very great, making identification difficult. After all, many of the features aiding identification are found on the exterior surface of this hard tissue (see left). Where this is relatively thin and the exterior sculpting only light the decorative forms can pass

Variability of preservation: *Tympanotomus* sp.: on the right a specimen of entire fossilisation with a thick shell whose exterior is heavily decorated with spiral rows of knotted ornament; on the left a specimen of steinkern or internal mould of great smoothness. Locality: Oligocene, Peissenberg/Upper Bavaria.

14

Preservation as hollow mould: *Melocrinus* sp.; this hollow mould of the stems of a sea-lily shows the impression of the exterior of the hard tissue with its central canal and radial sculpting. The original calcite of the tissue has been removed by successive solution. Locality: Lower Devonian, Bocksberg/Harz.

through onto the surface of the rock of the core while the shell itself disappears. If the shell closed tightly and so prevented any filling with sediment, but was itself subsequently dissolved, we speak of its preservation as a hollow mould (see above). Then we see only the impression made by the exterior of the hard (shell) tissue.

A large proportion of fossils are found in what are called concretions. These are concentrations of mineral substances around the fossilised form (such as pyritisations or calcifications), which are commonly harder than the surrounding rock. They usually have a different chemistry and a different colouring, and were produced either dur-

Preservation as concretion: *Osmeroides* sp.; this specimen of one of the (teleost) bony fishes is preserved in almost undistorted three-dimensional form. Locality: Lower Chalk, Pernambuco/Brazil.

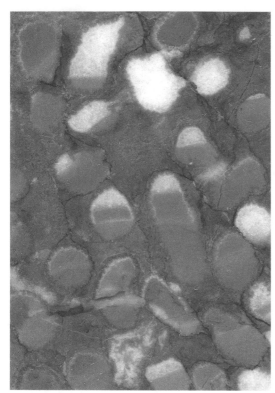

Fossils acting as a clinometer: The lower parts of the hollow chambers in these corals of the genus *Thecosmilia* have been filled in two stages with sediments of different colours, while the upper parts are filled with calcite crystallised out of solution. Locality: Sudelfeld/ Bavarian Calcareous Alps.

ing or after the formation of the fossil. In many cases the chemical nature of the creature itself or of its hard tissue was the cause of the formation of the concretion (see photo p.15). In one special case of concretion the fossils can act as a kind of spirit-level or clinometer. In this the lower part of a hollow space in the creature is filled with sedimentary particles while the upper part is filled by substances in solution or may even remain empty. The layer of sediment then shows us the attitude of the fossil during this filling. The upper part, in which the solutions have normally crystallised out, corresponded to the gas bubble which prevented the complete filling of the space. In many specimens this effect reveals the original attitude of the rock, showing the up and down directions (see above).

The system of naming fossils follows the same principles as that for naming living animals and plants. It attempts to be a classification that reflects the actual relationships in nature. Thus all members of each group share some characteristics. The species in modern biology is a group of interbreeding individuals; in palaeontology it can only be based upon common anatomies and occurences. At its simplest the hierarchy descends from phylum through class, order, family and genus (plural genera) to species. The animal kingdom itself is often divided into two sub-kingdoms, the protozoa or unicellular organisms, and the metazoa or multicellular organisms.

FOSSIL ANIMALS

Phylum Rhizopoda (Root foot)
Class Foraminiferida p.32
Class Actinopoda Subclass: Radiolaria p.34

Phylum Archaeocyatha p.36

Phylum Porifera (sponges): sessile, mostly marine animals; gelatinous soft parts, mostly about a skeleton of calcium carbonate, silica or spongin; skeletal elements made up of single spicules (monaxons), 3-pronged spicules (triaxons) or 4-pronged spicules (tetraxons); shape of body varied: tubular, goblet-, mushroom-shaped or layer-like. Range: Cambrian – Recent; pp.36-44.

Phylum Cnidaria (stinging animals): branching or solitary coelenterates (polyp); sessile or free moving with sting-cells.
Class Hydrozoa: colonial or solitary polyps, with organic body wall or aragonite deposited within the ectoderm, medusoid generation free swimming; gut never divided by septa. Range: Cambrian – Recent; p.46.

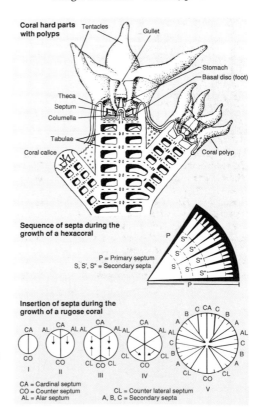

Coral hard parts with polyps — Tentacles, Gullet, Stomach, Basal disc (foot), Theca, Septum, Columella, Tabulae, Coral calice, Coral polyp

Sequence of septa during the growth of a hexacoral

P = Primary septum
S, S', S" = Secondary septa

Insertion of septa during the growth of a rugose coral

CA = Cardinal septum
CO = Counter septum
AL = Alar septum
CL = Counter lateral septum
A, B, C = Secondary septa

I II III IV V

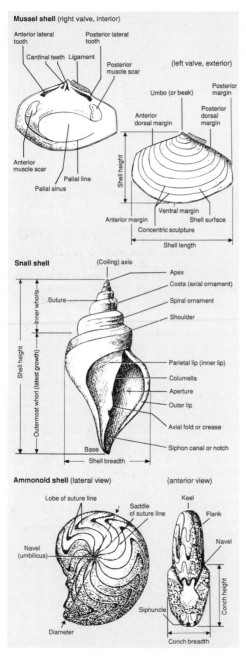

Mussel shell (right valve, interior)

Anterior lateral tooth

Posterior lateral tooth

Cardinal teeth   Ligament

Posterior muscle scar

(left valve, exterior)

Umbo (or beak)

Posterior margin

Anterior dorsal margin

Posterior dorsal margin

Shell height

Anterior muscle scar

Palial line

Palial sinus

Anterior margin

Ventral margin

Shell surface

Concentric sculpture

Shell length

Snail shell

(Coiling) axis

Apex

Costa (axial ornament)

Suture

Spiral ornament

Shoulder

Inner whorls

Parietal lip (inner lip)

Columella

Shell height

Outermost whorl (latest growth)

Aperture

Outer lip

Axial fold or crease

Base

Siphon canal or notch

Shell breadth

Ammonoid shell (lateral view)

(anterior view)

Lobe of suture line

Saddle of suture line

Keel

Flank

Navel (umbilicus)

Navel

Siphuncle

Conch height

Diameter

Conch breadth

Class Anthozoa (Corals): sessile, marine, solitary or colonial cnidaria with or without skeleton (calcareous, chitinous or calc-chitinous) gut partitioned by six, eight or more septa. Range: Ordovician – Recent; pp.46-58.

Phylum Mollusca (soft bodied animals): soft body, highly symmetrical bilaterally with an external calcareous shell (acting as a coat); body divisible into head, foot, mantle: mantle cavity containing paired gills.

Class (Lamellibranchata) Bivalvia (mussels): symmetrical soft body mantle and shell with two valves. Gills. Valves joined together by a dorsal ligament; inner side of valve with muscle scars. Range: Cambrian – Recent; pp.60-74.

Class Scaphopoda: molluscs with tubular form, unchambered; the shell is open at both ends: without gills, and with burrowing foot. Range: Ordovician – Recent; p.76.

Class Gastropoda (snails) shell unchambered, foot and head clearly distinguished from rest of body. Head with tentacles, mouth with radula (jaw apparatus). Range: Ordovician – Recent; pp.76-86.

Class Cephalopoda: free-swimming or crawling marine molluscs: mantle bilaterally symmetrical, head with 8 or 10 tentacles: mantle cavity on the underside; part of the mantle forms a funnel, through which water is drawn in and expressed in a strong current (moving the animal backwards). Mantle cavity with one or two pairs of gills; shell external in the Ammonoidea and Nautiloi-

...dea, straight, curved or planispiral and divided into chambers by septa through which a siphon (a gas-exchange organ) penetrates: only the anterior-most part (the living chamber) contains the soft-bodied parts of the animal. Range: Cambrian onwards; pp. 88-124.

Phylum Annelida (worms): bilaterally symmetrical structure to segmented body, nervous system of two cords. Range: Cambrian onwards; p.126.

Phylum Arthropoda (Joint-legged animals): bilaterally symmetrical segmented structure, jointed appendages, chitinous exoskeleton; includes three-quarters of all present day animals: pp.128-140.

Class Trilobita: three parts from front to rear, head (cephalon), body (thorax), tail (pygidium), divisible laterally into median lobe or axis and two lateral parts (pleura): on the underside of head two multijointed antennae and

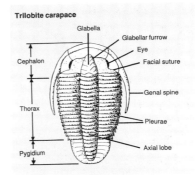

Trilobite carapace

up to four pairs of appendages (coxa). Range: Cambrian – Permian; pp.128-136.

Phylum Bryozoa (moss-animals) p.142.

Phylum Brachiopoda (lamp-shells) marine, most with a posterior pedicle for attachment: two articulating shells (valves), calcareous or chitinous, enclose the dorsal and ventral sides of

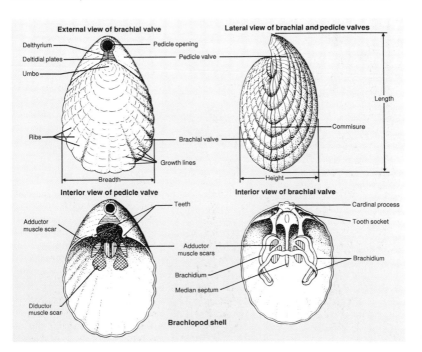

Brachiopod shell

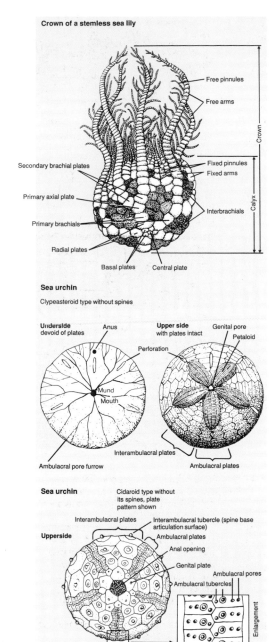

Crown of a stemless sea lily

Free pinnules

Free arms

Crown

Secondary brachial plates

Fixed pinnules
Fixed arms

Primary axial plate

Calyx

Interbrachials

Primary brachials

Radial plates

Basal plates   Central plate

Sea urchin

Clypeasteroid type without spines

Underside
devoid of plates   Anus

Upper side
with plates intact   Genital pore

Petaloid

Perforation

Mund
Mouth

Interambulacral plates

Ambulacral pore furrow   Ambulacral plates

Sea urchin   Cidaroid type without
its spines, plate
pattern shown

Upperside

Interambulacral plates   Interambulacral tubercle (spine base articulation surface)

Ambulacral plates

Anal opening

Genital plate

Ambulacral pores

Ambulacral tubercles

Enlargement

the animals, muscles attach to the inner sides of the valves. A brachial skeleton supports the brachia; articulate brachiopods completely enclosed by shell (with hinge teeth in the pedicle valve and sockets in the brachial valve). Shell shape, structure and the nature of the brachial skeleton used in classification. Range: Cambrian onwards; pp.144-154.

Phylum Echinodermata
(spiny-skinned animals): marine forms; in the larval stage bilaterally symmetrical; in the adult stage a fivefold radial symmetry; skeleton (internal skeleton) produced by secretion (of calcite).

Class Cystoidea: ball to pear-shaped, with the mouth on the upper surface of the body which is sessile and fixed, plates of the theca with differently shaped pores. Range: Cambrian – Devonian; p.56.

Class Blastoidea: theca is flower-bud like with the mouth on the underside of the body and with an anchoring stem. Theca composed of 15 plates; without pores. Ambulacral fields long and in life furnished with tube feet. Range: Ordovician – Permian; p.156.

Class Crinoidea (sea lilies): body composed of stem, calyx and arms. Mostly sessile; all echinodermata are marine: the stem serves to anchor the animal, calyx houses the intestine, arms employed to gather food. Originally dominantly bottom dwellers. Range: Silurian – Recent; pp.156-162.

Class Echinoidea (sea urchins): rounded to flattened echinoderms with skeletons of calcite, with stem, regular forms with 5-rayed symmetry, mouth and arms on upper surface, irregular form with bilateral secondary symmetry, mouth in anterior, arms towards the posterior. Range: from the Ordovician; pp.164-168.

Phylum Hemichordata
Class Graptolithida: Range: Ordovician – Carboniferous; p.170.

Phylum Vertebrata (backboned animals): anatomy divisible into head, trunk and tail; possess a cartilaginous or bony skeleton, true brain, dorsal nerve cord, multi-layered epiderm, muscular heart, paired lensed eyes, internal skeleton and paired limbs.
Class Agnatha: fishlike animals, without jaws, endocranium fused with endoskeleton. Range: Middle Silurian – Recent; p.172.
Class Aphetohyoidea (placoderms): Range: Upper Silurian – Lower Permian; p.172.
Class Chondrichthyes (cartilaginous fish): skeleton of cartilage; calcified in parts, lacking swim bladder and lungs, skin with placoid scales or bony plates, 5-7 pairs of gill openings, mostly marine. Range: Middle Devonian – Recent; p.174.
Class Osteichthyes (bony fish): in the course of development, growing ossification of the vertebrae, ribs, scales, gill cover and paired pectoral and pelvic fins: possessing swim bladder. Range: Lower Devonian – Recent; pp.176-182.
Class Amphibia: juvenile forms aquatic, adults terrestrial in habit: thin layered skin, with flexible bone; first vertebrae (atlas, epistropheus) not differentiated. Range: from Upper Devonian; p.184.
Class Reptilia: breathing lungs, skin with additional cuticle layer; first two cervical vertebrae allow better carriage of the head; lower jaw articulating against the quadrate bone; teeth uni-

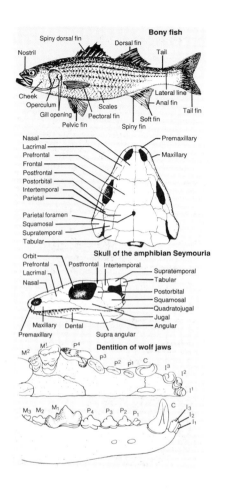

Bony fish
Spiny dorsal fin — Dorsal fin — Tail
Nostril
Cheek — Lateral line
Operculum — Anal fin
Gill opening — Scales — Tail fin
Pectoral fin — Soft fin
Pelvic fin — Spiny fin

Nasal — Premaxillary
Lacrimal
Prefrontal — Maxillary
Frontal
Postfrontal
Postorbital
Intertemporal
Parietal
Parietal foramen
Squamosal
Supratemporal
Tabular

Skull of the amphibian Seymouria
Orbit
Prefrontal — Postfrontal — Intertemporal — Supratemporal
Lacrimal — Tabular
Nasal — Postorbital
— Squamosal
— Quadratojugal
— Jugal
Maxillary — Dental — Angular
Premaxillary — Supra angular

Dentition of wolf jaws

form – little differentiated; skull roof closed or with openings in temporal region. Range: from Upper Carboniferous; pp.186-194.
Class Mammalia: possessing breathing lungs, hair and heart; secondary jaw joint between the dental and squamosal bones; nasal and brain capsules, articulation of vertebrae with cartilaginous discs; teeth differentiated by function: inscisors (I), canines (C), premolars (P), molars (M); body temperature constant. Range: since the Triassic; pp.196-208.

FOSSIL PLANTS

Plants generally lack hard tissues that may become fossilised, but common plant fossils include leaves, stems and roots. Seeds, fruits and even flowers do occur, however, and microscopic spores and pollen are abundant. Amongst the most numerous vegetable fossils are the simplest – the algae. Modern plant classification depends upon many attributes of which only the cellular or anatomical organisation can be found in the fossils. A brief note on the different categories of plants occuring in the fossil record is given below.

Bacteria: unicellular, rarely found as fossils; but exceptional preservation occurs in ancient cherts and evaporites.

Algae: a very large and varied group, aquatic and terrestrial. Many are photosynthetic, unicellular or multicellular and complex. Many are colonial. Reproduction is by spores. Major contributors to limestone and other rock genesis; pp.212-214.

Fungi: filamentous bodies with spore-bearing growths in some forms which may be large; others microscopic. Fungal activity may be revealed as minute borings in host fossils; p.216.

Mosses: small plants with slender leafy axes, erect or prostrate, which may or may not have uniseriate branches: reproduce by spores: very rare as fossils; p.214.

Vascular plants: stems (axes), leaves and roots well-differentiated with vascular tissue for the translocation of water and nutrients and for support: reproduction by spores or seeds. Non-flowering forms include the leafless club- and spike-mosses with small spore-bearing structures at apices of certain branches. Horsetails have whorls of branches and fertile appendages; well-defined nodes and internodes give a jointed appearance. Axes are woody. Ferns have fleshy prostrate or underground stems and hairlike rootlets; the leaves are the dominant structures. Spores may develop on special spikes or on segments of leaves. Seed-bearing plants have vascular tissues in roots, stems and leaves. Reproduction is by seeds borne within fruits, or in cones or strobili as in conifers, cycads and the maidenhair tree; pp.216-244.

THE HISTORY OF LIFE ON EARTH

THE ORIGIN OF LIFE AND ITS FIRST PRIMITIVE FORMS

The history of life on earth can be divided into two roughly defined periods of time which represent different stages of what we call life. The first of these timespans was one of chemical evolution and began with the birth of this planet some 5,000 million years ago. After the original fire-ball had cooled down and the first volatile atmosphere, consisting of helium and hydrogen, had dispersed, the earth's crust was formed. A second atmosphere arose as a gaseous mixture of hydrogen, ammonia, methane, carbon dioxide and water vapour were released by the earth's violently active volcanoes. After a phase of further cooling, the water vapour condensed and the earth was flooded with deluges of rain. Most of this water evaporated again but a relatively minor part of it collected in small seas and lakes. As numerous experiments in the laboratory have shown, it was possible for both simple and complicated organic molecules to have formed in such an atmosphere. A small proportion of these compounds reached the surface of the earth in the rainfall and were oncentrated in the seas. This created the starting point for further development. More and more complicated compounds were formed in the watery olution of the primeval oceans. Energy was supplied by ultraviolet and radioactive radiation, electrical discharges and volcanic activity, so that amino-acids, nucleic acids and membrane-like sheets of condensates were produced. Once deoxyribonucleic (and ibonucleic) acids had been formed, with the capacity to reproduce themselves exactly in a system of protein production, life had begun. This period of chemical evolution can be said to have ended with the occurrence of the first living cells.

The first cells appeared some 3,500 million years ago and marked the beginning of what may be called organic or biochemical evolution. To understand the proper significance of objects discovered from this period, we must bear in mind that fossils can be found preserved in a physical, chemical, or organic state. The oldest objects are, as one would expect, "chemo-fossils". The rocks of the Onverwacht Series in South Africa, about 3,400 million years old, have yielded traces of hydrocarbons whose origin must have been biological, as can be determined from their isotopic characteristics. The somewhat younger rocks of the Figtree Series, also from South Africa, contain spherical and filamentary bodies which are thought to belong to the algae and bacteria. The oldest calcareous algal layers (stromatolites) have been found in the sedimentary rocks of Rhodesia (2,800 million years), and the lime-bearing deposits of these can be attributed to the activity of photosynthetic blue-green algae. The siliceous layers of the Gunflint Series in Canada (1,900 million years) provided specimens not only of a micro-flora of prokaryotes (cells lacking nuclei as in purple bacteria, chloro-bacteria, blue algae) but also preserved amino acids. These fossils belonged to the prokaryotes (no nuclear membrane, asexual

reproduction) – genuine living organisms, capable of feeding themselves and of photosynthesis.

Whereas bacterial photosynthesis takes place in the absence of air and gives off no free oxygen, plant photosynthesis in the blue-green algae, using carbon dioxide, water and energy, produced the glucose and free oxygen necessary for respiration. Since not all the glucoses were consumed for respiration, and photosynthesis continued to produce free oxygen, a surplus gradually accumulated in the atmosphere. During this time, about 1,900 to 1,600 million years ago, an oxygen atmosphere was formed with a protective layer of ozone. This layer absorbed a large proportion of the ultraviolet radiation harmful to life, but also inhibited the processes of abiogenic, organic synthesis, as the ionising radiation became cut off. At the beginning of this period stromatolites and phytoplankton were still dominant. But in the rocks at Bitter Springs, Australia, 1,100 million years old, a micro-flora containing chlorophytes and fungi in addition to prokaryotes has been found. These newer forms are the first in which the presence of a cell nucleus, with indications of mitotic division, has been demonstrated. It is clear that, by this period at the latest, eukaryotes – organisms with nuclear and cell membranes, and a sexual reproduction process – must have existed. From the Precambrian levels of rocks in Europe and Asia have come specimens of what are called acritarches (probably belonging to the dinoflagellates) and sporomorphs. Sponge spicules have been discovered in rock layers in Northern Territory, Australia. These are the only indication of the existence of organisms which fed on others and possessed a multi-layered structure.

All the more surprising, then, is the occurrence in the youngest Precambrian of the Ediacara (South Australia) fauna (600 million years ago). Their structure shows them to have been highly organised, possessing organs and probably feeding on phytoplankton. Only the imprints of their bodies have been preserved, but on the basis of their similarity to the younger fossil groups of the cnidaria, they are classed among the jellyfish, octocorals, pennatularia or annelids. Some have been treated as belonging to the arthropods or the echinoderms. These organisms, with their multi-cellular structure, their organs and bodies containing a hollow space, show the typical characteristics of metazoa. No calcium carbonate-based skeleton was developed, although there was sufficient carbonate in solution in the seas. Perhaps none was needed for stability or protection in their mode of existence.

THE DEVELOPMENT OF LIFE FROM THE CAMBRIAN TO THE QUATERNARY

Cambrian: blue-green algae as rock elements; preserved only as marine fossils, no indication of terrestrial life; all basic groups of invertebrates already existent; trilobites as global index fossils and representatives of faunal groupings.

Ordovician/Silurian: in the Silurian are the first terrestrial plants; signs of tropical climate, also of glaciations and occurrence of brackish and fresh water; development of silica-bearing sponges, first occurrence of rugose and tabulate corals, also as reef-builders together with stromatoporoids; flourishing of nautiloids, further development of trilobites, occurrence of eurypterida; first peak of development of ostracoda, first appearance of bryozoa, main groups of articulate brachiopods, also of echinoderms; vertebrates including agnatha, acanthodians, placoderms and first bony fishes; graptolites as index fossils.

Devonian: in Lower or Middle Devonian psilophytes give way to lycopodia and horsetails (equisetinae), first appearance of ferns; reef formation with sponges, stromatoporoids, tabulate and rugose corals, first land snails, first occurrence of ammonoids, i.e. goniatites; terrestrial arthropods including insects, spiders, scorpions and mites; flourishing of brachiopods, further development of sea-urchins, starfish; fishes including agnatha, acanthodians, placoderms, cartilaginous fishes and bony fishes; development of first amphibians from crossopterygii; corals, goniatites, conodonts, ostracods and brachiopods as index fossils.

Carboniferous: land-masses with luxuriant plant growth, flourishing of lycopods, horsetails and ferns, first occurrence of gymnosperms and conifers, formation of hard coals; rock-forming large foraminifera, first freshwater molluscs, spread of goniatites, bryozoa as reef-builders, extinction of graptolites; development of bony and cartilaginous fishes, flourishing of amphibians (labyrinthodonts), first appearance of basic forms of reptiles (cotylosaurs); foraminifera (fusulinids), corals, goniatites and conodonts as marine index fossils; plants as terrestrial index fossils.

Permian: occurrence of conifers and first ginkgos; decline of stromatoporoids, tabulate corals, trilobites, eurypterids, blastoids; bryozoa and sponges as reef-builders; smooth-shelled goniatites, brachiopods including the groups of the productids, spiriferids, strophomenids; first appearance of dragonflies, neuroptera and beetles; among fishes dominance of ray-finned fishes; first appearance of reptiles and thecodonts with mammal-like features; goniatites and conodonts as marine index fossils, plants as terrestrial index fossils.

Triassic: rock-forming marine algae, decline of lycopods and horsetails, growth of modern ferns including mattoniacea, osmundacea, dipteridacea, cycadea; first hexacorals; reefs in low latitudes (Tethyan) regions, among brachiopods flourishing of terebratula-cea; among molluscs development of pteriids, myophoriids, pholadomyids; among snails extinction of bellerophon-tids and murchisoniids, first occurrence of naticacea and littorinacea; among ammonoids flourishing and extinction of ceratitacea; first belemnites; decline of brachiopods, extinction of conodonts and labyrinthodonts; first appearance of tortoises, ichthyosaurs, dinosaurs, mammals; calcareous algae, molluscs, ammonoids, brachiopods, tetrapods as index fossils.

Jurassic: predominance of gymnosperms including conifers, flowering cycads and ginkgos; rock-forming radiolaria, first plankton-like foraminifera; flourishing of sponges forming carpets and reefs, flourishing of molluscs including ostreids, venerids, corbulids, cyrenids; first pulmonate snails, flourishing of ammonites and belemnites, development of sepia and squids and cuttlefish; first irregular sea-urchins, among sea-lilies planktonic forms (*Saccocoma*); development of rhynchonellids and terebratulids among brachiopods; first modern bony fishes, flourishing of dinosaurs and pterosaurs (*Pterodactylus*), appearance of primeval bird forms, first turtles; ammonites as index fossils.

Cretaceous: first occurrence of angiosperms, together with modern conifers, cycads and last forms of cryptogamous plants; leaf remains of angiosperms in forms reminiscent of modern specimens, which are classed among the willows, plantains, fig-trees, magnolias and roses; decline of corals; molluscs including inoceramids and rudists, snails including *Actaeonella* and *Nerinea* as typical representatives; flourishing of heteromorphic ammonites; decline of brachiopods, renewed flour-ishing of bryozoa; all groups of recent echinoderms represented; dominance of genuine bony fishes, peak period of dinosaurs; slow rise of small-structured mammals and division into orders of marsupials and placentals; already existent, insectivores, small beasts of prey, prosimians and artiodactyls; end of Cretaceous, extinction of previously important groups such as globotruncanids, rudists, nerineids, actaeonellids, ammonites, belemnites, dinosaurs and pterosaurs; foraminifera, molluscs, ammonites, belemnites as index fossils.

Tertiary: dominance of angiosperms, formation of brown coal; appearance of deciduous woods, some evergreen, others with summer foliage only; rise of graminaceae, gradual development of modern plant distribution patterns; development of foraminifera, including giant forms such as *Nummulites* or *Assilina*; proliferation of species of molluscs and snails (also in fresh water); among crustaceans development of shrimps and prawns, and peak development of irregular sea-urchins, further development of insects; predominance of bony fishes; explosive growth of mammals, appearance of first humanoids; foraminifera, molluscs, snails, mammals as index fossils.

Quaternary: glaciations with alternating cold and warm periods; loss of areas of distribution for some plants; development of typical plant and animal communities in areas of forest or steppe grassy plain, such as forest and steppe elephants, palaeoloxodons and mammoths; development of hominids; plants (varying representation of pollen groups) and remains of rodents (voles and lemmings) important as index fossils.

Geological time-ranges of important groups of plants, invertebrates and vertebrates

Scale in millions of years	Eras	Geological systems	Divisions commonly recognized	Conifers	Gingko-trees	Flowering plants	Palm ferns	Seed ferns	Ancient ferns	Ferns	Lycopods	Horsetails	Algae, fungi, mosses	Bacteria, blue algae
	Cainozoic	Quaternary	Holocene											
			Pleistocene											
2,5		Tertiary	Pliocene Miocene Oligocene Eocene Palaeocene											
65														
	Mesozoic	Cretaceous	Upper											
			Lower											
136		Jurassic	Malm (White Jurassic)											
			Dogger (Brown Jurassic)											
190			Lias (Black Jurassic)											
		Triassic	Keuper											
			Muschelkalk											
225			Buntsandstein											
	Palaeozoic	Permian	Zechstein											
			Rotliegendes											
280		Carboniferous	Upper											
			Lower											
345		Devonian	Upper											
			Middle											
395			Lower											
		Silurian	Upper											
			Middle											
430			Lower											
		Ordovician	Upper								Psylophytes				
			Middle											
500			Lower											
		Cambrian	Upper											
			Middle											
570			Lower											
	Precambrian	Proterozoic												
4500		Archaean												

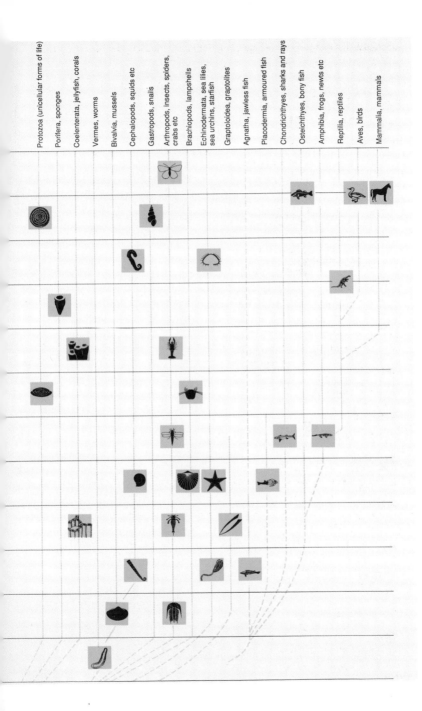

Protozoa (unicellular forms of life)

Porifera, sponges

Coelenterata, jellyfish, corals

Vermes, worms

Bivalvia, mussels

Cephalopods, squids etc

Gastropods, snails

Arthropods, insects, spiders, crabs etc

Brachiopods, lampshells

Echinodermata, sea lilies, sea urchins, starfish

Graptoloidea, graptolites

Agnatha, jawless fish

Placodermia, armoured fish

Chondrichthyes, sharks and rays

Osteichthyes, bony fish

Amphibia, frogs, newts etc

Reptilia, reptiles

Aves, birds

Mammalia, mammals

SOME TIPS
ABOUT FOSSIL
COLLECTING AS
A HOBBY

At some point your interest in fossils must have been aroused, whether by their aesthetic appeal or by a compulsion to compare these petrified forms with present-day plants and animals. Often it is a present of a fossil or a chance find by the roadside, a visit to one of the fossil shops or the infectious enthusiasm of collector friends and acquaintances which first sets you on the way to this hobby. Once you have caught the bug of fossil collecting, you should just give in to it and try to make the most of your obsession. Of course, anything can be overdone, but you will not get by in this hobby without a certain amount of planning and equipment. After you have seen the excellent specimens displayed in museums, perhaps you dream of making your own astonishing finds. If so, you should realise you will have to invest a great deal of patience, a deal of time, and some cash. For it is far more rewarding to make your own discoveries, rather than simply buying your collection. If you do not know the area in which you are going to start your collecting, get some tips from experienced collectors or take the chance to go out collecting with them. Not all rocks contain fossils. It would be useful to buy a geological and an accurate topographical map, so that you can get a geologist's general view of the distribution of rock strata which may be fossil-bearing, and so that you can recognise the places where lower levels of rock are exposed, even before you make your first trip. Keep a small diary and note in it the routes you

have taken, for experience will teach you that you cannot retain in your memory all the details that will be of value later. Even when you have chosen, say, a particular stone quarry as your destination, pay attention as you travel there to chance exposures produced by the digging out of foundations for a building, newly trenched drainage ditches, new excavations for roads and old quarry sites.

At all sites where you would like to search you should ensure that you have permission from some person in responsibility (chief engineer, foreman, site owner) both to enter the site and to dig there. Try to get permission in advance because in many cases it can only be obtained from a firm's central office. The quarry manager bears you no ill-will if he asks you what route you wish to take in the quarry and advises you which sections you should avoid, since he is responsible both to you and to his professional organisation if an accident should happen. Recently, mutual trust and respect has unfortunately been destroyed by irresponsible collectors who have entered sites illegally at weekends and made use of tools and machines found there to move larger quantities of rock to get at the fossils. In some areas collecting has been banned and access to many quarries prevented as a result. Do not disturb freshly constructed embankments unduly, and avoid all cultivated fields. It has been known for collectors to dig huge holes in the midst of standing crops, in order to get at ammonites beneath. Take care with important natural features, and in ature and landscape conservation reas. Even if you have got an owner's permission to dig some small holes, these should be filled in after your xploration.

Before setting out, you should ensure that you are adequately equipped. With stout clothing and footwear broken-in walking boots or wellingons, rain-gear), there will be less to distract you from the main business of finding the fossils. It is now very rare o find a rock exposure which is not overrun by collectors, where fossils which have been washed out of soft rock can simply be picked out. The best chances of finds are to be had by breaking open new material, after blasting in a quarry for example. For this you need a fairly heavy geological hammer, a chisel with a hand guard to protect the fingers, and heavy workinggloves. When working on softer rocks such as clays, marls and soft sandstones, a small pointed pick and a folding spade are useful. Similarly, a reasonably strong knife can help in splitting soft sedimentary rocks. With some old newspaper for wrapping, a felt-tip pen for marking the specimens, some plastic bags and old fruit crates for packing and transport, your equipment will be more or less complete. If you are working in a large-scale quarry or gravel pit, pay attention to the directions of the engineers or workmen, since the quarry and its dangerous spots are changing continually as the work progresses. Make sure you know the times of blasting and the shot signals. You might need to leave the quarry during blasting. In any case you should avoid hammering under vertical or overhanging surfaces, even with a safety helmet, or at least maintain a safe distance from them. It can be dangerous to do any unnecessary climbing or to approach too closely to steep drops. When you visit a quarry after prolonged rainfall, watch out particularly for rock slips since the softened material may still slide even after the rain has ceased.

It is always worthwhile to make a tour of inspection of the whole quarry because, while some levels of rock may be bare of fossils, others in different spots may contain a rich supply. Prepare a rough sketch of the exposure, so that on your next visit, even though more work has gone on there, you will find the fossil-bearing strata again more easily.

It is sensible to wear a pair of protective plastic goggles when splitting open rock fragments. Naturally you will be trying to release the fossils from the rock whole but do not be too depressed if, at the beginning, a number of specimens are broken; even a broken or neatly glued specimen will be of some value. Do not hesitate to take away fossils even when they are still largely covered in the surrounding rock, and save the task of basic and detailed preparation for work at home. Then you can work on them at your leisure with better tools and a suitable holding device. It is wise in the course of a larger scale programme of collecting in extensive exposures to make small storage depots for fossils related to particular strata. This makes selection simpler when packing, and it is helpful to be able to reconstruct the strata later. On your first expeditions, you will be tempted to take away even badly preserved specimens. Do not worry at this stage about taking too much material, you can always practise your preparation methods on it. You will soon, of necessity, become more selective. In the early stages of your hobby you will probably visit only one locality at a time; later you might explore several, and this will inevitably lead not only to an accumulation of specimens but possibly to the mixing up of the recovered material as well. It is therefore essential to pack specimens properly to avoid damage and to mark them conscientiously. Objects not likely to be damaged may be wrapped in newspaper, but more breakable finds should be packed in padded plastic boxes. Do not pack several specimens together because they can abrade or damage one another during transport. If you do not write some identification of the location and stratum where the object was found directly on to the wrapping paper, then at least you should enclose a note bearing the information with each specimen. It is worth having a coding system, which can also be recorded in your diary together with other points about the location and the circumstances of the find. This may sound pedantic, but experience has shown its worth: after a series of collecting trips, it is easy to overestimate the retentive capacities of one's memory. If they have been packed and arranged as suggested, your specimens will remain identifiable even after long expedi-

tions. The best way to transport smaller objects is to pack them in plastic bags or boxes and stow these together with the larger pieces in fruit crates padded with newspaper. When dealing with easily stored fossils not affected by drying out, the collector can wait several days before unpacking, reviewing and preparing his finds. More fragile pieces must sometimes, however, be impregnated with preservative solutions on the spot, if they are to survive the journey home in good condition.

To begin with, you may have difficulty in allocating many of your specimens to their correct zoological or botanical category; preparation may also prove unsuccessful. Try to get help from more experienced friends

An exposure in coarsely bedded Upper Jurassic (White Jura) at Mornsheim, Middle Franconia.

nd fellow collectors, whose acquaintance is well worth cultivating. Basic theoretical and practical knowledge can also be obtained at classes organised by local education authorities.

In most cases, the majority of likely locations for finds is well known among collectors. When you exchange specimens with them, you will also get to know the location of their finds from the data attached. The danger that likely locations might fall into the hands of fanatical collectors, who would exploit them mercilessly and leave them bare, can only be avoided by a measure of self-discipline and by the rapid exposure of any black sheep. Recently many locations have received far too many visitors because of publications in collectors' journals or through arranged group visits. Consequently, it is unlikely that much more will be found there for the next few years. Many of the specimens obtained at these spots have then appeared in the trade at exorbitant prices, and indeed there are some collectors who finance their group tours by laying sites to waste.

Those who wish to continue with their hobby will find that their expectations will rise; they may wish to concentrate on particular regions or particular groups of animals or plants. They will want to give their specimens their correct nomenclature, to identify them by genus and species, to catalogue them and to store them suitably. This last point can be met initially by using a cupboard or chest containing a good number of drawers. These should if possible be of differing depth to accommodate objects of varying size. Specimens can be stored and pro-tected from dust in plastic boxes with transparent lids. Pre-printed labels with space for location, formation, stratum, exact place of find, finder, genus and species can already be obtained from trade sources. In cataloguing, it is sensible to include the year date and a personal identification code for the location. When the number of specimens has grown, experienced collectors make out a separate file card for each one and these cards can be arranged by species and genus, so that there is easy access to every specimen.

If you specialise further, this present hand book will no longer suffice to identify all fossils. There are numerous specialist instructional books and scientific texts which can be consulted in public libraries. This facility has the advantage of allowing you to check whether a book's content is sufficient for your needs, and there are now a number of specialised book-dealers who stock a great range of geo-scientific literature. You can also learn more about your chosen specialisation by going to one of the numerous fossil and mineral exchanges, where all you may need as a collector is to be had. If you are still at a loss in identifying some of your finds and really cannot make further progress, you should visit a specialist institute or collection to ask their staff for help. Wherever possible, consult local museum curators for advice. Always make your specimens available to them if you think you have something interesting or new to science. Provided you do not arrive with your car-boot full of specimens to be identified, or with a basket of ill-sorted and unattributable finds, you will certainly receive an hospitable reception.

UNICELLULAR ORGANISMS
Sub-kingdom Protozoa Phylum Rhizopoda

Foraminifera [1-5] Class Foraminifera
Foraminifera are single-celled, usually marine Rhizopoda with shells (or tests)
containing one or more chambers. In life, threads of protoplasm emerge at the
end of the test or through holes in its wall. These threads form a network around
the test and are responsible for the intake and digestion of food. The test is
formed either from secretions from the protoplasm or by binding together foreign
bodies such as sand grains with organic adhesive substances. In the first case the
shell may consist of tectin, a substance similar to that of horn, or of calcium
carbonate. In the second case the walls of the test are described as hyaline
(glass-like, transparent), cryptocrystalline (porcelain-like), or calcareous grained.
The test diameter in foraminifera varies considerably, from 20μ to the 17cm of
large forms of the genus *Nummulites*. Important features for identification are the
structure, shape, sculpturing and size of the test. These are fine details which can
be observed only through the microscope. Most of the marine foraminifera led a
vagile or benthic existence, some were sessile, the remainder planktonic. Since
they occur in such great numbers and with such wide distribution the
foraminifera are among the best index fossils. They also provide information
about water temperature, depth and salt content on the basis of test size and the
relationship between pelagic and benthic forms. Because of their massed
assemblages foraminifera often make up entire masses of rocks.

The preparation of multiple specimens of the kind shown in Plate 1 is carried out
by mixing a sample of marl with water and hydrogen peroxide, to reduce the
sample to its component parts. The resulting suspension of sediment is filtered by
washing with water through sieves of varying mesh sizes and finally dried. The
foraminifera can then be picked out under the microscope.

1 Scattered specimens prepared from marine Miocene, Lower Bavaria, including genera
  Stilostomella, Robulus, Sigmoilopsis, Spiroplectamina and *Dentalina.* Magnification × 15
2 Green sandstone containing large foraminifera *Assilina exponens* and *Nummulites millecaput.*
  Eocene, Immenstadt/Germany. Diam. of individuals presented in true transverse section 3-4cm.
3 Polished section through ore-filled chamber walls of *Nummulites*, Eocene, Kressenberg/Germany.
  Diam. of shell 1.5cm.
4 Limestone containing shells of large foraminifera *Neoschwagerina,* Permian, Urals/Russia. Diam.
  of shells 1cm.
5 Limestone with specimens of *Nummulites* exposed by weathering, Eocene, Sebenico/Italy. Diam.
  of shells up to 3cm.

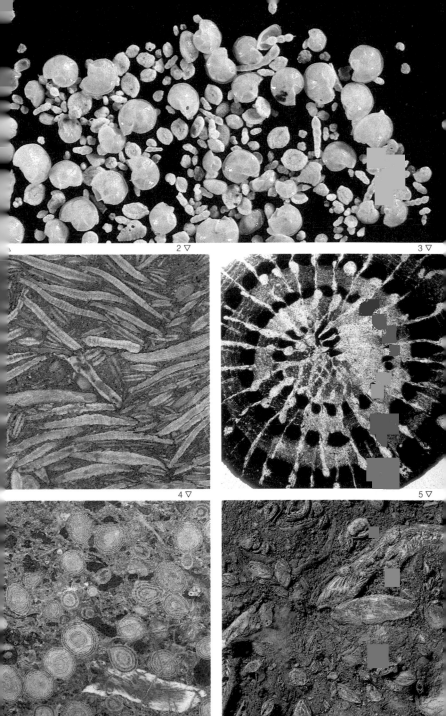

2 ▽   3 ▽

4 ▽   5 ▽

UNICELLULAR ORGANISMS
Subkingdom Protozoa Phylum Rhizopoda

Radiolaria Class Actinopoda Sub-class Radiolaria

Radiolaria are single-celled marine organisms with a diameter of 0.1-0.5mm. The body of an individual consists of a pseudochitinitic central capsule bearing pores. This capsule separates the inner layer of protoplasm from a surrounding outer layer. The pores of the capsule membrane may cover the whole surface or be grouped in a characteristic way on one part of the surface. The outer protoplasm in three layers can in particular forms reach such considerable thickness that the body of the radiolaria reaches a diameter of 25cm. The organism's buoyancy is provided by oil droplets enclosed in the central capsule and by extensions of the outer layer (pseudopodia). The skeleton, which is the form in which radiolaria are preserved, is accumulated around the central capsule, if present at all, and is composed of amorphous silica or strontium sulphate. Recent forms of radiolaria are found in all seas but never in fresh water. As buoyant planktonic organisms, radiolaria are easily carried along by ocean currents and winds, although they possess no means of propulsion. Particular groups characterise different depths of the oceans. Specially rich accumulations of their skeletons are found in deep-sea oozes in the Atlantic and Indian Oceans (at 3000-4000m). Because of the great numbers of individuals and their wide distribution they can be used in the relative determination of ages of rock just as well as foraminifera, and equally in the absence of larger fossils. Fossil radiolaria are classified according to the size and shape of the silica skeleton. Specimens have been found from as early as the Ordovician. Rocks which contain a high proportion of radiolaria are termed radiolarites. The skeleton remains they contain can be isolated by careful etching out with acid. Siliceous rocks known as "hornstone" radiolarites, of various colours, are found in and around European Alpine regions and represent sediments laid down in deep seas.

Assemblage of radiolaria, Eocene, Barbados. Among the wide variety of skeleton remnants are spherical forms belonging to the sub-order Spumellaria and funnel-shaped forms belonging to the sub-order Nasselaria. Magnification × 60.

ARCHAEOCYATHIDA
Sub-kingdom Metazoa Phylum Archaeocyatha

Archaeocyathida [1-4]
Archaeocyatha were marine organisms which colonised the warm shallows of the sea-bed during the Cambrian (Early to Middle Cambrian) period. Their goblet-shaped calcareous skeleton was anchored to the substrate by a root-like extension. On average the skeleton reached a height of 1-3cm and consisted of a single or double wall; if double, the walls were linked by vertical intermediate divisions. Specimens have also been discovered with dividing walls forming either bladder-like marginal structures or basal plates. Almost all of these structures had pores. Classification is based on the macro- and micro-structure of these elements. The wide distribution of Archaeocyatha resulted from the ability of the larva to swim about freely. They often formed carpet-like growths, but in combination with blue-green algae also built reefs. Lower Cambrian sedimentary rocks from Siberia have been divided into 11 zones of Archaeocyathids. They are also known in both eastern and western North America, and in Australasia.

SPONGES
Phylum Porifera
Fossil sponges usually occur singly, but may accumulate in reef-like structures. They may be preserved in silica or limestone, occurring in either shallow or deep water shales and limestones.

Cliona [5] Class Demospongia Order Hadromerida
CHARACTERISTICS: boring sponge which lives within the remains of lime-bearing organisms or in limestone rocks. It bores out tunnels branching in various patterns, which are interconnected in the manner of a pearl necklace. On the surface, however, only tiny openings are visible. The tunnels may be between 1 and 6mm in diameter. PROVENANCE: Devonian to Recent. DISTRIBUTION: world-wide.

Amphistomium [6] Class Demospongia Order Lithistida
CHARACTERISTICS: Variable in form, but commonly goblet-shaped; smooth surface covered with numerous openings surrounded by a rounded lip; thick interior and exterior walls; spicules lumpy in shape. PROVENANCE: Cretaceous. DISTRIBUTION: Europe.

1 *Cambrocyathus retesepta,* Lower Cambrian, Morocco. Transverse section: diam. 2cm.
2 *Archaeocyathus* sp., Middle Cambrian, Australia. Length: 2cm.
3 *Cambrocyathus retesepta* , Lower Cambrian, Morocco. Vertical section: height 2cm.
4 *Archaeocyathus atlanticus,* Lower Cambrian, Morocco. Transverse section: diam. 3cm.
5 Tunnels of *Clionida,* Malm, Neuburg/Danube/Germany. Tunnels preserved as result of subsequent sedimentary filling to give steinkern.
6 *Amphistomium aequabile,* Cretaceous, Misburg near Hanover/Germany. Diam. 10cm.

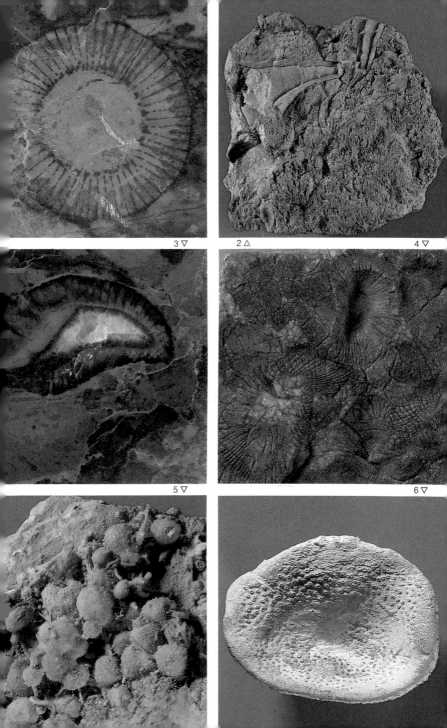

3 ▽   2 △   4 ▽

5 ▽   6 ▽

SPONGES
Phylum Porifera

Jereica [1/2] Class Demospongia Order Lithistida Sub-order Rhizomorina
CHARACTERISTICS: body may be shaped like a sphere, a club or cudgel, a spinning-top, a pear or a cylinder, sometimes with a long stem, perhaps smooth or with shallow, ring-shaped bulges; crown rounded or hollowed, carrying at its centre the apertures of the osculum of 2-5mm diameter; possibly also spherical swellings in the area of the crown. PROVENANCE: Upper Cretaceous. DISTRIBUTION: Europe.

A longitudinal section through the body of the sponge (Plate 2) shows the vertical arrangement of the channels through which water is ejected, beginning at the centre of the base and emerging on the upper surface. More or less at right angles to these are the radial canals, through which the water supply is drawn in. The skeleton of these siliceous sponges is made up of knotted and enlarged silica spicules combining to form an irregular framework. Recent lithistids have been found in marine deposits at water depths of 100-300m.

Verruculina [3] Class Demospongia Order Lithistida Sub-order Rhizomorina
CHARACTERISTICS: body variable in form including collared, beaker and bowl shapes; inner (or upper) surface bears wart-like openings rimmed with a rounded lip for expulsion of water, whilst lower (or outer) surface usually shows only simple pore-like ostia or prosopores (openings of intake canals); examples with only pore-like or only wart-like features are known; surfaces with the exception of these openings, are covered with a layer consisting of irregular desma. PROVENANCE: Upper Cretaceous. DISTRIBUTION: Europe.

Siphonia [4] Class Demospongia Order Lithistida Sub-order Tetracladina
CHARACTERISTICS: club-like with short or long stem and thicker upper section, vertex flattened or pointed, with deeply hollowed osculum; intake openings (ostia) on outer surface large and roundish, irregularly distributed; intake canals vertical to outer surface; exhalant canals central, vertical to axis, at edges bowed, opening into the osculum parallel to the outer wall; supporting skeleton formed of four-armed desma, surface layer of tetraxons. PROVENANCE: Upper Cretaceous to Tertiary. DISTRIBUTION: Europe. Flamborough/Yorkshire/England.

1 *Jereica tuberculosa,* Upper Cretaceous, Misburg/Germany. Height 15cm.
2 *Jereica polystoma,* Upper Cretaceous, Misburg/Germany. Height 11cm.
3 *Verruculina osculiferum,* Upper Cretaceous, Flamborough Head/England. Diam. 18cm.
4 *Siphonia tulipa,* Upper Cretaceous, Halberstadt/Germany. Height 19cm.

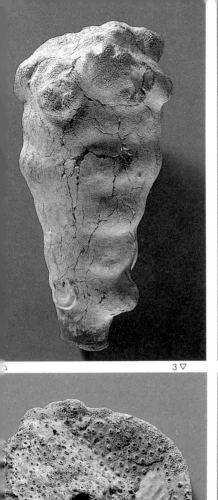

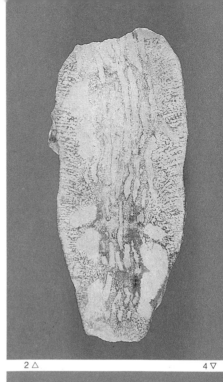

1

3 ▽

2 △

4 ▽

SPONGES
Phylum Porifera

Turonia [1] Class Demospongia Order Lithistida Sub-order Tetracladina
CHARACTERISTICS: body-shape variable, of rounded cone, pear or cylindrical shape, widening at top with ringed swellings; base carries root-like appendages; surface layer may be restricted to base, canal furrows may be found on top and base; ostia irregularly distributed over outer surface, diameter up to 3mm; crown rounded or sharply clipped off, with centrally placed inner ends of exhalant canals of up to 3mm diameter. PROVENANCE: Upper Cretaceous. DISTRIBUTION: Europe.

Astylomanon [2/3] Class Demospongia Order Lithistida
Sub-order Eutaxicladina
CHARACTERISTICS: restricted height, spherical or hemispherical in shape without root, outer surface divided by meridional ribs and furrows; carries large exhalant canals which are clearly marked particularly in the upper parts and open into a hollowed osculum, the inhalant canals are narrower and not so clearly marked; elements of skeleton consist of five- or six-armed desmas. PROVENANCE: Ordovician to Silurian. DISTRIBUTION: world-wide.

Cylindrophyma [4] Class Demospongia Order Lithistida
Sub-order Anomocladina
CHARACTERISTICS: cylindrical tube-like form, attached at lower surface, with tube-like central hollow space reaching down almost to the base, with inhalant canals normal to walls; skeleton composed of desmas with a thickened centre and 5-6 arms, in the thick surface layer monaxons also present. PROVENANCE: Jurassic. DISTRIBUTION: Europe.

Hydnoceras [5] Class Hexactinellidea Order Lyssacida
CHARACTERISTICS: large vase-shaped forms with 8 sides, along the longitudinal ribs bulbous or spiky extensions; the thin outer wall consists of a single layer of four-rayed skeletal elements which lie in one plane and form linking squares. PROVENANCE: Upper Devonian-Carboniferous. DISTRIBUTION: North America, Western Europe.

1 *Turonia* sp., Upper Cretaceous, Misburg/Germany. Height 9cm.
2 *Astylomanon verrucosum,* Silurian, Tennessee/USA. Width: 5cm. The weathered top surface shows the furrows leading to the central osculum.
3 Longitudinal section of *Astylomanon verrucosum* showing the broad canals leading to the osculum.
4 *Cylindrophyma* sp., Upper Jurassic, Kelheim/Germany. Height 7cm.
5 *Hydnoceras tuberosum,* Devonian, Cohocton/New York/USA. Height 23cm.

3 ▽　　　2 △　　　4 ▽

5 ▽

SPONGES
Phylum Porifera

Tremadictyon [1] Class Hexactinellidea Order Dictyida
CHARACTERISTICS: body of beaker or funnel shape, the prosopores are arranged in alternating rows; the skeleton consists of triaxons forming a regular lattice; the surface layer consists of four-rayed elements (stauractina) which lie in one plane and as a rule form linking squares; the base tends to thicken. PROVENANCE: Upper Jurassic – Recent. DISTRIBUTION: world-wide.

Laocetis [2] Class Hexactinellidea Order Dictyida
CHARACTERISTICS: body may be shaped like funnel, shell or tube, or branch like the twigs of a tree, the walls are thick and consist of three layers; the interior and exterior pores are arranged in vertical rows, the surface layer is composed of four-rayed skeletal elements forming linking squares. PROVENANCE: Jurassic to Tertiary. DISTRIBUTION: Europe, North Africa.

Rhizopoterion [3] Class Hexactinellidea Order Lychniscida
CHARACTERISTICS: a thick-walled sponge, whose body consists of a thickened branching root, a long stem and an umbrella- or trumpet-shaped upper part; the rounded oval canal exits are arranged in longitudinal furrows; the skeletal scaffold consists of triaxons which produce diagonal buttressing at the crossing point (*Lychnisca*) and bear spikes. Outer surface layer of silicified threads. PROVENANCE: Cretaceous. DISTRIBUTION: Europe.

The skeleton of Hexactinellidea always consists of tri-axial spicules of silica forming six rays. The whole skeleton adheres together in a fine glassy web. Recent specimens, by contrast to all other sponges, prefer a muddy substrate at depths between 200 and 500m, although examples have been found in the deep seas.

1 *Tremadictyon radicatum,* Upper Jurassic, southern Germany. Diam. of elongated prosopores 2mm.
2 *Laocetis fittoni,* Cretaceous, Neuburg/Danube/Germany. Height: c. 3cm.
3 *Rhizopoterion cervicornis,* Upper Cretaceous, Westfalia/Germany. Diam. 13cm.

2 △

3 ▽

SPONGES
Phylum Porifera

Coeloptychium [1/2] Class Hexactinellidea Order Lychniscida
CHARACTERISTICS: shaped like a mushroom with stem and cap; cap shape varies from disc-like form to funnel-like; on the underside radial folds spread out from the stem, and these may be covered by a surface layer either at the edge of the cap or over its whole surface; the ostia are located on the radial folds of the under-side of the cap, and the smaller exit pores in the radial furrows of the outer side; the skeleton consists of triaxons with diagonal buttressing at the crossing point, the surface layer consists of interwoven triaxonic spicules with six, five or four rays. PROVENANCE: Upper Cretaceous. DISTRIBUTION: Europe.

Eusiphonella [3] Class Calcispongia Order Pharetronida
CHARACTERISTICS: thick-walled, relatively small tubular form; several individuals grow together on common substrate; longitudinal furrows around edge of osculum, large canal exits; skeletal elements of calcite; spicules structured like tuning forks are typical. PROVENANCE: Jurassic. DISTRIBUTION: Europe.

Cypellia [4] Class Hexactinellidea Order Lychniscida
CHARACTERISTICS: goblet- or beaker-like shape, with stem and of large size; internal skeleton of interweaving canals, surface layer of four armed axons lying in one plane. PROVENANCE: Upper Jurassic. DISTRIBUTION: Europe.

Dictyocoelia [5] Class Calcispongia Order Sphinctozoa
CHARACTERISTICS: a calcareous sponge consisting of barrel-shaped segments joined together in a chain and linked by a central tube, which emerges at the osculum on the upper surface; the pore-bearing chambers are linked together and with the central tube and are separated by a wall-like filling, whose tissue consists of a primary cemented carbonate. PROVENANCE: Triassic, reefs in Wetterstein Limestone. DISTRIBUTION: Germany, Austria.

1/2 *Coeloptychium sulciferum,* Upper Cretaceous, Coesfeld/Westfalia/Germany. Diam. 8cm.
   1 Under-side of cap showing radial folds and large canal exits.
   2 Upper side of cap with surface layer.
3 *Eusiphonella bronnii,* White Jurassic, Nattheim/Germany. Height: 1.5cm.
4 *Cypellia rugosa,* Upper Jurassic, Forchheim/Germany. Diam. 11cm.
5 *Dictyocoelia manon,* Mieming Range/Austria. Specimens etched with acid. Diam. of central tube
   with its white infill 1cm.

CNIDARIA
Phylum Cnidaria Class Hydrozoa
Commonly found in shallow water limestones and shales, locally profuse and even in reef-like masses; Silurian-Cretaceous, rarely in younger formations.

Ellipsactinia [1] Order Hydroida
CHARACTERISTICS: colonial form growing as incrustation on substrate, either in flat layers, hemispheres or in stalked form; identifying feature (visible only in polished section) is structure of parallel carbonate layers (laminae) with radial tubes, furrows and warts (tubercles). PROVENANCE: Triassic to Cretaceous. DISTRIBUTION: Europe, Africa.

Millepora [2] Order Milleporida
CHARACTERISTICS: branching, crusted or conglomeratic forms, calcareous skeleton with system of canals, containing openings for admission of polyps for feeding or defence and of medusae. Also with transverse basal elements. PROVENANCE: Upper Cretaceous to Recent. DISTRIBUTION: world-wide.
Most important recent reef-building organism, symbiosis with green algae, not found deeper than 40m.

Stromatopora [3] Order Stromatoporoida
CHARACTERISTICS: a colonial form growing in layers or conglomerations, with a network structure composed of horizontal laminae and vertical pillars; interspersed among them are tiny vertical tubes sealed at the base, which have been interpreted as the chambers occupied by polyps. PROVENANCE: Ordovician to Permian. DISTRIBUTION: world-wide. Reef-builder from Silurian to Devonian.

Amphipora [4] Order Stromatoporoida
CHARACTERISTICS: branching colonial form; if central canal present, this may be sub-divided; internal skeleton net-like with irregular pillars, bubble-like chambers formed towards edges; dissepiments may be present. PROVENANCE: Silurian to Jurassic. DISTRIBUTION: Europe, North America, Africa, Asia. Torquay/Devon/England.

CORALS
Phylum Cnidaria Class Anthozoa
(see p. 48 for general description)

Isis [5] Order Gorgonacea
CHARACTERISTICS: branching octocorals with calcified axial centres and horny intermediate limbs, usually only calcified axes preserved. PROVENANCE: Eocene to Recent.

Acervularia [6] Order Rugosa
CHARACTERISTICS: thickly branching or colonial form with outer and inner walls, transverse basal elements as inverted cone; dissepiments between inner and outer walls divided into two zones, of which outer contains cavitated dissepiments, inner a flatter partitioning; a third layer within inner wall fuses with base; septa are finely toothed. PROVENANCE: Silurian. DISTRIBUTION: Europe. Welsh Marches (borderlands), English Midlands.

---

1 *Ellipsactinia ellipsoidea,* Upper Jurassic, Stramberg/Czechoslovakia. Laminae 0.5mm thick.
2 *Millepora* sp., Cretaceous, southern France. Branches up to 1.5cm thick.
3 *Stromatopora concentrica,* Middle Devonian, Torquay/England. Magnification × 1.3.
4 *Amphipora ramosa,* Middle Devonian, Schlade/Germany. Branches 4mm thick.
5 *Isis melitensis,* Pliocene, Sicily. Length: 8.5cm.
6 *Acervularia luxurians,* Silurian, Dudley/England. Diam. cupped forms c. 1cm.

3 ▽

2 △

4 ▽

5 ▽

6 ▽

CORALS
Phylum Cnidaria Class Anthozoa

Abundant at many levels in Palaeozoic and Mesozoic marine limestones. Colonial and solitary forms often found together. Reefal communities occur in the mid-Palaeozoic to Recent systems. Commonly associated with brachiopods, algae and bryozoa.

Zaphrentoides [1] Order Rugosa
CHARACTERISTICS: section of clearly marked septa on the inner side of the goblet-shaped calice, relatively small form, curved like animal horn; counter-septum long, smaller septal divisions arranged vertically in main septal area. PROVENANCE: Lower Carboniferous. DISTRIBUTION: Europe, North America.

Calceola [2] Order Rugosa
CHARACTERISTICS: slipper-shaped individual corals, triangular in outline, semi-circular in transverse section and on top surface; main septum on curved edge, counter-septum on straight edge of deep central hollow, upper surface with distinct median septum. PROVENANCE: Lower to Middle Devonian. DISTRIBUTION: Europe, Asia.

Haplothecia [3] Order Rugosa
CHARACTERISTICS: stick-like corals, walls between individual corallites weak or missing; main and subsidiary septa long enough to reach those of neighbouring corallites; septa on the inner edge of the large dissepimentarium thickened, septa-like stems of carinae with side extensions on both sides always beginning at same points. PROVENANCE: Devonian. DISTRIBUTION: Europe.

Eridophyllum [4] Order Rugosa
CHARACTERISTICS: densely packed stalked form, individual corallites joined by extensions to neighbours; ends of septa form an internal tube (aulo), septa gradually increasing in thickness and carinate on both sides, bases compounded of horizontal and slanting elements. PROVENANCE: Silurian to Devonian. DISTRIBUTION: Europe, North America. South Ontario/Canada; New York/USA.

• Favistella [5] Order Rugosa
CHARACTERISTICS: polygonal goblet-shaped forms, slender septa in tabular area, main septa reach to inner axis, subsidiary septa short, solid base, bent downwards at sides. PROVENANCE: Middle to Upper Ordovician. DISTRIBUTION: world-wide. South Ontario/Canada; New York, Ohio/USA.

Porpites [6] Order Rugosa
CHARACTERISTICS: a flattish form shaped like a spinning-top or disc with round outline; no separate base or dissepiments, at centre of upper surface shallow depression of conical shape; all septa bear feather-like lateral extensions, on under-side a button-like mass (point of attachment). PROVENANCE: Lower to Middle Silurian. DISTRIBUTION: Europe, North America. South Ontario/Canada; New York, Ohio/USA.

1 *Zaphrentoides edwardsiana*, Lower Carboniferous, Belgium. Height of goblet 4cm.
2 *Calceola sandalina*, Middle Devonian, Eifel/Germany. Index fossil. Length of form 3cm.
3 *Haplothecia pengellyi*, Devonian, Torquay/England. Polished section × 1.5.
4 *Eridophyllum vennori*, Silurian, Lake Huron/USA. Diam. of individual corallite 5mm.
5 *Favistella alveolata*, Silurian, Lake Huron/USA. Diam. of main upright section 7cm.
6 *Porpites porita*, Silurian, Gotland/Sweden. Diam. up to 2.5cm.

1

2 △

3 △

4 ▽

5 ▽

6 ▽

CORALS
Phylum Cnidaria Class Anthozoa

Goniophyllum [1] Order Rugosa
CHARACTERISTICS: pyramidal, rectangular in plan, flat-sided corals; flattened form consists of four triangular plates, main septa contained in marginal furrow (fossula), bases of tabulae and the chambered dissepiments tend to thicken. PROVENANCE: Middle Silurian. DISTRIBUTION: Europe.

Astrocoenia [2] Order Scleractinia
CHARACTERISTICS: clump-like colonial coral with polygonal upper calices, the edges of which are formed by septa which have coalesced as they spread outwards; septa formed from spiky individual elements arranged in rows to form palisades, older septa may be smooth or decorated with pearl-like chains; the columella is strongly pronounced and shaped like a plant pistil, free-standing in upper part. PROVENANCE: Upper Triassic to Recent. DISTRIBUTION: world-wide.

Thamnasteria [3] Order Scleractinia
CHARACTERISTICS: colonial coral of branching, clump-like or encrusting habit, upper calices shallow, septa of neighbouring individuals intergrown; septa bear pores, may be smooth or decorated with pearl-like chains or carry ribs running parallel to their edges. Columella present. PROVENANCE: Middle Triassic to Middle Cretaceous. DISTRIBUTION: Europe, Asia, Africa, North America. Steeple Ashton/Wiltshire/England.

Areacis [4] Order Scleractinia
CHARACTERISTICS: coenosteum between round corallites reticulated with spiny upper surface; primary septa in thin sheet form, joined at centre, where they carry thorn-like projections. PROVENANCE: Eocene. DISTRIBUTION: Europe.

Cyathophora [5] Order Scleractinia
CHARACTERISTICS: colonial corals, individual corallites (members) joined by coenosteum, upper calices round and raised, septa short, dissepiments horizontal between septa, no columella. PROVENANCE: Jurassic to Cretaceous. DISTRIBUTION: Europe.

Stylosmilia [6] Order Scleractinia
CHARACTERISTICS: a branching form with thick members, ribs (continuations of septa beyond edge of upper calice) limited to upper part of outside edge; columella thin, linked to septa by spiky continuations, septa reaching to centre, the remaining 18 septa shorter. PROVENANCE: Middle Jurassic to Lower Cretaceous. DISTRIBUTION: Europe, North Africa.

1 *Goniophyllum pyramidale,* Middle Silurian, Gotland/Sweden. Length of upper side 2.5cm.
2 *Astrocoenia decaphyllia,* Upper Cretaceous, Linderhof/Germany. Diam. of corallite 2mm.
3 *Thamnasteria serrata,* Upper Jurassic, Nattheim/Germany. Diam. of single corallite 1cm.
4 *Areacis michelini,* Eocene, Paris/France. Diam. of single corallite 5mm.
5 *Cyathophora bourgeti,* Upper Jurassic, Nattheim/Germany. Diam. of corallite 6mm.
6 *Stylosmilia suevica,* Upper Jurassic, Nattheim/Germany. Diam. of corallite up to 5mm.

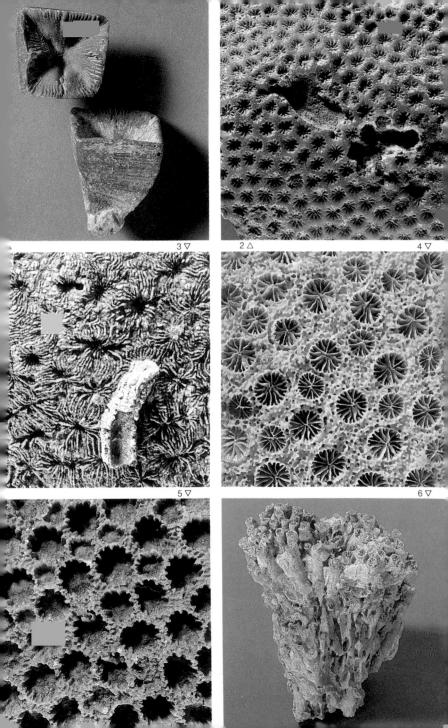

3 ▽

2 △

4 ▽

5 ▽

6 ▽

CORALS
Phylum Cnidaria Class Anthozoa

Stylina [1] Order Scleractinia
CHARACTERISTICS: colony forming, corallites joined by coenosteum, which carries ribs and basal chambering, edges of calices raised, septa smooth, 16 to 24 in number, with or without columella. PROVENANCE: Upper Triassic to Lower Cretaceous. DISTRIBUTION: Very widespread; Europe, North and South America.

Enallhelia [2] Order Scleractinia
CHARACTERISTICS: branching form with narrower or thicker branches, raised calices sometimes arranged alternately along broad side of branches; septa arranged in four- or six-fold symmetry, costae limited to upper outer rim of calice, columella present. PROVENANCE: Middle Jurassic to Lower Cretaceous. DISTRIBUTION: Europe, Asia, South America.

Microphyllia [3] Order Scleractinia
CHARACTERISTICS: colony-forming, corallites arranged in rows divided by longitudinal small ridges, these correspond to walls which are reinforced by transverse elements; septa are interrupted, carrying pores and lateral pearl-chain-like decoration, centre of calice small. PROVENANCE: Upper Jurassic. DISTRIBUTION: Europe, Asia.

Cyclolites [4] Order Scleractinia
CHARACTERISTICS: solitary coral, circular or elliptical in plan, lower side shows growth rings, upper side arched, septa with pores, also on exterior and at sides with pearl-chain-like thickened elements, narrow vertical depression. PROVENANCE: Upper Cretaceous to Recent. DISTRIBUTION: Europe, Asia, North Africa.

Stylophyllum [5] Order Scleractinia
CHARACTERISTICS: cylindrical to sub-cylindrical forms; septa isolated or linked at sides, mostly directed inwards and of spiny form; dissepiments within walls horizontal, no columella. PROVENANCE: Upper Triassic. DISTRIBUTION: Europe.

Montlivaltia [6] Order Scleractinia
CHARACTERISTICS: solitary coral, usually tall, of conical or cylindrical shape, septa toothed, striped or granular, within walls numerous dissepiments, adult specimens with up to 250 septa, columella only weakly developed or absent. PROVENANCE: Middle Triassic to Cretaceous. DISTRIBUTION: world-wide. Middle Jurassic of Dorset, Wiltshire, Yorkshire/England.

1 *Stylina limbata*, Upper Jurassic, Nattheim/Germany. Diam. of calice 2mm.
2 *Enallhelia compressa*, Sinabrunn/Swabian Alps/Germany. Diameter of calice 2mm.
3 *Microphyllia soemmeringi*, Upper Jurassic, Nattheim/Germany. Magnified ×1.5.
4 *Cyclolites macrostoma*, Upper Cretaceous, Gosau/Austria. Diam. 6cm.
5 *Stylophyllum paradoxum*, Upper Triassic, Austria. Diam. 3cm.
6 *Montlivaltia zitteli*, Upper Jurassic, Nattheim/Germany. Diam. 6.5cm.

CORALS
Phylum Cnidaria   Class Anthozoa

Aplosmilia   Order Scleractinia
CHARACTERISTICS: colony-forming, usually two calices are developed on the branches by a process of intratentacular fusion, calices round or elliptical; thick, smooth septa strongly pronounced; calices joined or separated only by coenosteum, which allows the costae to be seen clearly only in the upper part of the exterior; columella is slender, standing leaf-life vertically in the long axis of the calice; few dissepiments within calice, no epitheca. PROVENANCE: Upper Jurassic to Lower Cretaceous. DISTRIBUTION: Europe, Asia Minor.

The first Scleractinia (Cyclocorallia) occur in the Lower Triassic. The peaks of their development are found in the Jurassic and Cretaceous chalk reefs of Europe. Recent coral reefs have been built up from a network of scleractinian corals (Acroporidae and Poritidae), octocorals of the genera *Heliopora* and *Tubipora*, and hydrocorals (*Millepora*). The structure of these reefs is consolidated by the action of calcium carbonate-secreting organisms such as red algae and bryozoa.

CORALS
Phylum Cnidaria Class Anthozoa

Thecosmilia [1] Order Scleractinia
CHARACTERISTICS: branching form with thick limbs, united in a ring, with up to 3 cups per arm produced by fission, edges of septa finely serrated, decorated with pearl-chain-like elements on lateral surfaces, columella deep set, outer walls of branches and calices usually destroyed. PROVENANCE: Middle Triassic to Cretaceous. DISTRIBUTION: world-wide. Dorset, Central England, Yorkshire; East Scotland.

Placosmiliopsis [2] Order Scleractinia
CHARACTERISTICS: a short-stemmed form, the growth of the calice in one direction produces fan-like shape, numerous massive septa with ribs (costae), laterally granular, lightly serrated on outer edge; columella appears as lengthwise wall standing vertically in direction of central depression of calice, no outer walling, occasional arching dissepiments. PROVENANCE: Upper Cretaceous. DISTRIBUTION: Europe.

Diploctoenium [3] Order Scleractinia
CHARACTERISTICS: initial element fan-shaped, as in *Placomiliopsis*, but then extended sideways in curved form; massive septa with ribs of two or three different sizes, upper and outer edge of septa finely toothed, sides marked as with pearl-chain-like elements and arched striping, columella continuous as lengthwise plate-like element. PROVENANCE: Middle to Upper Cretaceous. DISTRIBUTION: Europe, North Africa, Caribbean.

Heterocoenia [4] Order Scleractinia
CHARACTERISTICS: plate- or branch-like form, indistinct boundaries between individual corallites, septa thicken into club shape towards centre by deposits in central zone, corallites linked by leaf-like granular coenosteum, no columella. PROVENANCE: Cretaceous. DISTRIBUTION: Europe, North America.

Heliolites [5] Order Tabulata
CHARACTERISTICS: massive corals, coenenchym between the small slender corallites, which carry 12 thorn-like septa, tabulae complete. PROVENANCE: Middle Ordovician to upper Middle Devonian. DISTRIBUTION: world-wide. Dudley, Shropshire, Torquay/England.

Peplosmilia [6] Order Scleractinia
CHARACTERISTICS: individual corals, thick septa with ribs, edges of septa finely toothed, lateral surfaces at right angle to outer edge, granular but combining to form feathered stems at upper edge, columella thick and lamellar. PROVENANCE: Upper Jurassic to Middle Cretaceous. DISTRIBUTION: Europe.

1 *Thecosmilia trichotoma,* Upper Jurassic, Nattheim/Germany. Diam. of cup up to 2cm.
2 *Placosmiliopsis salisburgensis,* Upper Cretaceous, St Gilgen/Austria. Height, 4cm.
3 *Diploctoenium contortum,* Upper Cretaceous, Gosau/Austria. Height: 3.5cm.
4 *Heterocoenia grandis,* Upper Cretaceous, Gosau/Austria. Magnified × 1.5.
5 *Heliolites porosa,* Devonian, Torquay/England. Polished section, magnified × 2.
6 *Peplosmilia latona,* Cretaceous, France. Height: 4cm.

3 ▽   2 △   4 ▽

5 ▽   6 ▽

CORALS
Phylum Cnidaria Class Anthozoa

Favosites [1] Order Tabulata
CHARACTERISTICS: corallites polygonal, directly adjacent to each other without intervening coenosteum, side walls covered with pores, septa arranged in longitudinal rows of spines, tabulae complete. PROVENANCE: Upper Ordovician to Middle Devonian. DISTRIBUTION: world-wide. Dudley, Wenlock Edge, Torquay/England.

Michelinia [2] Order Tabulata
CHARACTERISTICS: forming clumps or flat discs or segments of spheres, narrowing towards base; outer walls bear large, spiny extensions (as supports), corallites polygonal, directly adjacent to each other with raised rims, pores on walls irregularly distributed, septa prominent as vertical rows of spines, tabulae composed of several elements and thin-walled. PROVENANCE: Upper Devonian to Permian. DISTRIBUTION: world-wide. South Wales; Avon, Gloucestershire, Lancashire/England.

Catenipora [3/4] Order Tabulata
CHARACTERISTICS: corallites are small, roundish, oval, or elliptical, usually arranged in single row in form of palisade; these palisades branch out to form a coarse network of honeycomb appearance; if septa are present, these are vertical spines arranged in 12 rows; the tabulae are horizontal and gently arched, walls carry no pores, corallites of uniform size. PROVENANCE: Middle Ordovician to Upper Silurian. DISTRIBUTION: North America, Europe, Asia, Africa.

The Order Tabulata is composed exclusively of colony-forming corals, which first occur in the Ordovician and become extinct in the Permian. As reef-builders they are familiar in the Ordovician, Silurian and Devonian of North America; rugose and tabulate corals together with algae and stromatoporoids make up the Devonian reefs in the Schiefergebirge of the Rhineland. The Palaeozoic corals required similar conditions to the recent corals (Scleractinia): a suitable substrate, as free as possible of sand and mud; moving sea-water with an adequate supply of oxygen and good water circulation, with a minimum temperature of about 18˚C; and sufficient light penetration to support symbiosis with algae, suggesting a maximal depth of water up to 35m.

1 *Favosites favosus.*, Silurian, Illinois/USA. Diam. of corallite 4mm.
2 *Michelinia favosa,* Devonian, Tournai/Belgium. Diam. of clump 11cm.
3 *Catenipora escharoides,* Silurian debris, Merseburg/Germany. Magnified × 1.2.
4 *Catenipora catenularius,* Silurian, Gotland/Sweden. Magnified × 2.

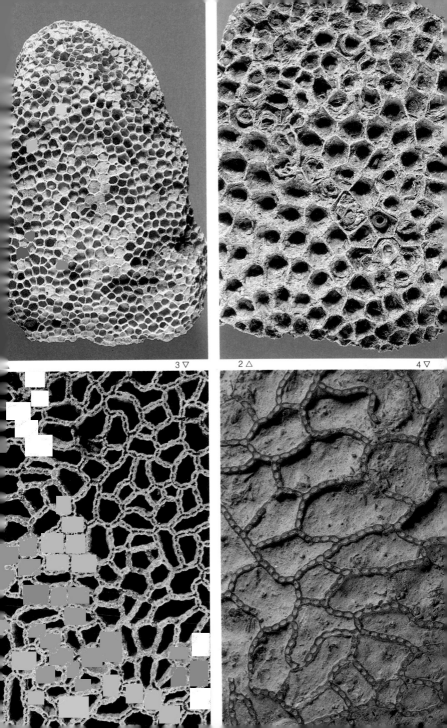

3 ▽   2 △   4 ▽

BIVALVES
Phylum Mollusca Class Bivalvia
A highly varied and successful group, abundant locally in marine and non-marine rocks. Forming complex communities on sea or lake floors.

Nucula [1] Order Nuculoidea Family Nuculidae
CHARACTERISTICS: shell rounded or lengthways extended triangle, pallial line without sinus, dentition taxodont, fine radial ribbing, inner edge very finely serrated. PROVENANCE: Lower Cretaceous to Recent. DISTRIBUTION: world-wide. Upper Jurassic, Dorset; Upper Cretaceous, Berkshire, Norfolk/England.

Cardiola [2] Order Praecardioida Family Praecardiidae
CHARACTERISTICS: thin, equivalve shell of bulbous shape, pronounced beak (or umbo) at hinge, with triangular, striped surface, exterior bears numerous radial ribs. PROVENANCE: Upper Silurian to Devonian. DISTRIBUTION: Europe; North America. Silurian, North Wales.

Anadara [3] Order Arcoida Family Arcidae
CHARACTERISTICS: shell rounded to sub-trapezoidal, ribbed exterior, inner edge strongly serrated, beak bent over to rear, below this a triangular or oblong cardinal area, closing valve has obliquely placed serrations at edge and is gently arched. PROVENANCE: Oligocene to Recent. DISTRIBUTION: world-wide.

Idonearca [4] Order Arcoida Family Cucullaeidae
CHARACTERISTICS: thick, subtrapezoidal shell; densely packed fine ribbing, rear edge of shell cut off at angle, beak inclined towards front, cardinal area has furrows interrupted by sharp bends, the teeth below the beak lie obliquely, the long teeth at the sides lie horizontally and are directed downwards and to the side. PROVENANCE: Jurassic to Eocene. DISTRIBUTION: Europe, North America.

Glycymeris [5] Order Arcoida Family Glycymerididae
CHARACTERISTICS: a thick shell of circular outline, with triangular depressed ligament furrow and relatively small beak; short teeth, set at an angle, become rarer towards the centre, upper surface may be smooth or ribbed, inner edge crenulate. PROVENANCE: Tertiary to Recent. DISTRIBUTION: world-wide. Upper Greensand, east Devon; Eocene, Hampshire, Isle of Wight; Pliocene, East Anglia/England.

Mytilus [6] Order Mytiloida Family Mytilidae
CHARACTERISTICS: thin-shelled, valves pointed at front, broadened at rear, beak at front; extended narrow ligament, closing edge at front notched; upper surface smooth or with radial ribs. PROVENANCE: Pliocene to Recent. DISTRIBUTION: North America, Northern Europe. Red Crag, East Anglia/England.

1 *Nucula incrassa,* Upper Cretaceous, Owl Creek/USA. Length: 3cm.
2 *Cardiola interrupta,* Silurian, Dvorek/Czechoslovakia. Diam. 1.5cm.
3 *Anadara fichteli,* Miocene, Lower Rhine/Germany. Length: 3cm.
4 *Idonearca crassatina,* Eocene, Jouchery/France. Length: 8cm.
5 *Glycymeris philippi,* Upper Oligocene, Moers/Lower Rhine/Germany. Length: 6cm.
6 *Mytilus californicus,* Pleistocene, Newport Bay/USA. Length: 11cm.

3 ▽   2 △   4 ▽

5 ▽   6 ▽

BIVALVES
Phylum Mollusca   Class Bivalvia

Lithophaga [1] Order Mytiloida Family Mytilidae
CHARACTERISTICS: shell elongated or cylindrical, narrowing towards rear, beak just behind front end, surface smooth or finely striated, ligament deep set.
PROVENANCE: Miocene to Recent. DISTRIBUTION: world-wide. Lower Jurassic, Glamorgan/Wales, Somerset/England; Upper Jurassic, Wiltshire/England.

Pinna [2] Order Mytiloida Family Pinnidae
CHARACTERISTICS: a shallow infaunal mollusc of triangular, paddle-like shape, front end carries beak, small muscle cavity towards anterior, large muscle attachment point towards rear end, ventral edge has long opening to permit passage of byssus, long ligament, without teeth, surface covered with spiny scales.
PROVENANCE: Lower Carboniferous to Recent. DISTRIBUTION: world-wide. Lower Jurassic, Yorkshire, Dorset/England.

Rhaetavicula [3] Order Pterioida Family Pteriidae
CHARACTERISTICS: outline irregular oval with wing-like extensions on both valves, front wing smaller; left valve convex with vertical ribbing, right valve somewhat smaller, flat and without ribs, below the beak a notched tooth and tooth lamellae, below the smaller wing (auricle) the byssus opening. PROVENANCE: Upper Triassic. DISTRIBUTION: Europe; North America. Westbury on Severn/Gloucestershire/England; Barry/South Wales.

Hoernesia [4] Order Pterioida Family Bacevelliidae
CHARACTERISTICS: outline elongated, trapezoidal; left valve convex, with prominent beak, right valve slightly convex or even concave, valve edges not in same plane, rear wing longer than forward wing, but both only minor features; hinge shows hollows for ligament attachment, one or more front teeth and one long back tooth. PROVENANCE: Triassic to Middle Jurassic. DISTRIBUTION: Europe, Asia.

Hippochaeta [5/6] Order Pterioida Family Isognomonidae
CHARACTERISTICS: a thick-shelled form, in outline tongue-shaped or rectangular with rounded corners, front edge usually shows curved indentation; hinge area has numerous ligament attachment hollows located on platforms separated by furrows; byssus opening below the beak. PROVENANCE: Eocene to Pliocene. DISTRIBUTION: world-wide.

1 *Lithophaga avitensis,* Miocene, Leibnitz/Germany. Length: 7.5cm. A boring mollusc which penetrates the rock with chemical secretions.
2 *Pinna* sp., Miocene, Oberschwärzenbach/Germany. Length: 13cm. Buries pointed forward end in soft sediment.
3 *Rhaetavicula inaequiradiata*, Upper Triassic, Wendelstein/Germany. Length: 4cm.
4 *Hoernesia socialis*, index fossil from Muschelkalk, Bayreuth/Germany. Length: 6cm.
5/6 *Hippochaeta maxillata,* Oligocene, Weinheim/Germany. Width: 9cm.

3 ▽   2 △   4 ▽

5 ▽   6 ▽

BIVALVES
Phylum Mollusca Class Bivalvia

Cataceramus [1] Order Pterioida Family Inoceramidae
CHARACTERISTICS: outline round to oval, extended towards rear, left valve more arched than right, dorsal edge straight and longer than ventral, pronounced concentric ribbing with fine striping, shell greater in length than height. PROVENANCE: Upper Cretaceous. DISTRIBUTION: world-wide.

Posidonia [2] Order Pterioida Family Posidoniidae
CHARACTERISTICS: outline roughly oval, thin-shelled, valves only slightly convex with sides of unequal length, but almost equivalvular; beak not pronounced, hinge-line straight, hinge without teeth, very small wings, upper surface bears concentric ribbing. PROVENANCE: Lower Carboniferous to Upper Jurassic. DISTRIBUTION: North America; Eurasia. Devon, North Staffordshire, Yorkshire, Lancashire/England.

Chlamys [3] Order Pterioida Family Pectinidae
CHARACTERISTICS: right valve more arched than left, both bear deep radial ribbing and concentric growth rings, on the right valve ribs are wider than intervening spaces; wings approximately equal, front auricle or ear has small byssus opening. PROVENANCE: Jurassic to Recent. DISTRIBUTION: world-wide. Jurassic, Dorset, Yorkshire/England; Upper Cretaceous, Warminster/Wiltshire/England.

Camptochlamys [4] Order Pterioida Family Pectinidae
CHARACTERISTICS: valves slightly convex, greater in height than width; front auricle with byssus opening is longer than rear; sculpturing consists of concentric growth rings and radial ribbing. PROVENANCE: Triassic to Recent. DISTRIBUTION: world-wide.

Monotis [5] Order Pterioida Family Monotidae
CHARACTERISTICS: thin-shelled, outline roughly oval, strong radial ribbing, no auricle at rear, at front right auricle or wing smaller than left, closure edge straight. PROVENANCE: Upper Triassic. DISTRIBUTION: world-wide.

Plicatula [6] Order Pterioida Family Plicatulidae
CHARACTERISTICS: outline roughly oval, right valve more convex than left, even early growth rings strongly pronounced, slender or broad ribs and spines shown towards edges; small cardinal area, ligament hollow sharply pointed triangle. PROVENANCE: Middle Triassic to Recent. DISTRIBUTION: world-wide. Middle Jurassic, Dorset/England; Upper Cretaceous, Folkestone/England.

1 *Cataceramus regularis,* left valve, Upper Cretaceous, Gosau/Austria. Length: 9cm.
2 *Posidonia becheri,* index fossil Lower Carboniferous, Nassau/Germany. Length: 4cm.
3 *C. (Pecten) gigas,* Miocene, Ortenburg/Germany. Length: 15cm.
4 *Camptochlamys michaelensis,* Upper Jurassic, Malton/England. Length: 9cm.
5 *Monotis haueri,* Upper Triassic, Iran. Length: 4cm.

6 *Plicatula pectinoides*, Middle Triassic, Nancy/France. Length: 3cm.

3 ▽　　2 △　　4 ▽

5 ▽　　6 ▽

BIVALVES
Phylum Mollusca   Class Bivalvia

Spondylus [1] Order Pterioida Family Spondylidae
CHARACTERISTICS: both valves noticeably convex, cardinal area of right valve broad and triangular; teeth short and thick; pronounced radial ribbing, which also carries spines or other extensions; usually found on surface of substrate. PROVENANCE: Jurassic to Recent. DISTRIBUTION: world-wide. Lower Cretaceous, South-east England and East Midlands.

Plagiostoma [2] Order Pterioida Family Limidae
CHARACTERISTICS: roughly oval, convex shell with peak inclined to rear; wings only indistinctly formed, pointed beaks widely separated, pronounced lunule, hinge line either without teeth or with no more than two; upper surface smooth or very finely striated or gently ribbed. PROVENANCE: Middle Triassic to Upper Cretaceous. DISTRIBUTION: world-wide. Middle Jurassic, Malton/Yorkshire/England; Cretaceous, Broadstairs, Kent/England.

Palaeanodonta [3] Order Unionida Family Anthracosiidae
CHARACTERISTICS: small fresh-water molluscs of variable shell form; front end recognisable by pronounced lunule, edge smoothly curved from beak to rear, hinge without teeth, hinge line may be straight or curved. PROVENANCE: Permian. DISTRIBUTION: Russia, South Africa, Norway.

Unio [4] Order Unionida Family Unionidae
CHARACTERISTICS: valves of equal side length, covered with horny layer, dorsal edge clearly prolonged, at edge parallel growth rings, closure schizodont, very variable. PROVENANCE: Triassic to Recent. DISTRIBUTION: Europe, Africa. Middle Jurassic, East Yorkshire, East Midlands/England; Cretaceous, Hastings, Kent/England.

Myophoria [5] Order Trigonioida Family Myophoridae
CHARACTERISTICS: a rounded triangle in shape, with diagonal or marginal longitudinal ridge; spaces between occasional ribs smooth, slightly concave; right valve with triangular tooth. PROVENANCE: Lower to Upper Triassic. DISTRIBUTION: Europe, Asia.

Trigonia [6] Order Trigonioida Family Trigoniidae
CHARACTERISTICS: rounded triangle in outline, front edge curved, rear edge prolonged or sharply cut off, beak pronounced, area behind it bears radial ribbing, sides rising to peak with concentric ribs, which end clearly before longitudinal ridge; left valve has divided triangular tooth and two others, right valve has two teeth placed at angle in V-shape. PROVENANCE: Middle Triassic to Upper Cretaceous. DISTRIBUTION: world-wide. Middle Jurassic, Gloucestershire/England; Upper Jurassic, Dorset, Yorkshire/England.

1 *Spondylus spinosus,* Upper Cretaceous, Quedlinburg/Germany. Length: 5.5cm.
2 *Plagiostoma lineata,* Middle Triassic, Muschelkalk, Würzburg/Germany. Height: 11cm.
3 *Palaeanodonta* sp., Permian, Nizhny-Novgorod/Russia. Length: 2cm.
4 *Unio eseri,* Miocene, Oberkirchberg/Germany. Length: 7cm.
5 *Myophoria kefersteini,* index fossil, Upper Triassic, Raibl/Austria. Length: 5cm.
6 *Trigonia latezonatum,* Dogger (Middle Jurassic), Bielefeld/Germany. Length: 11cm.

3 ▽   2 △   4 ▽

5 ▽   6 ▽

BIVALVES
Phylum Mollusca Class Bivalvia

Pseudosmiltha [1] Order Veneroida Family Lucinidae
CHARACTERISTICS: a large, flat, rounded shell with a narrow, upright beak, the surface concentrically ribbed or smooth, usually without teeth; no dorsal area, long narrow muscle attachment scars at front, inside edges smooth. PROVENANCE: Eocene to Miocene. DISTRIBUTION: Europe, Asia.

Megacardita [2] Order Veneroida Family Carditidae
CHARACTERISTICS: thick-shelled, rounded beak sharply inclined to front, right valve has one small front tooth, and at back a long, obliquely angled cardinal tooth, deep radial ribbing. PROVENANCE: Miocene. DISTRIBUTION: Europe.

Pachythaerus [3] Order Veneroida Family Crassatellidae
CHARACTERISTICS: front rounded in outline, but rear edge at different angle, first somewhat elongated and then cut off straight, ribs extend outwards at an angle from this edge, cardinal tooth on left valve stands at acute angle towards front. PROVENANCE: Upper Cretaceous to Upper Eocene. DISTRIBUTION: North America, Europe.

Astarte [4] Order Veneroida Family Astartidae
CHARACTERISTICS: outline rounded with concentric ribbing; beak small, to front a small lunula, to rear longer cardinal area; laterally weakly developed teeth and angled cardinal teeth. PROVENANCE: Lower Jurassic-Recent. DISTRIBUTION: world-wide. Lower-Middle Jurassic, Yorkshire, Dorset; Pliocene, Suffolk/England.

Trachycardium [5] Order Veneroida Family Cardiidae
CHARACTERISTICS: thick, convex shell of oval outline with radial ribbing, which extends into spines or scales; cardinal teeth of unequal size, shell usually greater in height than length. PROVENANCE: Eocene to Recent. DISTRIBUTION: Europe, America.

Mactra [6] Order Veneroida Family Mactridae
CHARACTERISTICS: thin shell of rounded triangular shape; cardinal tooth of right valve of inverted V-shape, both cardinal teeth of left valve approximately V-shaped. PROVENANCE: Eocene to Recent. DISTRIBUTION: world-wide.

Arcupaginola [7] Order Veneroida Family Tellinidae
CHARACTERISTICS: flat shell, rear edge marked by rib extending from beak, two cardinal teeth on both valves. PROVENANCE: Pleistocene to Recent. DISTRIBUTION: Europe, North Africa.

Congeria [8] Order Veneroida Family Dreissenidae
CHARACTERISTICS: smooth thick shell of rounded or rectangular form with depressed beak, hinge without teeth, below the beak a triangular hollow for the front adductor muscle and to the rear of this (below the hinge line) attachment point for the byssus. PROVENANCE: Lower Oligocene to Pliocene. DISTRIBUTION: Europe, Western Asia. (continued over)

1 *Pseudosmiltha gigantea*, Eocene, Paris/France. Length: 9.5cm.
2 *Megacardita jouanetti*, Miocene, Pulgram/Czechoslovakia. Length: 6cm.
3 *Pachythaerus sulcata*, Eocene, Barton/England. Length: 3.5cm.
4 *Astarte herzogii*, Lower Cretaceous, SW Africa. Length: 4cm.
5 *Trachycardium galacticum*, Eocene, Salzburg/Austria. Length: 3.5cm.
6 *Mactra ponderosa*, Miocene, Maryland/USA. Length: 6cm.
7 *Arcupaginola benedini*, Pliocene, Antwerp/Holland. Length: 5cm.
8 *Congeria subglobosa*, Pliocene, Wolfendorf/Austria. Breadth: 8cm.
9 *Corbicula gravesii*, Eocene, Cuise la Motte/France. Length: 4cm.

4 ▽   2 △   5 ▽   3 △   6 ▽

7 ▽   8 ▽   9 ▽

BIVALVES
Phylum Mollusca Class Bivalvia

Circomphalus [1] Order Veneroida Family Veneridae
CHARACTERISTICS: thick shell of triangular to rounded outline with pronounced concentric ribs which extend towards the front from the central rib of the rear edge; in front of the beak small sunken lunule, and behind these the cardinal area teeth of left valve larger than those of right, edge of mantle has small hollowed out section (pallial sinus). PROVENANCE: Miocene to Recent. DISTRIBUTION: Europe, West Africa.

Rzehakia [2] Order Veneroida Family Rzehakiidae
CHARACTERISTICS: a small form with an elongated egg-shaped outline, no side teeth at closure, left valve has 3 cardinal teeth, right 2; front muscle attachment area bounded by rib. PROVENANCE: Middle to Upper Miocene. DISTRIBUTION: Europe.

Megapitaria [3] Order Veneroida Family Veneridae
CHARACTERISTICS: large, rounded to triangular shell, beak inclined to front, exterior smooth or with fine concentric lamellation, lunule slightly raised, 3 cardinal teeth on each valve, sharply angled pallial sinus. PROVENANCE: Pliocene to Recent. DISTRIBUTION: Central America.

Sphaera [4] Order Veneroida Family Fimbriidae
CHARACTERISTICS: thick, bulbous shell, pronounced beak turned inwards; exterior has heavy concentric ribs, front lateral tooth on left valve fused with first cardinal tooth. PROVENANCE: Lower Cretaceous. DISTRIBUTION: Europe.

Borer Mollusc [5] Order Myoida Family Teredinidae
CHARACTERISTICS: cavities produced by fossil "ship worm" and their infilling; usually produced in wood by mechanical movement of both valves.

Pleuromya [6] Order Pholadomyoida Family Pleuromyidae
CHARACTERISTICS: short leading edge noticeably rounded off with less gape than at elongated rear edge, no tooth at closure; a projection below beak of each valve, these interlock with each other, rear edge of right valve overlaps that of left; fine concentric ribbing. PROVENANCE: Triassic to Lower Cretaceous. DISTRIBUTION: world-wide. Lower and Middle Jurassic, Lincolnshire, Yorkshire/England.

Pholadomya [7] Order Pholadomyoida Family Pholadomyidae
CHARACTERISTICS: elongated oval in shape with extended rear edge, uniform valves always gape at rear, ribbed concentrically and/or radially. PROVENANCE: Upper Triassic to Recent. DISTRIBUTION: world-wide. Lower and Middle Jurassic, Dorset, Yorkshire/England.

1 *Circomphalus plicata,* Pliocene, Asti/Italy. Length: 5.5.cm.
2 *Rzehakia gümbeli,* Miocene, Simbach/Germany. Length: 2cm.
3 *Megapitaria squalida,* Pleistocene, Mexico. Length: 7cm.
4 *Sphaera corrugata,* Lower Cretaceous, Atherfield/England. Length: 9cm.
5 *Teredo* sp., Cretaceous, Aachen/Germany. Diam. of cavity: 5mm.
6 *Pleuromya jurassi,* Middle Jurassic, Bayeux/France. Length: 7cm.
7 *Pholadomya murchisonii,* Piezchnow/Poland. Length: 8cm.

Corbicula [9] Family Corbulidae (continued from p. 68)
CHARACTERISTICS: shell round to oval; both valves carry 3 cardinal teeth and long, jagged lateral teeth; no openings in edge of mantle (= no pallial sinus).
PROVENANCE: Upper Cretaceous to Recent. DISTRIBUTION: Europe, Asia, Africa. Hampshire, Isle of Wight/England.

2 △ 4 ▽

3 △ 5 ▽

6 ▽

7 ▽

BIVALVES
Phylum Mollusca Class Bivalvia

Paradiceras [1] Order Hippuritoida Family Diceratidae
CHARACTERISTICS: large form with unequal valves bearing horn-like twisted beaks thick shell; rear cardinal tooth of smaller right valve large and curved in parallel with hinge-line, separated from front cardinal tooth by horseshoe-shaped hollow; cardinal tooth of right also horseshoe-shaped; ligament runs along furrow of beak PROVENANCE: Upper Jurassic. DISTRIBUTION: Europe, Russia.

Plagioptychus [2] Order Hippuritoida Family Caprinidae
CHARACTERISTICS: thick shell, firmly attached to substrate by beak of right valve; right valve has one tooth, usually low in profile and distorted, occasionally conical or even long and straight; left valve convex with beak turned inwards and bearing canals in the middle layer, has a small front tooth and larger rear one; interior space divided by vertical wall. PROVENANCE: Upper Cretaceous. DISTRIBUTION: Europe, North Africa.

Hippurites [3-6] Order Hippuritoida Family Hippuritidae
CHARACTERISTICS: shell of conical or cylindrical shape, left valve forms lid, right valve large and fixed at back; right surface smooth or with longitudinal ribs, usually interspersed by two furrows; double-walled, with a thick outer and thinner inner layer; interior structure includes two small pillars, a hollow for the rear myophore of the left valve and the hollow for the rear closure tooth of this valve, the closure fold, the cardinal tooth, the hollow for the front (closure) tooth of the left valve and the imprint of the front adductor muscle. The exterior of the left valve has pores which open into radial canals within the shell running towards the edge; at the edge there are two openings located above the pillars of the right valve; the lower side of the left valve shows two closure teeth, an attachment projection for the rear adductor muscle, the closure fold and the hollow for the closure tooth of the right valve. The arrangement of the teeth and hollows on both valves as well as that of the ligaments shows that the lid could only be raised a small amount, to provide a supply of water. The two pillars in the right valve are interpreted as original siphons for the intake and expulsion of water, especially in combination with the oval apertures in the left valve. It is assumed that water circulation could take place through the pores and canals without raising the lid. PROVENANCE: Upper Cretaceous. DISTRIBUTION: Europe, North Africa, Asia, North America.

1 *Paradiceras bavaricum,* Upper Jurassic, Kelheim/Germany. Height: 12cm (steinkern preservation)
2 *Plagioptychus aguilloni,* Upper Cretaceous, Brandenberg/Austria. Height: 8cm.
3-6 *Hippurites* sp., Upper Cretaceous, Gosau/Austria.
  3 Right and left valves from the side
  4 Internal view of right valve with its pillars and hollows
  5 Lid (left valve)
  6 Cross-section of right valve, polished.

3 ▽   2 △   4 ▽

5 ▽   6 ▽

BIVALVES
Phylum Mollusca Class Bivalvia

Crassostrea [1-3] Order Pterioida Family Ostreidae
CHARACTERISTICS: valves always greater in height than breadth, usually of triangular form extended towards apex and paddle-like in shape, exterior bears scale-like growth markings, ventral edge often irregular and wavy, not in uniform plane. Left valve more strongly arched and attached to substrate on lower side, small notches or wrinkles on both sides of hinge-line; large muscle imprint close to rear edge and closer to ventral edge than to closure, ligamental attachment area triangular with noticeable growth markings. PROVENANCE: Lower Cretaceous to Recent. DISTRIBUTION: world-wide.

Arctostrea [4] Order Pterioida Family Ostreidae
CHARACTERISTICS: sickle-shaped in outline, both flanks parallel and falling steeply away from central ridge; on the exterior of both valves ribs forking at ends with fine wrinkles along their length, these ribs run out into the sharply delineated folds of the flanks; on the ridges of the folds further folded extensions; edge of shell runs in zig-zag as result of sharp V-forms of the folds at the margin. PROVENANCE: Upper Cretaceous. DISTRIBUTION: world-wide.

Lopha [5/6] Order Pterioida Family Ostreidae
CHARACTERISTICS: thick shell, elongated towards rear; pronounced radial folds which become lower towards front and rear edges, edges of valves interlock in clear zig-zag pattern; attached by left, more strongly arched valve. PROVENANCE: Triassic to Recent. DISTRIBUTION: world-wide. Middle Jurassic, Dorset; Upper Cretaceous, Folkestone/Kent/England.

1-3 *Crassostrea crassissima,* Miocene, Tarragona/Spain. Height: 18cm.
  1 Exterior of right valve
  2 Interior of left valve
  3 Interior of right valve.
4 *Arctostrea colubrina,* Upper Cretaceous, Crimea/Ukraine. Diam. of arc: 15cm.
5/6 *Lopha cristagalli,* Middle Jurassic, Swabian Alps/Germany. Length: 13cm.
  5 View of exterior of right valve
  6 Interior view of left valve showing muscle scar.

1

2 △

3 △

4 ▽

5 ▽

6 ▽

SCAPHOPODS (TUSK-SHELLS)
Phylum Mollusca   Class Scaphopoda
Burrowing molluscs, a few centimetres long, found in shallow water marine deposits. Earliest forms rare; very common in some Palaeogene sands.

Dentalium [1] Family Dentaliidae
CHARACTERISTICS: tooth-shell or tusk-shell are the names given to the tube-like, tapering unchambered calcium carbonate shell of scaphopods. PROVENANCE: Silurian to Recent. DISTRIBUTION: world-wide. Eocene, Hampshire/England.

SNAILS
Phylum Mollusca   Class Gastropoda
Occur in rocks of all ages from Cambrian onwards, in almost all habitats. Especially prominent in Cainozoic marine and fresh-water faunas.

Bellerophon [2] Order Archaeogastropoda   Family Bellerophontidae
CHARACTERISTICS: shell helical in form, with or without umbilicus, each turn of the spiral is broad, having selenizone on back, surface shows growth lines, aperture broad, partly overlapping shell spiral. PROVENANCE: Silurian to Lower Triassic. DISTRIBUTION: world-wide. Lower Carboniferous, North England.

Pleurotomaria [3] Order Archaeogastropoda   Family Pleurotomariidae
CHARACTERISTICS: shell conical or top-like in form, spirals flattened on exterior and ornamented with tubercles; selenizone at centre of spiral. PROVENANCE: Lower Jurassic to Lower Cretaceous. DISTRIBUTION: world-wide. Lower Jurassic, Dorset/England.

Ptychomphalus [4] Order Archaeogastropoda   Family Pleurotomariidae
CHARACTERISTICS: flattish shell, trochoid spiral in form, suture of shell join overlaps the edge of each previous spiral; underside convex, with fine longitudinal striping, umbilicus hidden by callus. PROVENANCE: Lower Jurassic. DISTRIBUTION: Europe.

Ditremaria [5] Order Archaeogastropoda   Family Pleurotomariidae
CHARACTERISTICS: flattish shell, trochoid spiral in form, diameter of spiral chamber increases rapidly; surface has rib-like bulges which are pronounced on interior, below the edge of the spiral is a groove which is clearly visible only on the last turn. PROVENANCE: Middle to Upper Jurassic. DISTRIBUTION: Europe.

Discohelix [6] Order Archaeogastropoda   Family Euomphalidae
CHARACTERISTICS: shell planispiral in form, turns of spiral overlap one another slightly, tubercle-like nodes at edges, cross-section of spiral chamber roughly rounded or squared. PROVENANCE: Middle Triassic to Upper Cretaceous. DISTRIBUTION: world-wide.

1 *Dentalium dentale,* Pleistocene, Rhodes/Greece. Length: 6cm.
2 *Bellerophon umbilicalis,* Lower Carboniferous, Belgium. Diam. 4cm.
3 *Pleurotomaria bessina,* Dogger, Bayeux/France. Width: 6cm.
4 *Ptychomphalus cirroideus,* Lower Jurassic, Upper Franconia/Germany. Diam. 3.5cm.
5 *Ditremaria discoidea,* Upper Jurassic, Kelheim/Germany. Diam. 4.5cm.
6 *Discohelix ferox* (upper right and lower left of plate, among other species), Lower Jurassic, Hochfelin/Germany. Diam. 2.5cm.

1

3 ▽   2 △   4 ▽

5 ▽   6 ▽

SNAILS
Phylum Mollusca   Class Gastropoda

Euomphalus [1] Order Archaeogastropoda Family Euomphalidae
CHARACTERISTICS: shell planispiral, each turn gradually increasing in size, joined only at sides, lower surface with broad umbilicus; the flatter upper surface depressed towards the centre is sharply divided by the central marginal rib from the rounded lower surface. PROVENANCE: Silurian to Middle Permian. DISTRIBUTION: world-wide. Silurian, Dudley/Shropshire/England.

Platyceras [2] Order Archaeogastropoda Family Platyceratidae
CHARACTERISTICS: shell tilts to one side like a pointed cap, initially turns of spirals enclosed within each other, but later ones extend successively; edges of aperture irregularly curved to correspond to the surface of the sea-lilies, to which these snails were parasitically attached by the posterior mouth section. PROVENANCE: Silurian to Middle Permian. DISTRIBUTION: world-wide. Carboniferous Limestone, northern England; Devonian, New York and southwest England.

Cyclonema [3] Order Archaeogastropoda Family Cyclonematidae
CHARACTERISTICS: a thick shell, conical in shape, no umbilicus, turns of spiral divided by deep sutures, ribs on spiral separated by concave furrows, aperture roughly rounded in shape. PROVENANCE: Ordovician to Carboniferous. DISTRIBUTION: Europe, North America. Upper Ordovician, Girvan/Scotland.

Tectus [4] Order Archaeogastropoda Family Trochidae
CHARACTERISTICS: shell a cone of no great height, densely packed spirals are flat and narrow, outer surface marked with deeply notched spiral strips, lower surface with rough granular spiral marking, short spindle with obvious fold. PROVENANCE: Upper Cretaceous to Recent. DISTRIBUTION: Europe.

Pustulifer [5] Order Mesogastropoda Family Coelostylinidae
CHARACTERISTICS: a large conical shell with distinct spiral formation, concave turns of spiral separated by seams and bearing an upper and lower row of nodes, aperture rounded or rectangular. PROVENANCE: Middle Triassic to Middle Jurassic. DISTRIBUTION: Europe.

Dicosmos [6] Order Archaeogastropoda Family Neritopsidae
CHARACTERISTICS: shell without umbilicus, usually smooth, last turn of spiral embraces all others but for small section at very tip, aperture semicircular with an inner lip. PROVENANCE: Middle to Upper Triassic. DISTRIBUTION: Europe, Indonesia.

1 *Euomphalus pentangulatus,* Lower Carboniferous, Kildare/Ireland. Diam. 6cm.
2 *Platyceras aequilateralis,* Lower Carboniferous, Crawfordsville/USA. Diam. 3cm.
3 *Cyclonema soetenichensis,* Middle Devonian, Eifel/Germany. Height: 4.5cm.
4 *Tectus lucasianus,* Oligocene, Vicenza/Italy. Height: 3.5cm.
5 *Pustulifer pustulina,* Middle Triassic, Alps/Germany. Height: 11cm.
6 *Dicosmos maculatus,* Middle Triassic, southern Tirol/Italy. Diam. 6cm.

3 ▽   2 △   4 ▽

5 ▽   6 ▽

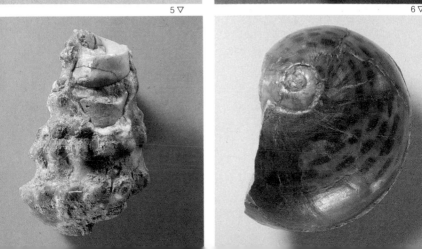

SNAILS
Phylum Mollusca   Class Gastropoda

Trachynerita [1/2] Order Archaeogastropoda   Family Neritidae
CHARACTERISTICS: thick shell of moderate size; a small number of strongly arched whorls separated by channel-like sutures, with one or two rows of nodes below the suture; the spindle has an S-curve, the aperture is basically round but angled at the top. PROVENANCE: Middle Triassic to Middle Jurassic. DISTRIBUTION: Europe, eastern Asia, South America.

Turritella [3] Order Mesogastropoda   Family Turritellidae
CHARACTERISTICS: shell a pronounced elongated cone, with arched whorls separated by deep sutures, outer edge of aperture curved outwards, edge of aperture extended beyond suture, aperture roundish, spindle edge on lower surface broadened. PROVENANCE: Cretaceous to Recent. DISTRIBUTION: Europe, Africa, Japan, Australia. Lower Cretaceous and Eocene, Hampshire and the Isle of Wight/England.

Terebralia [4] Order Mesogastropoda   Family Potamididae
CHARACTERISTICS: shell a somewhat extended cone, spiral whorls have furrows or axial ribs and are separated by depressed sutures, aperture bears teeth; a short, folded spindle at an angle to the main axis, last spiral clearly folded over. PROVENANCE: Upper Cretaceous to Recent. DISTRIBUTION: Europe, East Africa, Iran, Australia.

Glauconia [5] Order Mesogastropoda   Family Thiaridae
CHARACTERISTICS: shell fairly large and conical, whorls divided by sutures marked as little more than lines, 2-4 rows of nodes on each whorl; lower surface flat, but tending also to form cone similarly marked spirally; edge of aperture curves outward. PROVENANCE: Cretaceous. DISTRIBUTION: Europe, North Africa.

Nerinea [6/8] Order Mesogastropoda   Family Nerineidae
CHARACTERISTICS: large shell a long, extended cone, last whorl makes up ¼ of total length, whorls concave, lower surface also a flattened cone, aperture shows a spout-like form and also folds at spindle, under surface and outer surface. PROVENANCE: Lower Jurassic to Upper Cretaceous. DISTRIBUTION: Europe, North Africa, North and South America.

In Plate 8, of *Nerinea buchi*, the whorls, filled with sediment, on both sides of the spindle axis show the narrowing produced by the internal folds of the shell on lateral and upper surfaces, and these, together with the shape and markings of the exterior, are a significant characteristic.

1/2 *Trachynerita depressa,* Triassic, Marmolata/Italy. Diam. 5cm.
3 *Turritella terebralis,* Lower Miocene, France. Length: 8cm.
4 *Terebralia lignitarum,* Miocene, Serbia. Length: 6.5cm.
5 *Glauconia conoidea,* Cretaceous, Brandenberg/Austria. Height: 4cm.
6/7 *Nerinea tuberculosa,* Upper Jurassic, Verdun/France. Height: 8cm.
  6 Lateral view
  7 Longitudinal section.
8 *Nerinea buchi,* longitudinal section, Upper Cretaceous, Tirol/Austria.

3 ▽

2 △ 4 ▽

5 ▽

6 ▽

7 ▽

8 ▽

SNAILS
Phylum Mollusca   Class Gastropoda

Crucibulum [1/2] Order Mesogastropoda Family Calyptreidae
CHARACTERISTICS: shell conical, apex sub-central, radial ribbing, aperture rounded; inner whorl lamellae broad, tending to funnel shape, joined at sides to inner surface of shell. PROVENANCE: Miocene. DISTRIBUTION: Europe, West Indies, North America.

Capulus [3] Order Mesogastropoda Family Capulidae
CHARACTERISTICS: this specimen identified as *Capulus* belongs probably to a Palaeozoic spiral type known as "capuloid", which would now be classified as a platycerate in modern terms (see p.78). PROVENANCE: Silurian to Recent.
DISTRIBUTION: Lochkov/Czechoslovakia; Lower Pliocene, Essex/England.

Helicaulax [4] Order Mesogastropoda Family Aporhaidae
CHARACTERISTICS: medium-sized, spindle-shaped shell; whorls carry axial or radial ribs; spindle short; aperture generally narrow but broadening at centre; rear groove runs almost to tip of shell, where it is bent round; wing of outer edge has broad first stage, is then suddenly narrowed, only to broaden again later, and ends in an extension which is inclined to the rear and forms a sharp point.
PROVENANCE: Cretaceous. DISTRIBUTION: Europe, North America, West Africa.

Pelicaria [5] Order Mesogastriopoda Family Struthiolariidae
CHARACTERISTICS: medium large shell, whorls divided by deep grooves, convex, covered with delicate knotted shapes or marked with spiral stripes and growth lines. Aperture a rounded pentagon with a thickened outer edge rolled back on itself; this edge shows a more prominent centre section between the upper and lower indentation; grooved spindle concave; last whorl always ends in protruding umbilicus. PROVENANCE: Oligocene to Recent. DISTRIBUTION: New Zealand.

Dilatilabrum [6] Order Mesogastriopoda Family Strombidae
CHARACTERISTICS: a large shell with only brief spiral section, whorls short set with spikes at edges, final whorl has a sharp, jagged edge; aperture narrow with short, curved outer lip, and deep indentation; spindle itself is straight but set at an angle to the main axis. PROVENANCE: Eocene. DISTRIBUTION: Europe.

3 ▽   2 △   4 ▽

5 ▽   6 ▽

SNAILS
Phylum Mollusca Class Gastropoda

Barycypraea [1] Order Mesogastropoda Family Cypraeidae
CHARACTERISTICS: shell rounded or angular with largest section in front (or upper) third, central area of rear side marked by swellings and depressions, brownish in colour, aperture has gentle S-shaped curve, last tooth at aperture set apart from others. PROVENANCE: Upper Oligocene to Upper Pliocene. DISTRIBUTION: Middle East, Indonesia.

Natica [2] Order Mesogastropoda Family Naticidae
CHARACTERISTICS: moderately large shell of roughly spherical shape, whorl forms not pronounced, umbilicus fairly broad, ends in a thickening of the spindle which somewhat restricts the umbilicus, semicircular aperture with straight outer edge. PROVENANCE: Palaeocene to Recent. DISTRIBUTION: Europe, North Africa, Japan, Australia. Pliocene, Essex/England.

Volutispina [3] Order Neogastropoda Family Volutidae
CHARACTERISTICS: a large coiled shell forming a cone, whorls in distinctly separated stages with axial ribs, which end in spikes at the shoulder-edges of the turns; growth lines and spiral striping may also give a finely meshed surface sculpturing; final whorl of greater height, as is aperture, which forms a sharp point at the junction of suture and last whorl edge, and also narrows towards the base; the spindle is twisted and carries several clear folds. PROVENANCE: Upper Cretaceous to Recent. DISTRIBUTION: Europe, North Africa, South America. Eocene, Hampshire/England.

Chelyconus [4] Order Neogastropoda Family Conidae
CHARACTERISTICS: a moderately large shell with conical or concave conical whorls, smooth on exterior, edge of final whorl rounded, outer surface has weakly developed spiral threads and marked swelling at siphon, aperture somewhat compressed at top but lower becomes broader with moderate opening, parietal edge shows wide spiral groove. PROVENANCE: Eocene to Recent. DISTRIBUTION: Europe, West Indies, North America.

Trochactaeon [5/6] Order Cephalaspidea Family Actaeonidae
CHARACTERISTICS: a thick shell with a short, conical spine, in outline egg- or spindle-shaped or cylindrical, numerous spiral turns only weakly divided from each other, aperture broader towards base, axis has three spindle folds. PROVENANCE: Lower Cretaceous to Upper Cretaceous. DISTRIBUTION: Europe, North Africa, Asia Minor.

1 *Barycypraea murisimilis,* Miocene, Java. Height: 6cm.
2 *Natica redempta,* Miocene, Milulov/Czechoslovakia. Height: 3cm.
3 *Volutispina* sp., Oligocene, location of find not known. Height: 5cm.
4 *Chelyconus ventricosus,* Miocene, Vöslau/Austria. Height: 4cm.
5/6 *Trochactaeon* sp., Upper Cretaceous, Brandenberg/Austria. Height: 8cm.
  5 Top view of shell
  6 Sectioned specimen.

3 ▽　　2 △　　4 ▽

5 ▽　　6 ▽

SNAILS
Phylum Mollusca   Class Gastropoda

Lymnaea [1] Order Basommatophora Family Lymnaeidae
CHARACTERISTICS: a thin shell of pointed egg shape with a sharp apex, the spiral chambers are convex and increase in size relatively rapidly; the aperture is broad and ovoid, with a sharp outer edge; the spindle is twisted, with the edge folded back on itself. PROVENANCE: Palaeocene to Recent. DISTRIBUTION: Europe, North Africa, Asia. Pleistocene, Red Crag, Ilford/Essex/England.

Planorbarius [2] Order Basommatophora Family Planorbidae
CHARACTERISTICS: size of shell ranges from moderate to large, shaped like thick disc, both upper and lower sides are depressed towards centre and the lower has a deep-set umbilicus; there are up to four rounded whorls gradually increasing in size with clear growth rings and less distinct spiral markings; the aperture is rounded or elliptical in shape and the lower part of its edge protrudes. PROVENANCE: Upper Eocene to Recent. DISTRIBUTION: Europe.

Abida [3] Order Stylommatophora Family Chondrinidae
CHARACTERISTICS: shell is elongated or pointed ovoid in shape and up to 20mm in height; flattish whorls of low profile with growth rings at an angle to axis; the aperture is of rounded egg shape and has an angular lamella, whilst the inner lip has 2-4 lamellae, the spindle edge two and there are several palatal lamellae. PROVENANCE: Middle Eocene to Recent. DISTRIBUTION: Europe.

Archaeozonites [4] Order Stylommatophora Family Zonitidae
CHARACTERISTICS: shell a somewhat rounded cone shape; whorls convex, with oblique growth rings, separated by distinct sutures, an embryonic screw-like thread bears radial ribbing; the roundish aperture is broader than high; with open umbilicus, up to 4.5cm in diameter. PROVENANCE: Middle Eocene to Lower Pliocene. DISTRIBUTION: Europe.

Triptychia [5] Order Stylommatophora Family Clausiliidae
CHARACTERISTICS: shell is of elongated spindle form, with anti-clockwise coiling, the early whorls are smooth, later ones have axial ribbing; the aperture has a point at the top, but is rounded at the bottom, with three lamellae (upper, lower and sub-columellar lamellae). PROVENANCE: Upper Oligocene to Upper Pliocene. DISTRIBUTION: Europe.

Pseudochloritis [6] Order Stylommatophora Family Helicidae
CHARACTERISTICS: a substantial shell with dome-like profile, whorls gradually increasing in size, somewhat distorted S-shaped growth markings and microscopically small dimpling; edge of aperture noticeably folded back on itself, with a parietal callus, umbilicus slightly covered by edge of spindle, aperture somewhat round with extension at top. PROVENANCE: Lower Miocene to Middle Pliocene. DISTRIBUTION: Europe.

1 *Lymnaea dilatata*, Upper Miocene, Mundringen/Germany. Height: 2.7cm.
2 *Planorbarius cornu-mantelli*, Miocene, Württemberg/Germany. Diam. 3.5cm.
3 *Abida antiqua*, Miocene, Steinheim/Germany. Height: 1cm.
4 *Archaeozonites conicus*, Miocene, Neudorf/Czechoslovakia. Height: 2.7cm..
5 *Triptychia grandis*, Miocene, Mörsingen/Germany. Height: 3cm.
6 *Pseudochloritis robusta*, Lower Miocene, Tuchorschitz/Czechoslovakia. Height: 2.2cm.

3 ▽   2 △   4 ▽

5 ▽   6 ▽

CEPHALOPODS
Phylum Mollusca   Class Cephalopoda

Varied, robust fossils, common in marine limestones and shales, especially in Mesozoic of Europe. Rapid evolution of some groups makes them useful in biostratigraphy.

Orthoceras [1] Order Orthocerida Family Orthoceratidae
CHARACTERISTICS: long, straight, cylindrical shells, whose exterior is covered with fine striations; siphuncle located close to centre of chamber or may be slightly towards the ventral side, siphuncular necks are short and straight, connecting ring is cylindrical; the living chamber narrows about halfway along its length and has two ventral and one dorsal furrow. PROVENANCE: Middle Ordovician. DISTRIBUTION: Europe. Silurian, Shropshire/England and North Wales.

Actinoceras [2] Order Actinocerida
This longitudinal section of the shell shows the centrally positioned siphuncle and the chambers subsequently filled with calcium carbonate. In contrast to the siphuncle in *Orthoceras*, here the septal necks are tipped towards the exterior at the point of narrowing and the connecting rings also swell outwards. This structure is reminiscent in appearance of a pearl necklace. During the animal's life the calcareous siphuncle contained a complicated system of vessels used for the exchange of gases between the chambers.

Michelinoceras [3] Order Orthocerida Family Orthoceratidae
CHARACTERISTICS: a type with an elongated, quasi-cylindrical, thin shell. The sutures are straight, perpendicular to axis of shell, the living chamber is very long and the siphuncle is more or less central; in life the siphuncle contains no calcareous deposits but some are found in the chambers of the shell. The connecting rings are cylindrical, the septal necks straight. PROVENANCE: Lower Ordovician to Upper Triassic. DISTRIBUTION: North America, Europe, Asia, Australia. Lower Carboniferous, Somerset, northern England, South Wales.

A newer classification gathers the various orders Orthocerida, Endocerida, Actinocerida, Discosorida, Tarphycerida, Oncocerida and Nautilida all together as Palcephalopoda and members of the group of nautiloids in its broader sense. They are differentiated, on the basis of their common descent from the Silurian cephalopods (bactritids), from the ammonoidea together with the coleoidea (sepias, octopus and squids, belemnites) as a sub-class of Neocephalopoda.

1 Shells of *Orthoceras* sp., Middle Ordovician, Sweden. Length: 7cm.
2 *Actinoceras* sp., Silurian, Kuchelbad near Prague/Czechoslovakia. Length: 10cm.
3 *Michelinoceras* sp., chambers with outer shell removed, Ordovician, Sweden. Length: 6cm.

CEPHALOPODS
Phylum Mollusca Class Cephalopoda

Archiacoceras [1] Order Oncocerida Family Archiacoceratidae
CHARACTERISTICS: shell curved in short horn-like shape, curvature of ventral side distinct; dorsal side concave, with septal furrow, relatively large siphuncle towards edge; internal structure of siphuncle consists of radially arranged lamellae which meet at a central longitudinal axis. PROVENANCE: Middle Devonian. DISTRIBUTION: Europe.

Cyrtendoceras [2] Order Endocerida Family Cyrtendoceratidae
CHARACTERISTICS: a longish shell curved into a horn shape, ventral side convex, dorsal side concave, narrow chambering in close succession; external sculpturing consists of ribs bearing parallel raised welts; inner tube of siphuncle is narrow and cylindrical; the endocone (space between inner and outer tubes) is simple, ring-like in cross-section; siphuncle located towards ventral side. PROVENANCE: Middle Ordovician. DISTRIBUTION: Europe.

Cinctoceras [3] Order Discosorida Family Mandaloceratidae
CHARACTERISTICS: shell tends to short conical shape with only slight curvature, cross-section of aperture T-shaped, outer wall carries numerous fine cross-ribs, dorsal side somewhat flattened, short and broad. PROVENANCE: Middle Silurian. DISTRIBUTION: Europe.

Cameroceras [4] Order Endocerida Family Endoceratidae
CHARACTERISTICS: a long, straight shell circular or oval in cross-section; siphuncle located towards edge, in mature specimens occupying half the width of the chamber; suture simple with a weak ventral lobe. Classification based on fragmentary remains. PROVENANCE: Middle to Upper Ordovician, Middle Silurian. DISTRIBUTION: world-wide.

Lituites [5] Order Tarphycerida Family Lituitidae
CHARACTERISTICS: early chambers rolled into plane spiral, whorls may or may not be joined but are never closely in contact with one another on dorsal side, later chambers do not form part of spiral but lie in a straight line or have very slight curve; in adult specimens the aperture has two projecting lobes (or lappets) at the sides, the siphuncle subcentral to subdorsal. PROVENANCE: Middle Ordovician. DISTRIBUTION: Europe.

1 *Archiacoceras subventricosum*, Middle Devonian, Gerolstein/Germany. Greatest width: 10cm.
2 *Cyrtendoceras imperiale*, Middle Ordovician, Vyscocilka/Czechoslovakia. Greatest width: 4.5cm.
3 *Cinctoceras imperiale*, Middle Silurian, Karlstein/Czechoslovakia. Greatest width: 4.5cm.
4 *Cameroceras incognitum*, Middle Silurian, Reval/Estonia. Greatest width: 4.5cm.
5 *Lutuites lituus*, Öland/Sweden. Length of incomplete specimen: 9cm.

3 ▽   2 △   4 ▽

5 ▽

NAUTILOIDS
Phylum Mollusca Class Cephalopoda Order Nautilida
Exclusively marine floating forms, never abundant as fossils. Some forms very large.

Germanonautilus [1] Family Tainoceratidae
CHARACTERISTICS: shell moderately involute, cross-section of whorl rounded or square, usually broader than tall; rear side divided by shallow depression, outer edges slope towards rear, suture has shallow rear lobe and deeper marginal lobes; siphuncle placed roughly centrally. PROVENANCE: Triassic. DISTRIBUTION: Europe, North America, Asia, Africa.

Temnocheilus [2] Family Koninckioceratidae
CHARACTERISTICS: shell evolute, with broad, perforated umbilicus, cross-section of whorl trapezohedral; broad, flattened rear side, outer edge set with row of somewhat elongated knots. Ventral, dorsal and marginal lobes well developed; siphuncle small, located sub-centrally. PROVENANCE: Lower Carboniferous to Permian. DISTRIBUTION: Europe, North America; Indiana, Ohio.

Aturia [3/4] Family Aturriidae
CHARACTERISTICS: shell with narrow umbilicus, tending to discus shape with rounded rear side, suture with broad, flattened ventral saddle, marginal lobe running to point, broad umbilical lobe; broad dorsal saddle divided by deep, narrow lobe; siphon placed towards edge of dorsal side, with funnel-like siphuncular chambers. PROVENANCE: Palaeocene to Miocene. DISTRIBUTION: world-wide.

Aulaconautilus [5] Family Paracenoceratidae
CHARACTERISTICS: compact shell with narrow umbilicus, sides smooth and convex, sloping towards rear; broad, flattish ventral side with ribs lengthways; sutures with shallow rear lobe, deep, broad marginal lobe and saddle on shoulder of umbilicus. PROVENANCE: Upper Jurassic. DISTRIBUTION: Europe.

Cenoceras [6] Family Nautilidae
CHARACTERISTICS: form of shell disc or sphere-like, shell where preserved shows longitudinal striping and growth lines. Suture has flat rear and lateral lobes, siphuncle usually central, never marginally located. PROVENANCE: Upper Triassic to Middle Jurassic. DISTRIBUTION: world-wide. Middle and Upper Jurassic, Dorset, Midlands and Yorkshire/England.

1 *Germanonautilus bidorsatus,* Upper Muschelkalk, Franconia/Germany. Diam. 12cm.
2 *Temnocheilus biangulatus,* Carboniferous Limestone, Kildare/Ireland. Diam. 6.5cm.
3 *Aturia aturi,* Miocene, Bordeaux/France. Formation of siphonal chambers.
4 *Aturia lingulata,* Eocene, Germany. Diam. 6cm.
5 *Aulaconautilus picteti,* Upper Jurassic, Koniakau/Czechoslovakia. Diam. 9cm.
6 *Cenoceras* sp., Dogger, Wasseralfingen/Germany. Diam. 5cm.

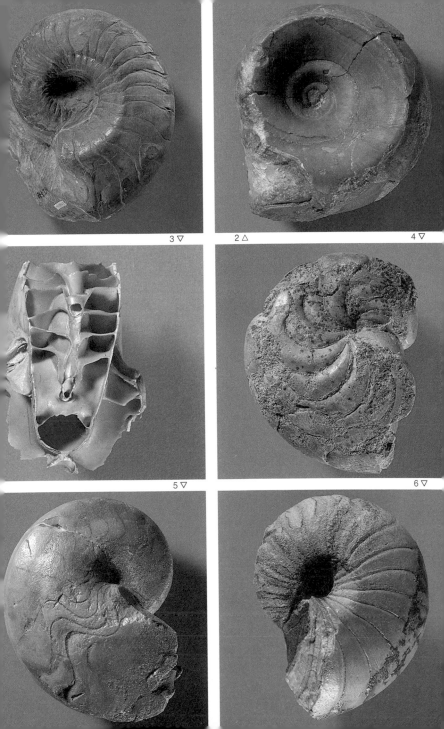

3 ▽   2 △   4 ▽

5 ▽   6 ▽

NAUTILOIDS
Phylum Mollusca Class Cephalopoda Order Nautilida

Cenoceras [1] Family Nautilidae
Description as for Plate 6, page 92.

AMMONOIDS
Phylum Mollusca Class Cephalopoda Order Ammonoidea
Highly varied and locally abundant Palaeozoic and Mesozoic floating creatures; rapidly evolving, they are important in biostratigraphy.

Clymenia [2] Family Clymeniidae
CHARACTERISTICS: shell rolled into flattened disc, spiral gradually increases in height, smooth-surfaced, occasionally with fine growth lines. Chamber cross-section elliptical with rounded or narrow outer side. Siphuncle located on inner edge. Only marginal and inner lobes present. PROVENANCE: Upper Devonian. DISTRIBUTION: Europe, North Africa, Asia. South Devon/England.

Tornoceras [3] Family Tornoceratidae
CHARACTERISTICS: shell of rounded disc or spherical shape with small, dot-like umbilicus; encircling shell periodic depressions as if shell constricted, these laterally concave, but convex on rear side; external lateral lobe juts back at acute angle, inner lateral saddle of simple arch shape extends to edge of whorl. PROVENANCE: Middle Devonian to Upper Devonian. DISTRIBUTION: Europe, North Africa, North and South America. Torbay/Devon/England.

Cheiloceras [4] Family Cheiloceratidae
CHARACTERISTICS: involute shell of compact, rounded disc form, no visible umbilicus, arched growth lines folded back on rear side, suture with flattened, undivided exterior lobes and shallow lateral lobes, some depressions as if shell constricted. PROVENANCE: Upper Devonian. DISTRIBUTION: Europe, North Africa, Western Australia; New York/North America.

Adrianites [5] Family Agathiceratidae
CHARACTERISTICS: shell of rounded disc or spherical shape, with narrow umbilicus, surface marked with fine longitudinal striping intersected by even finer cross stripes at right angles. Goniatitic suture-line (see 1, p.96) with 20-30 lobes showing almost identical structure. PROVENANCE: Middle Permian. DISTRIBUTION: world-wide.

Imitoceras [6] Family Cheiloceratidae
CHARACTERISTICS: shell of spherical or flattened disc shape, with narrow umbilicus, total of eight lobes present, of which only three visible, the narrow external lobe and two lateral lobes at margin, tending towards point. PROVENANCE: Upper Devonian to Lower Carboniferous. DISTRIBUTION: Europe, Asia, North Africa, USA.

1 *Cenoceras semistriatum,* Lower Jurassic, Franconia/Germany. Diam. 18cm.
2 *Clymenia laevigata,* Upper Devonian, Fichtelgebirge/Germany. Diam. 12cm.
3 *Tornoceras intermedium,* Upper Devonian, Morocco. Diam. 3cm.
4 *Cheiloceras verneuli,* Upper Devonian, Nehden/Germany. Diam. 2.5cm.
5 *Adrianites* sp., Permian, Timor Island/Indonesia. Diam. of left specimen 3cm.
6 *Imitoceras rotatorium,* Lower Carboniferous, Indiana/USA. Diam. 8cm.

3 ▽

2 △

4 ▽

5 ▽

6 ▽

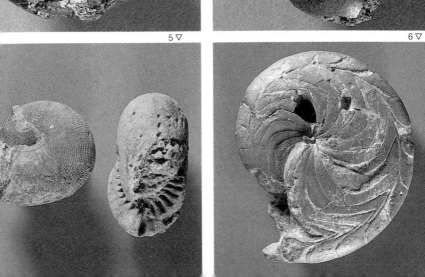

AMMONOIDS
Phylum Mollusca Class Cephalopoda Order Ammonoidea

Goniatites [1] Family Goniatitidae
CHARACTERISTICS: spherical, usually smooth-surfaced shell with small, narrow umbilicus; external lobe clearly divided into two, first lateral saddle of suture-line noticeably angular, total of eight lobes present. PROVENANCE: Lower Carboniferous. DISTRIBUTION: Europe, Asia, North Africa, North America. Carboniferous limestone, northern England.

Pericyclus [2] Family Goniatitidae
CHARACTERISTICS: shell thickened disc in shape with broad umbilicus; ribs unseparated, with gentle curve on sides, concave on outer edge. Constricted depressions along line of back, narrow outer lobe. PROVENANCE: Lower Carboniferous. DISTRIBUTION: Europe, Asia, North Africa. Lancashire/England.

Tropites [3/4] Family Tropitidae
CHARACTERISTICS: evolute shell with deep umbilicus and broadly rounded outer side, which has a sharply defined edge paralleled by two furrows; ribs inclined forward, tending to divide at outer edge; umbilical knots usually present. Ammonitic (i.e highly sinuous) suture. PROVENANCE: Middle Upper Triassic. DISTRIBUTION: Alps, Himalaya, Timor, Alaska, California.

Propinacoceras [5] Family Medlicottiidae
CHARACTERISTICS: flat, disc-like shell, outer edge has median furrow, on both sides of which is row of symmetrical nodes. First lateral saddle short, not sub-divided in vicinity of ventral side, bipartite sub-lobes present. PROVENANCE: Middle Permian. DISTRIBUTION: Europe, Asia, Africa.

Choristoceras [6] Family Choristoceratidae
CHARACTERISTICS: markedly evolute shell, later turns of whorl often detached, chamber cross-section squarish with rounded corners, ribs arranged radially may intersect one of marginal furrows, also decorated with knots at outer edge. Goniatitic to ceratitic suture-line. PROVENANCE: Upper Triassic. DISTRIBUTION: Alps, Timor, California, Nevada.

1 *Goniatites* sp., Lower Carboniferous, Morocco. Diam. 3cm.
2 *Pericyclus bailyi*, Carboniferous limestone, Ireland. Diam. 8cm.
3/4 *Tropites subullatus*, Aussee/Austria. In 3 partially preserved shell, Diam. 6cm, in 4 no shell remains. Diam. 4cm.
5 *Propinacoceras beyrichi*. Permian, Sicily. Diam. 4.5cm.
6 *Choristoceras marshi,* Upper Triassic, Salzburg/Austria. Diam. 4cm.

3 ▽   2 △   4 ▽

5 ▽   6 ▽

AMMONOIDS
Phylum Mollusca Class Cephalopoda Order Ammonoidea

Flexoptychites [1] Family Ptychitidae
CHARACTERISTICS: initial turns of whorl spherical, later disc-shaped; oval shell with abruptly depressed umbilicus; sloping sides convex, with sickle-like ribs weakly developed at outer edge, ammonitic suture. PROVENANCE: Middle Triassic. DISTRIBUTION: Alps, Balkans, Himalaya.

Joannites [2] Family Ptychitidae
CHARACTERISTICS: involute, disc-shaped shell with smooth surface, constrictions at regular intervals; arched suture running forwards, ammonitic, with clearly divided lobes and saddles. PROVENANCE: Middle to Upper Triassic. DISTRIBUTION: Alps, Balkans, Himalaya, Timor.

Juvavites [3] Family Haloritidae
CHARACTERISTICS: involute shell, thickened disc or spherical in shape with rounded rear side, ribs fork at centre-line of side and continue beyond outer edge with or without break, ammonitic suture. PROVENANCE: Middle Upper Triassic. DISTRIBUTION: Alps, Sicily, Himalaya, Timor, Indochina.

Flemingites [4] Family Flemingitidae
CHARACTERISTICS: flattened disc-shaped, evolute shell; ribs finely laminated, but on sides clearly sickle-shaped, becoming convex on rounded outer side. Suture ceratitic (see 6 below). PROVENANCE: Lower Triassic. DISTRIBUTION: Madagascar, Timor, Idaho, Montana.

Otoceras [5] Family Otoceratidae
CHARACTERISTICS: involute shell with convex faces which run to a point at outer edge; because of projecting shoulder of umbilicus and sharp angle of outer edge cross-section of final turns of whorl is triangular; outer edge has distinct central ridge and small ridges on each side; deep umbilicus, ammonitic suture. PROVENANCE: Lower Triassic. DISTRIBUTION: Himalaya, Eastern Greenland, Alaska.

Ceratites [6] Family Ceratitidae
CHARACTERISTICS: evolute shell with strongly pronounced ribs which develop distinct nodes close to outer edge and in middle of sides; ribs seldom extend beyond outer edge; all lobes jagged at base; ceratitic suture-line. PROVENANCE: Triassic. DISTRIBUTION: Germany, Spain, France, Romania, Sardinia.

1 *Flexoptychites flexuosus,* Middle Triassic, Yugoslavia. Diam. 12cm.
2 *Joannites klipsteini,* Middle Triassic, Aussee/Austria. Diam. 9cm.
3 *Juvavites sandbergeri,* Upper Triassic, Timor. Diam. 6cm.
4 *Flemingites densistriatus,* Lower Triassic, Timor. Diam. 4.5cm.
5 *Otoceras woodwardi,* Lower Triassic, Himalaya. Diam. 4cm.
6 *Ceratites nodosus,* Würzburg/Germany. Diam. 10cm.

3 ▽   2 △   4 ▽

5 ▽   6 ▽

AMMONOIDS
Phylum Mollusca   Class Cephalopoda   Order Ammonoidea

Discoceratites [1] Family Ceratitidae
CHARACTERISTICS: shell relatively flat and discus shaped, with narrow umbilicus, chamber cross-section of considerable height, living chamber somewhat less than half of one turn in size. Saddles of simple arched shape, lobes jagged at base, suture-line ceratitic. Surface usually smooth, narrow outer edge rounded or sharply pointed. PROVENANCE: Triassic. DISTRIBUTION: Germany, France.

Holcophylloceras [2] Family Phylloceratidae
CHARACTERISTICS: smooth, involute shell with flattened faces and rounded outer edge; constrictions visible both on steinkern and actual shell have sharply angled edges; fine ribbing on outer half of face, saddles of suture-line usually with two secondary lobes, but with three in specimens from later geological period. PROVENANCE: Middle Jurassic to Lower Cretaceous. DISTRIBUTION: world-wide.

Calliphylloceras [3] Family Phylloceratidae
CHARACTERISTICS: smooth, involute shell with flattened faces and rounded outer edge; regular, curved constrictions on steinkern, showing as protrusions on surface of shell mostly in outer half of whorl; first and second saddles of suture-line usually triple, remainder double. PROVENANCE: Lower Jurassic to Lower Cretaceous. DISTRIBUTION: world-wide.

1 *Discoceratites semipartitus*, Würzburg/Germany. Diam. 30cm.
2 *Hocophylloceras silesiacum,* Upper Jurassic, Stramberg/Czechoslovakia. Diam. 13cm.
3 *Calliphylloceras capitanioi*, Lower Jurassic, Bad Ischl/Austria. Diam. 9cm. Suture marked in Indian ink to show the larger, triple saddle close to the outer edge: the smaller double ones can be traced towards the centre.

1

2 ▽

3 ▽

AMMONOIDS
Phylum Mollusca   Class Cephalopoda   Order Ammonoidea

Macroscaphites [1] Family Macroscaphitidae
CHARACTERISTICS: shell tends to unroll, initial whorls spiral in one plane, living chamber extended in straight line, last section bends back to form hook; simple, radial ribs are intersected by irregular constrictions. PROVENANCE: Lower Cretaceous. DISTRIBUTION: southern and central Europe, North Africa.

Macroscaphites belongs to the heteromorphic ammonites of the Lower Cretaceous

Spiroceras [2] Family Spiroceratidae
CHARACTERISTICS: shell usually in form of open spiral, but contorted or corkscrew-like specimens are also known; simple ribs, less pronounced at inner edge, interrupted by smooth band at outer edge, along which 2 rows of nodes or spikes are located on both sides at the ends of the ribs. PROVENANCE: Middle Jurassic. DISTRIBUTION: Europe, North Africa.

Aegocrioceras [3] Family Ancyloceratidae
CHARACTERISTICS: shell forms spiral, whorls of which not closely in contact; clearly marked ribs of simple form, with spikes on the outer edge of the initial turns. PROVENANCE: Lower Cretaceous. DISTRIBUTION: Northern Europe.

Mariella [4] Family Turrilitidae
CHARACTERISTICS: close whorls of shell form rising spiral, oblique ribs weakly developed, each one bearing a pair of upper and lower (lateral) knots, nodes all equally pronounced and spaced. PROVENANCE: Cretaceous. DISTRIBUTION: Europe, North Africa, Madagascar.

Myloceras [5] Family Labeceratidae
CHARACTERISTICS: initial whorl in open spiral, later more closely in contact, straight living chamber finally bends to end in hook, in cross-section flattening of sides noticeable, outer edge flattened or rounded; ribs may extend beyond outer edge or sometimes end at edge in thorn-like shape. Suture-line with bipartite saddles and tripartite lobes. PROVENANCE: Lower Cretaceous. DISTRIBUTION: East Africa, Madagascar.

1 *Macroscaphites yvani,* Provence/France. Length including living chamber 13cm.
2 *Spiroceras bifurcatum,* Middle Jurassic, Württemberg/Germany. Greatest diameter of chamber 5cm.
3 *Aegocrioceras semicinctum* , Stadthagen/Germany. Diam. 11cm.
4 *Mariella oehlerti,* Cenoman/Mozambique. Diam. of larger whorl 8cm.
5 *Myloceras serotinum,* Lower Cretaceous, Mozambique. Diam. 11cm.

2 ▽

3 ▽

4 ▽

5 ▽

AMMONOIDS
Phylum Mollusca   Class Cephalopoda   Order Ammonoidea

Parapsiloceras [1] Family Psiloceratidae
CHARACTERISTICS: evolute shell with numerous whorls, cross-section of chamber elliptical; inner whorls show fine striping and constrictions, outer whorls are smooth, gradually increasing in height. PROVENANCE: Lower Jurassic. DISTRIBUTION: Europe.

Charmassiceras [2] Family Scholtheimiidae
CHARACTERISTICS: involute shell, whorls rapidly increase in size, chamber cross-section elliptical; pronounced ribs, divided close to inner edge, interrupted at outer edge. PROVENANCE: Lower Jurassic. DISTRIBUTION: Europe.

Arietites [3] Family Arietitidae
CHARACTERISTICS: large, evolute shell, outer edge sharply ridged with accompanying furrows on both sides, simple ribs, cross-section squarish with rounded corners. PROVENANCE: Lower Jurassic. DISTRIBUTION: Europe, Himalaya, South America.

Oxynoticeras [4] Family Oxynoticeratidae
CHARACTERISTICS: flat disc-like shell with sharply ridged outer edge; surface smooth or marked with fine ribs which fork at seam between whorls and are inclined forwards at outer edge. PROVENANCE: Lower Jurassic. DISTRIBUTION: Europe, North Africa.

Crucilobiceras [5] Family Eoderoceratidae
CHARACTERISTICS: evolute shell with dense ribbing extending around the outer edge and interspersed at regular intervals with thicker ribs which end in spikes at the outer edge. Whorls of living chamber flattened laterally. PROVENANCE: Lower Jurassic. DISTRIBUTION: Europe.

Liparoceras [6] Family Liparoceratidae
CHARACTERISTICS: whorls rapidly increase in height, with deep umbilicus, ribbing may be fine or relatively coarse and run around the outer edge, with two rows of nodes towards each margin, joined by ribs. PROVENANCE: Lower Jurassic. DISTRIBUTION: Europe, North Africa, Indonesia.

1 *Parapsiloceras polycyclum,* Lower Jurassic, Wolfgangsee/Austria. Diam. 16cm.
2 *Charmassiceras hercynicum,* Lower Jurassic, Harz/Germany. Diam. 14cm.
3 *Arietites bucklandi,* Lower Jurassic, Württemberg/Germany. Diam. 15cm.
4 *Oxynoticeras oxynotum,* Lower Jurassic, Göppingen/Germany. Diam. 4.5cm.
5 *Crucilobiceras* sp., Lower Jurassic, Dorset/England. Diam. 7cm.
6 *Liparoceras striatum,* Lower Jurassic, Cheltenham/England. Diam. 7cm.

3 ▽

2 △

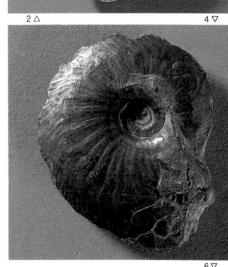

4 ▽

5 ▽

6 ▽

AMMONOIDS
Phylum Mollusca Class Cephalopoda Order Ammonoidea

Dactylioceras [1] Family Dactylioceratidae
CHARACTERISTICS: evolute shell with circular chamber cross-section; ribs slightly inclined forward, running over outer edge, either simple or forking at outer end. PROVENANCE: Lower Jurassic. DISTRIBUTION: Europe, North Africa, Japan.

Harpoceras [2] Family Hildoceratidae
CHARACTERISTICS: flat shell with tall mouth opening, outer edge sharply ridged; sickle-shaped ribs densely packed, increasing in thickness towards outer edge; aperture with lateral lappets or ears. PROVENANCE: Lower Jurassic, index fossil. DISTRIBUTION: Europe, North Africa, Iran, Japan, Indonesia. Lower Jurassic, Yorkshire/England.

Hildoceras [3] Family Hildoceratidae
CHARACTERISTICS: evolute shell of disc shape, outer edge with three ridges (keels); outer ridges separated from centre by furrows; a furrow in the middle of the lateral face cuts across the sickle-shaped ribbing, ribs more pronounced towards outer edge. PROVENANCE: Lower Jurassic. DISTRIBUTION: Europe, North Africa, Anatolia, Caucasus, Iran, Japan. Lower Jurassic, Dorset/England.

Pseudoliceras [4] Family Hildoceratidae
CHARACTERISTICS: flat shell with tall aperture and concave outer edge; sickle-shaped ribs clearly separated. PROVENANCE: Lower Jurassic. DISTRIBUTION: Europe.

Grammoceras [5] Family Hildoceratidae
CHARACTERISTICS: disc-shaped, evolute shell with moderate or broad umbilicus; numerous ribs of slightly curved sickle shape; whole outer edge sharply ridged. PROVENANCE: Lower Jurassic. DISTRIBUTION: Europe, North Africa, Caucasus, Iran.

Leioceras [6] Family Graphoceratidae
CHARACTERISTICS: involute shell of flattened disc shape with ridged outer edge; fine, densely packed ribs of sickle shape. PROVENANCE: Middle Jurassic, index fossil. DISTRIBUTION: Europe, North Africa, Caucasus, Iran.

1 *Dactylioceras tenuicostatum,* Lower Jurassic, Whitby/England. Diam. 9cm.
2 *Harpoceras subplanatum,* Lower Jurassic, Altdorf/Germany. Diam. 9cm.
3 *Hildoceras semicosta,* Lower Jurassic, Le Clapier/France. Diam. 5cm.
4 *Pseudoliceras lythense,* Lower Jurassic, place found unknown. Diam. 6.5cm.
5 *Grammoceras aalense,* Lower Jurassic, Ries/Germany. Diam. 5cm.
6 *Leioceras opalinum,* Middle Jurassic, Salzgitter/Germany. Diam. 7.5cm.

3 ▽   2 △   4 ▽

5 ▽   6 ▽

AMMONOIDS
Phylum Mollusca   Class Cephalopoda   Order Ammonoidea

Hammatoceras [1] Family Hammatoceratidae
CHARACTERISTICS: shell moderately involute, tending to evolute, chamber cross-section triangular, outer edge ridged; ribs on inner edge of face are short, leading to row of knots, from which further ribs extend towards outer edge. PROVENANCE: Lower Jurassic. DISTRIBUTION: Europe, North Africa, north-west Canada, South America.

Glochiceras [2] Family Haploceratidae
CHARACTERISTICS: small, flat shell with narrow umbilicus and usually smooth or slightly ribbed surface, ear-like extensions to aperture. PROVENANCE: Upper Jurassic. DISTRIBUTION: Europe, Russia, Mexico, Japan.

Taramelliceras [3] Family Oppeliidae
CHARACTERISTICS: involute shell with narrow umbilicus and broad, rounded outer edge; ribs have knots at ends and divide at middle of face, row of nodes at outer edge. PROVENANCE: Upper Jurassic. DISTRIBUTION: Europe, Africa.

Stephanoceras [4] Family Stephanoceratidae
CHARACTERISTICS: squat chamber in cross-section. Simple ribs run from inner edge to middle of side, ending in slightly raised nodes, from which they divide and run over outer edge. PROVENANCE: Middle Jurassic. DISTRIBUTION: Europe, North Africa, Iran, Canada, South America.

Macrocephalites [5] Family Macrocephalitidae
CHARACTERISTICS: large, involute forms with deep narrow umbilicus; whorl has sharply pronounced ribs which form close to the umbilicus and run unbroken over the outer edge. PROVENANCE: Middle Jurassic. DISTRIBUTION: Europe, North Africa, Russia, Madagascar, New Guinea.

Cosmoceras [6] Family Cosmoceratidae
CHARACTERISTICS: shell of thickened disc shape with moderately broad umbilicus, outer edge flattened; ribs run to nodes close to umbilicus or in middle of face, then fork and run over outer edge. PROVENANCE: Middle Jurassic. DISTRIBUTION: world-wide.

1 *Hammatoceras subinsigne,* Lower Jurassic, La Verpilliere/France. Diam. 5.5 cm.
2 *Glochiceras lingulatum,* Oxford, Franconia/Germany. Diam. 3cm.
3 *Taramelliceras holbeini,* Upper Jurassic, Swabian Alps/Germany. Diam. 10cm.
4 *Stephanoceras umbilicum,* Middle Jurassic, Württemberg/Germany. Diam. 7cm.
5 *Macrocephalites macrocephalus,* Middle Jurassic, Reutlingen/Germany. Diam. 11cm.
6 *Cosmoceras duncani,* Middle Jurassic, Calvados/France. Diam. 7cm.

3 ▽

2 △

4 ▽

5 ▽

6 ▽

AMMONOIDS
Phylum Mollusca   Class Cephalopoda   Order Ammonoidea

Kepplerites [1] Family Cosmoceratidae
CHARACTERISTICS: moderately evolute shell, inner whorls have furrow or flattened outer edge with small nodes, from which ribs divide, outer edge of later whorls rounded; ribs at inner edge of face at first simple in form, but close to centre become denser, gathered into small groups. PROVENANCE: Middle Jurassic. DISTRIBUTION: Northern hemisphere, Romania, Anatolia.

Lamberticeras [2] Family Cardioceratidae
CHARACTERISTICS: moderately evolute shell, chamber cross-section triangular with rounded corners; S-shaped ribs, some of which fork at middle of face, where additional ribs also begin; outer edge pointed, but with indistinct ridge only. PROVENANCE: Middle Jurassic. DISTRIBUTION: Europe, Russia.

Parkinsonia [3] Family Parkinsoniidae
CHARACTERISTICS: flat disc-shaped shell with broad umbilicus; ribs curve towards front, and towards outer edge are divided into two branches, which are intersected at edge by narrow, smooth band. PROVENANCE: Middle Jurassic. DISTRIBUTION: Europe, North Africa, Caucasus, Iran.

Reineckeites [4] Family Reineckiidae
CHARACTERISTICS: thick disc-shaped shell with broad umbilicus; ribs inclined forward, forking at middle of face, intersected at outer edge by smooth, narrow furrow; aperture with lateral ears. PROVENANCE: Middle Jurassic. DISTRIBUTION: Europe, North Africa.

Indospinctes [5] Family Perisphinctidae
CHARACTERISTICS: medium large to large shell with broad umbilicus; sides of outer whorls flattened in comparison with those of inner whorls; on inner edge of whorls main ribs clearly marked, but towards outer edge they become less distinct and divide into several irregularly arranged secondary ribs; there are irregular constrictions; living chamber less densely ribbed. PROVENANCE: Middle Jurassic. DISTRIBUTION: Europe.

Ataxioceras [6] Family Perisphinctidae
CHARACTERISTICS: flat disc-shaped shell with moderately broad umbilicus, high aperture, irregular constrictions; ribs divided both at inner and at outer edge. PROVENANCE: Upper Jurassic. DISTRIBUTION: Europe, Caucasus, Iran.

1 *Kepplerites keppleri,* Middle Jurassic, Bad Boll/Germany. Diam. 4cm.
2 *Lamberticeras* sp. Middle Jurassic, Calvados/France. Diam. 7cm.
3 *Parkinsonia parkinsoni,* Middle Jurassic, Dorset/England. Diam. 11cm.
4 *Reineckeites eusculptus,* Middle Jurassic, Normandy/France. Diam. 7.5cm.
5 *Indospinctes* sp., Middle Jurassic, Orion/France. Diam. 10cm.
6 *Ataxioceras eudiscinum,* Upper Jurassic, Nusplingen/Germany. Diam. 11cm.

3 ▽

2 △

4 ▽

5 ▽

6 ▽

AMMONOIDS
Phylum Mollusca   Class Cephalopoda   Order Ammonoidea

Parapallasiceras [1] Family Perisphinctidae
CHARACTERISTICS: small shell with broad umbilicus; ribs usually fork from middle of chamber face, but interspersed with simple ribs, ribbing continues over outer edge, which has partial furrow; constrictions and ears present at aperture, living chamber without ribs. PROVENANCE: Upper Jurassic. DISTRIBUTION: Germany.

Virgatosphinctes [2] Family Perisphinctidae
CHARACTERISTICS: large, moderately evolute shell with roundish chamber cross-section; ribs weakly developed, split into two or three branches, occasionally form groups or grow broader with wider separation. PROVENANCE: Upper Jurassic. DISTRIBUTION: Europe, North Africa, Himalaya, Australia, Mexico.

Aspidoceras [3] Family Aspidoceratidae
CHARACTERISTICS: moderately evolute shell with deep, broad umbilicus, chamber cross-section usually square with rounded corners; faces with short, straight ribs, which end at both umbilicus and outer edge in thickened nodes; outer edge rounded, without ridge. PROVENANCE: Middle to Upper Jurassic. DISTRIBUTION: Europe, North Africa, Iran, Caucasus.

Polyptychites [4] Family Olcostephanidae
CHARACTERISTICS: shell with broad or moderately broad umbilicus, squat chamber cross-section; rib-like nodes at umbilicus, dividing into single- or double-branched ribs towards outer edge. PROVENANCE: Lower Cretaceous. DISTRIBUTION: Europe, California, Mexico. Lower Cretaceous, Specton/Yorkshire/England.

Neocomites [5] Family Beriasellidae
CHARACTERISTICS: shell with tall aperture and flattened sides; ribs initially turned in on themselves, but later dividing from slight umbilical nodes or towards outer edge, in juvenile forms ribs end in vicinity of smooth outer edge with thickened portion, but in adult specimens continue over outer edge. PROVENANCE: Lower Cretaceous. DISTRIBUTION: southern and central Europe, North Africa, Madagascar.

Holodiscus [6] Family Holodiscidae
CHARACTERISTICS: small shell with chamber cross-section in broadened circle or square with rounded corners; oblique, rib-like thickenings with nodes on sides or slightly detached run out at an angle to become fine, curved ribs of simple or branching form. PROVENANCE: Lower Cretaceous. DISTRIBUTION: central and southern Europe.

1 *Parapallasiceras praecox,* Upper Jurassic, Neuburg/Germany. Diam. 6cm.
2 *Virgatosphinctes broilii,* Upper Jurassic, Tibet. Diam. 9cm.
3 *Aspidoceras hypselum,* Upper Jurassic, Balingen/Germany. Diam. 11cm.
4 *Polyptychites keyserlingi,* Lower Cretaceous, Bückeburg/Germany. Diam. 7.5cm.
5 *Neocomites weissi,* Lower Cretaceous, Hanover/Germany. Diam. 10.5cm.
6 *Holodiscus fellax,* Lower Cretaceous, Basses Alpes/France. Diam. 5.5cm.

3 ▽   2 △   4 ▽

5 ▽   6 ▽

AMMONOIDS
Phylum Mollusca   Class Cephalopoda   Order Ammonoidea

Leoniceras [1] Family Tissotiidae
CHARACTERISTICS: involute shell shaped like discus, relatively narrow and abruptly depressed umbilicus; no ribbing, smooth-surfaced with exception of some indistinct knots on the outer edge of whorls; inner side of face convex, outer side slightly concave with clear ridging formed by depression around outer edge; initial whorls may show a delicate ribbing. PROVENANCE: Upper Cretaceous. DISTRIBUTION: France, North Africa, Madagascar.

Hoplites [2] Family Hoplitidae
CHARACTERISTICS: moderately evolute shell, chamber cross-section greater in height than width, rectagular to trapezoid; strong ribs, concave at front edge, originate from umbilical node and run to thickenings at outer edge; thickenings are spaced alternately on each side of the outer edge, which has a depressed furrow. PROVENANCE: Lower Cretaceous. DISTRIBUTION: Europe, Mexico; Folkestone, Kent.

Knemiceras [3] Family Engonoceratidae
CHARACTERISTICS: chamber cross-section may be rounded or laterally flattened; faces may be flat or rounded off towards outer edge; ribs pronounced, with relatively wide separation; they originate in thickened umbilical nodes, may branch at the mid-point of the face, end in thicker sections at the outer edge or continue beyond; suture with deeply serrated lobes and less deeply serrated saddles. PROVENANCE: Lower Cretaceous. DISTRIBUTION: southwest Europe, North Africa, Syria, Iran, Ecuador, Peru.

1 *Leoniceras segnis,* Upper Cretaceous, Arabia. Diam. 12cm.
2 *Hoplites dentatus,* Lower Cretaceous, Wassy/France. Diam. 8.5cm.
3 *Knemiceras syriacum,* Lower Cretaceous, Iran. Diam. 7cm.

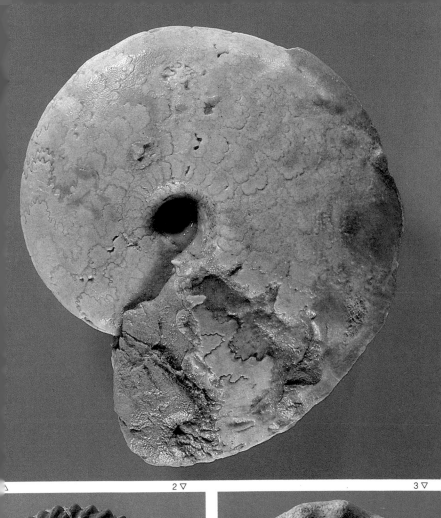

AMMONOIDS
Phylum Mollusca   Class Cephalopoda   Order Ammonoidea

Placenticeras   Family Placenticeratidae

CHARACTERISTICS: in adult stage moderately large to large shell with narrow umbilicus and high, slightly convex flanks, outer edge pointed, but in last whorl often rounded off, surface smooth or with delicate, sickle-shaped marking. In juvenile stages this type has a rounded outer edge with nodes extended lengthways along both sides; similar lengthwise nodes close to the umbilicus are displaced during growth on to the faces. Suture-line ammonitic, both saddles and lobes deeply cleft. PROVENANCE: higher layers of Upper Cretaceous. DISTRIBUTION: France, Germany, Poland, Madagascar, Southern India, Mexico, USA.

Specimens from South Dakota, an area rich in finds, are amongst the most sought after, and expensive, items of the trade because of their excellent state of preservation, the reddish iridescence of their layer of mother of pearl and their intricate suture showing white.

This extremely intricate suture with its deeply cleft saddles and lobes is only to be found in ammonites from the Cretaceous. This genus *Placenticeras* has also provided indications of the likely predators of the original creatures. A specimen from the Cretaceous of South Dakota, with a diameter of 30cm, shows the marks of bites on its shell. On the basis of the depth, size and spacing of these marks it was possible to reconstruct a tooth structure which proved that a sea lizard of the genus *Mosasaurus* had repeatedly tried to hold the ammonite fast with its teeth and to swallow the animal inside. Similarly, chewed up shell remains of the ammonite genus *Scaphites* have been found among the fossilised contents of the stomach of plesiosaurs (sea reptiles with extraordinary swimming ability), discovered in the Upper Cretaceous of North America.

Plancenticeras meeki, Upper Cretaceous, South Dakota/USA. Diam. 25cm. See also Plate p.2.

AMMONOIDS
Phylum Mollusca Class Cephalopoda Order Ammonoidea

Aptychi [1-4]

CHARACTERISTICS: calcitic forms which, when preserved in pairs, are so reminiscent of bivalves that they may be confused with them. They are distinguished and classified according to size, shape, sculpturing and structural detail. They may be preserved singly or in pairs, often occurring in great numbers in alpine rocks or found in association with ammonite shells. In this last case they usually cover the aperture of the shell or are found within the shell itself.

PROVENANCE: Lower Jurassic to Lower Cretaceous.

Finds of ammonite shells, whose living chambers contained aptychi, led to early interpretations of these features as the organically formed hard elements of the animal itself. Since the aptychi in pairs often fit the end of the living chamber so exactly as to close it, they were seen for a long time as the closure element of the ammonite shell. This assumption was reinforced by the occurrence of a head-shield in recent nautilus forms, which closes the mouth of the shell like a lid when the soft body is withdrawn into the shell. It was not until recently that the majority of the aptychi were interpreted as the calcareous component of the ammonite lower jaw, on which is found an inner, horny layer called the anaptychus. This interpretation was supported by the results of systematic searching and fortunate finds of beak-like upper jaws together with aptychus and anaptychus from many genera. Aptychi were then shown to be no more than outer calcareous deposits on the anaptychus. These were already familiar from deposits in the Upper Devonian up to the Upper Jurassic. The limited thickness of the horny layer and the unlikelihood of its preservation accounts for the fact that at first no connection was made between these parts of the body. Various basic types of aptychi correspond to different families of Ammonoidea. Where aptychi occur in great numbers together in the alpine rocks of the Upper Jurassic and Lower Cretaceous, this led to the term "aptychi layers".

1 *Laevaptychus longus,* impression; Upper Jurassic, Treuchtlingen/Germany. Length: 7cm.
2 *Lamellaptychus,* found in haptocerate and phyllocerate ammonites; Upper Jurassic, Solnhofen/Germany. Length: 3.5cm.
3/4 *Laevaptychus,* found in aspidocerate ammonites; Upper Jurassic, Eichstätt/Germany. Length: 8cm.
   3 Steinkern impression
   4 Exterior.

2 △

3 ▽

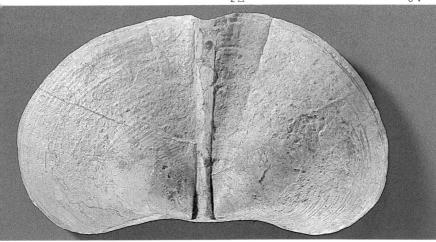

4 ▽

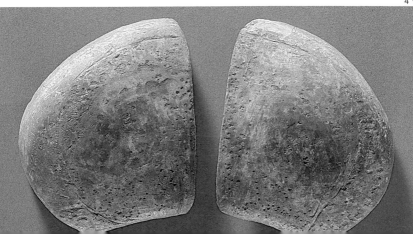

SQUIDS AND CUTTLEFISH
Phylum Mollusca Class Cephalopoda
These rare fossils may accompany the Mesozoic ammonite faunas.

Acanthoteuthis [1/2] Order Teuthoidea
CHARACTERISTICS: Teuthoidea are squid-like, ten-armed, marine cephalopods, in which the rostrum and phragmocone are, in contrast to the belemnites, only vestigially developed. As in *Sepia* they possess a horny, bilaterally symmetrical, internal skeleton which supports the soft body and was partially calcified. This group is known from the Lower Jurassic onwards. Usually only the horny, calcified internal skeleton is preserved, but there have been rarer finds of impressions of the soft body and of fossil ink-sacs.

Aulacoceras [3] Order Aulacocerida
CHARACTERISTICS: in contrast to the belemnites this group of cephalopods did not have a fully developed proostracum. They had a long, tube-like living chamber to accommodate the soft body. The septa are widely separated, the siphon always located on the ventral side, while the rostrum has longitudinal furrows.

BELEMNITES
Phylum Mollusca Class Cephalopoda Order Belemnitida
Common in certain Jurassic and Cretaceous formations, these extinct forms occur with the ammonites.

Hibolites [4]
CHARACTERISTICS: belemnites belong to the group Coleoidea. They are cuttlefish, in which a part of the external shell was replaced by soft tissue and the shell was transposed within the soft body. In the belemnites the hard body-elements, generally forming a straight shell, are divided into rostrum, chambered phragmocone and proostracum. The phragmocone is hollow and shaped like a sharply pointed cone; it is inserted point first into the rostrum, and through it passes the siphon. Classification is based on size, shape and structural detail. Like present-day squids, belemnites probably lived in shoals. In addition to the smaller forms, specimens with a rostrum of over 1.5 metres have been found in the Lower and Middle Jurassic formations. Common in British Jurassic. Commonly only the rostrum is preserved.

1/2 *Acanthoteuthis* sp., Upper Jurassic, Solnhofen/Germany.
  1 Preserved internal skeleton; length 20cm:
  2 Impression of head-section with its tentacles set with small hooks; length 8cm.
3 *Aulacoceras sulcatum,* Upper Triassic, Timor. Length: 12cm.
4 *Hibolites* sp., section through rostrum and chambered phragmocone, Lower Jurassic, Treuchtlingen/Germany. Length: 11cm. See also 4, p.122.

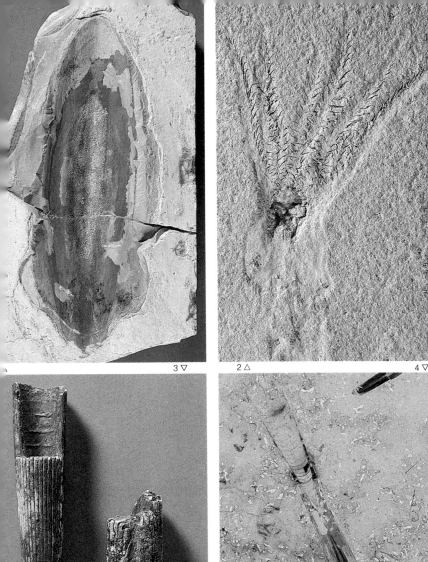

3 ▽ 2 △ 4 ▽

BELEMNITES
Phylum Mollusca   Class Cephalopoda   Order Belmnitida

Dactyloteuthis [1]
CHARACTERISTICS: rostrum flattened front and back, shaped like finger, with indistinct furrow on ventral side; lower end of rostrum always rounded off-centre never pointed. PROVENANCE: Lower-Middle Jurassic. DISTRIBUTION: Europe, Russia. Dorset, Yorkshire/England.

Duvalia [2]
CHARACTERISTICS: rostrum flattened front and back, with dorsal furrow, cross-section wider on ventral side than on dorsal, no ventral furrow; lower end o rostrum either rounded or pointed, point closer to dorsal side. PROVENANCE: Middle Jurassic to Lower Cretaceous. DISTRIBUTION: Europe.

Passaloteuthis [3]
CHARACTERISTICS: rostrum slightly flattened ventrally, shaped like tethering peg o stake, but with relatively blunt point, two short dorsoventral furrows originating a point. PROVENANCE: Lower Jurassic. DISTRIBUTION: Germany, Britain.

Hibolites [4]
CHARACTERISTICS: long, slender forms of moderate or large size, oval in cross-section; rostrum lanceolate, with distinct ventral furrow running along broadest section of rostrum. PROVENANCE: Middle Jurassic to Upper Jurassic. DISTRIBUTION: Europe.

1 *Dactyloteuthis digitalis,* Lower Jurassic, Neumarkt/Germany. Length of both specimens: 6cm.
2 *Duvalia lata,* Cretaceous, Berchtesgaden/Germany. Length: 6.5cm.
3 *Passaloteuthis vulgaris,* Lower Jurassic, Whitby/England. Length of specimen with phragmocone: 10cm.
4 *Hibolites semihastatus,* Upper Middle Jurassic, Bad Boll/Germany. Length: 17cm.

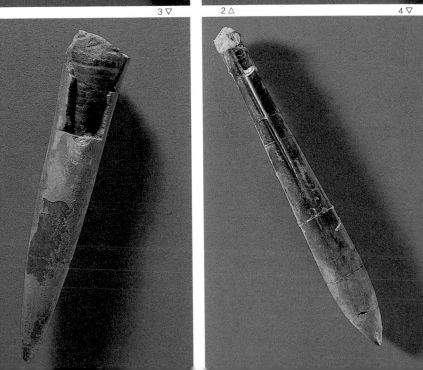

3 ▽   2 △   4 ▽

BELEMNITES
Phylum Mollusca Class Cephalopoda Order Belmnitida

"Belemnite Battlefields" [1]

The belemnoids lived close to the surface in the prehistoric seas, presumably similarly to modern squid in schools or shoals. One theory holds that, since the shells of the living creatures were extremely light (corresponding roughly to the weight of the internal skeleton of *Sepia*) and only increased in weight after fossilisation by mineral transfer, these parts could drift in the sea currents after the animals had died and were carried to form part of the sediments deposited close to shore in shallow waters. Here they were hydrodynamically arranged in regular patterns according to their buoyancy and exterior form. The accumulation of masses of these rostra, or "corpses" as they may be called, in rock beds led to a comparison with a battlefield.

Megateuthis [2]

CHARACTERISTICS: very large forms with rostra up to 1.5 metres in length, divided by recent research into two sub-genera.

Megateuthis: large forms with long epirostrum, furrowed, hollow, with blunt point, although juvenile form short and conical in shape. PROVENANCE: Middle Jurassic. DISTRIBUTION: Germany, France.

Mesoteuthis: smaller forms, without epirostrum, conical rostra slightly flattened at sides, point blunt, 2 dorsolateral furrows. PROVENANCE: Lower Jurassic to Middle Jurassic. DISTRIBUTION: Germany.

1 Belemnite battlefield with specimens of the genera *Dactyloteuthis, Cuspiteuthis* and *Salpingoteuthis;* Lower Jurassic, Salzgitter/Germany. Length of specimens between 4 and 11cm.
2 Top: juvenile form of *Megateuthis*, length 16cm; Centre: holorostrum (rostrum and epirostrum) of *Megateuthis*, inhabited by serpulae (see pp.126, 127), length 50cm; Bottom: phragmocone of *Megateuthis,* length 11cm. All specimens from the Middle Jurassic, Bad Boll/Germany.

2 ▽

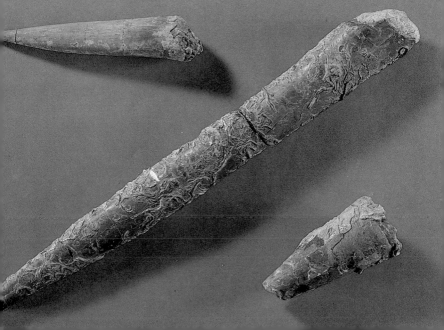

SEGMENTED WORMS
Phylum Annelida

Generally very rare, these fossils are locally abundant in the Mesozoic and Cainozoic rocks.

Annelida [1-5]

The annelids are regarded as the group from which the arthropods originated on the basis of their segmentation, their characteristic nervous sytem and their larval development. The first forms which may be termed annelids because of their segmentation come from the Upper Precambrian Ediacara series of Southern Australia. Other important finds were made in the Middle Cambrian shales of British Columbia (Burgess Pass). As a result of favourable fossilisation condition exceptional examples of bristle worms have been preserved there, which show all the details such as mouth-bristles, antennae and segmented body. From the Cambrian on, specimens have also been found of chitinous or calcified jaw structures (called scolecodonts), occurring as isolated elements. Bristle worms are preserved in the Upper Jurassic limestone of Solnhofen as body impressions still associated with their scolecodonts. These special circumstances of preservation are exceptional and usually it is the calcareous tube-like living chambers of the sedentary polychaetes (Sedentaria, without jaws) which are preserved. This type of shell consists in cross-section of two concentric layers and its surface may be smooth or sculptured, while it may also have a lid to close it. Normally it is attached to a substrate. These living-chamber tubes of the Sedentaria are found from the Cambrian onwards.

1 A rock consisting of living-tubes (serpulids) and so named serpulite, from the Upper Jurassic, Hanover/Germany.
2 Spiral shells, *Rotularia spirula*, from the Eocene, Italy. Diam. up to 2cm.
3 Irregularly formed tube or "shell" of *Serpula grandis,* from the Middle Jurassic, Blumberg/Germany, implanted on oyster shell. Diam. 5cm. Common in British Jurassic.
4 *Serpula grandis,* Middle Jurassic, attached to belemnite rostrum (arrowed).
5 *Ctenoscolex procerus,* fossil polychaete from the lithographic limestone at Solnhofen/Germany, showing clear segmentation.

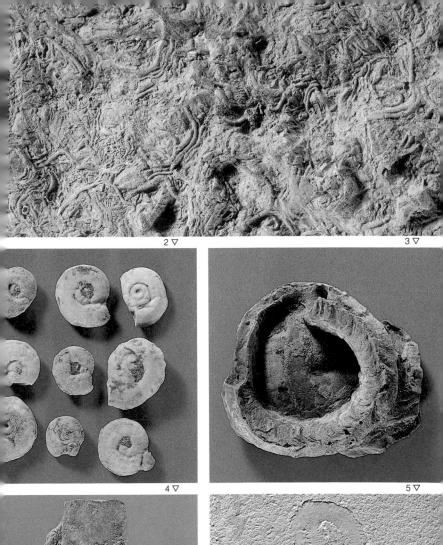

2 ▽   3 ▽

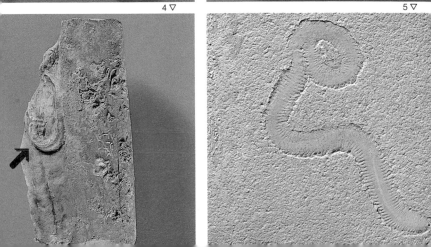

4 ▽   5 ▽

TRILOBITES
Phylum Arthropoda   Class Trilobita
Marine fossils in which cephalon, segments and pygidium usually became separated. A dominant form of palaeozoic benthos.

Agnostus [1] Order Agnostida Family Agnostidae
CHARACTERISTICS: a small trilobite, whose head- and tail-covers are similarly constructed. A median longitudinal furrow is found in front of the bipartite glabella. The axis of the pygidium with its three lobes ends before the rear edge. The thorax consists of only two segments. The pygidium has a short spine on each of the rear edges. There are no eyes or facial sutures. PROVENANCE: Upper Cambrian. DISTRIBUTION: Europe, North America, Siberia, China, Australia. Nuneaton/Warwickshire/England.

These trilobites, reaching a maximum body length of 1cm, are excellent index fossils for the Upper Cambrian. Since they have no eyes, it is assumed that they were burrowing creatures, feeding on microscopic organisms.

Ellipsocephalus [2] Order Redlichiida Family Ellipsocephalidae
CHARACTERISTICS: body outline oval with broadening towards front, glabella also broader towards front but angular and pointed. Cheek corners rounded, 12 segment thorax, small but broad pygidium, narrow eye-ridges, facial suture opisthoparian. PROVENANCE: Lower to Middle Cambrian. DISTRIBUTION: Europe, Morocco.

Paradoxides [3] Order Redlichiida Family Paradoxididae
CHARACTERISTICS: forms of moderate to large size; glabella with 2-4 pairs of side furrows, thickening towards front to become cudgel-shaped and extending to edge of cephalon. Large eyes, facial suture opisthoparian; thorax has 16-21 segments, is deeply furrowed, with spines increasing in length towards rear; small, somewhat elongated pygidium of few segments, with or without spines. Cephalon semi-circular, with long cheek spines. PROVENANCE: Middle Cambrian. DISTRIBUTION: Europe, eastern North America, South America, North Africa, Northern Australia. North and South Wales, Warwickshire/England.

Conocoryphe [4] Order Ptychopariida Family Conocoryphidae
CHARACTERISTICS: body outline oval, cephalon semicircular, with cheek spines; glabella narrows towards front, with 3 pairs of oblique side furrows and also 2 divergent furrows at front edge, which mark the pre-glabellar area; no eyes; thorax of 14 segments, pleura end abruptly, deeply furrowed; pygidium small with 6-8 segments; rear marginal band clearly marked. PROVENANCE: Middle Cambrian. DISTRIBUTION: North America, Europe, Asia.

1 *Agnostus pisiformis,* Upper Cambrian, Sweden. Length of pygidium: 0.5cm.
2 *Ellipsocephalus hoffi,* Middle Cambrian, Jinec/Czechoslovakia. Length: 3cm.
3 *Paradoxides latus,* Middle Cambrian, Jinec/Czechoslovakia. Length: 19cm.
4 *Conocoryphe sulzeri,* Middle Cambrian, Jinec/Czechoslovakia. Length: 5.5cm.

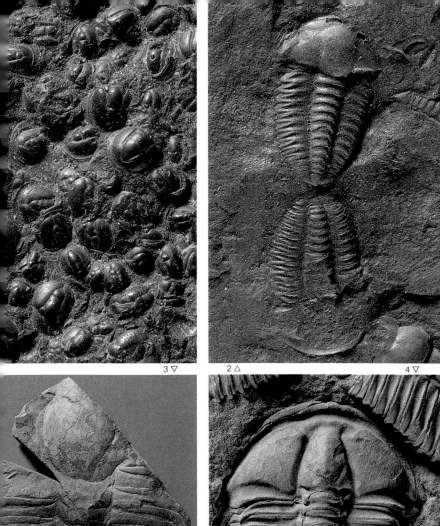

3 ▽   2 △   4 ▽

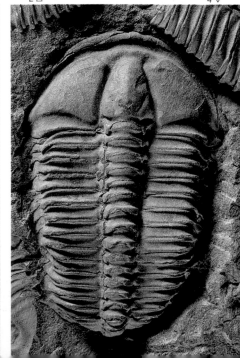

TRILOBITES
Phylum Arthropoda Class Trilobita

Ptychoparia [1] Order Ptychopariida Family Ptychopariidae
CHARACTERISTICS: body outline of elongated egg shape, cephalon semicircular
with clearly marked front edge and cheek spines; glabella narrows slightly toward
front, with 4 side furrows, front of glabella shows shallow welts diverging; thorax
of 12-17 segments; pygidium of 5 segments half as long and broad as cephalon.
PROVENANCE: Middle Cambrian. DISTRIBUTION: Czechoslovakia.

Peltura [2] Order Ptychopariida Family Olenidae
CHARACTERISTICS: cephalon of bean-shaped outline, with rounded cheeks, spines
usually absent or only weakly developed; glabella occupies one third of cephalon,
with 2 or 3 pairs of oblique side furrows, eye-ridges indistinct, facial suture
opisthoparian; thorax of 12 segments, axial section usually broader than pleura,
these with short spines pointing to rear; small pygidium with 2 or 3 pairs of
pleura, edge smooth or set with short spines. PROVENANCE: Upper Cambrian.
DISTRIBUTION: Europe, Eastern Canada. North and South Wales.

Asaphus [3] Order Ptychopariida Family Asaphidae
CHARACTERISTICS: cephalon and pygidium have no clear edge strip/band; glabella
broadens in area on front of eyes, runs centrally up to front edge of cephalon;
cheek corners usually rounded; conical eyes clearly marked, somewhat protruding
thorax normally of 8 segments, axis of pygidium laterally segmented, sides
smooth or weakly segmented. PROVENANCE: Lower Ordovician. DISTRIBUTION:
North-west Europe; North Wales, Welsh Borderland.

Isotelus [4] Order Ptychopariida Family Asaphidae
CHARACTERISTICS: head cover triangular with rounded corners, glabella somewhat
broader in front of protuberant eyes; cheek corners rounded or angular, with
short spines; no clear marginal band in cephalon or pygidium; thorax of 8
segments, axis broader than pleura; broad pygidium axis dies away towards rear,
pleural areas of pygidium not clearly marked or only by fine grooves.
PROVENANCE: Middle to Upper Ordovician. DISTRIBUTION: Northern Europe,
Greenland, Siberia, China. Ohio, Ontario, New York/North America.

1 *Ptychoparia striata,* Middle Cambrian, Jinec/Czechoslovakia. Length: 8cm.
2 *Peltura scarabaeoides,* Andrarum/Norway. Length of cephalon up to 1cm.
3 *Asaphus expansus,* Lower Silurian, St Petersberg/Russia. Width of larger specimen in rolled
   position, shown at top: 4.5cm.
4 Remains of cast skins of *Isotelus* sp., Ordovician, Oklahoma/USA. Length of one specimen: 5cm.

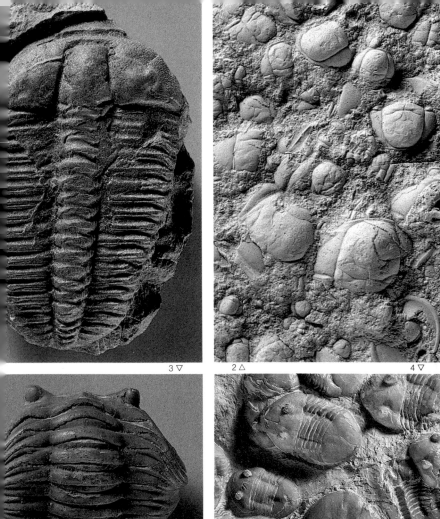

3 ▽

2 △

4 ▽

TRILOBITES
Phylum Arthropoda Class Trilobita

Cornuproetus [1] Order Ptychopariida Family Proetidae
CHARACTERISTICS: cephalon half-oval, with moderately long cheek spines, eyes located on sides of broad glabella base, narrower frontal section of glabella in contact with outer edge of cephalon, which is marked by a furrow, broad occipital ring; facial suture opisthoparian; thorax of 9 or 10 segments, the axis of which narrows slightly towards rear, axis as broad as or broader than the pleura which may have blunt or pointed terminations; surface of pygidium less than half circle, with broad axis with blunt termination, reaching almost to the rear edge, pleural areas of pygidium marked by 4-6 parallel lines which bend towards rear at the margins. PROVENANCE: Silurian to Upper Devonian. DISTRIBUTION: Europe, North Africa. New York, Pennsylvania, Ohio/North America.

Pseudogygites [2] Order Ptychopariida Family Asaphidae
CHARACTERISTICS: cephalon with broad marginal band, cheek corners end in spines; glabella broadens towards front in pear shape, but at centre narrows down over ¾ of length of middle of cephalon, a further ¼ occupied by pre-glabellar area; eyes located at level of narrowest section of glabella; thorax of 8 segments, axis of thorax roughly as wide as pleural elements; pygidium has distinct marginal band, axis clearly pronounced, pleural areas sub-divided by numerous ribs reaching to edge. PROVENANCE: Middle Ordovician. DISTRIBUTION: Canada, Ontario, Newfoundland.

Illaenus [3] Order Ptychopariida Family Illaenidae
CHARACTERISTICS: eyes clearly distinguished from glabella only at rear by furrow, glabella broadens in front of eyes but narrows again close to front edge of cephalon, cephalon half oval, thorax of 10 segments; axis and pleural areas of pygidium marked by fine lines, pygidium as large as or only slightly smaller than cephalon. PROVENANCE: Ordovician. DISTRIBUTION: world-wide. Shropshire, Worcestershire and Herefordshire/England.

Aulacopleura [4] Order Ptychopariida Family Aulacopleuridae
CHARACTERISTICS: cephalon kidney-shaped in outline, with clear marginal band and cheek spines; glabella of same length as pre-glabellar area, half length of cephalon, 2 or 3 pairs of glabellar side furrows, of which rear one runs at angle to occipital furrow; eyes with orbital ridges on both sides at level of front section of glabella; pre-glabellar area and sides of cheeks have grainy surface; thorax of between 12 and 22 segments; pygidium small, with 6 or 7 axial rings. PROVENANCE: Silurian. DISTRIBUTION: Czechoslovakia.

1 *Cornuproetus cornutus,* Middle Devonian, Gerolstein/Germany. Length: 2.4cm.
2 *Pseudogygites latimarginatus,* Middle Ordovician, Canada. Length: 6.5cm.
3 *Illaenus esmarkii,* Lower Silurian, Sweden. Specimens in rolled position. Length of individual shown at top (thorax and pygidium): 5cm.
4 *Aulacopleura koninckii,* Silurian, Motol/Czechoslovakia. Length: 2cm.

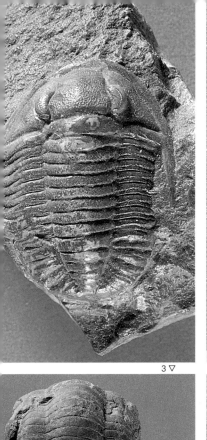
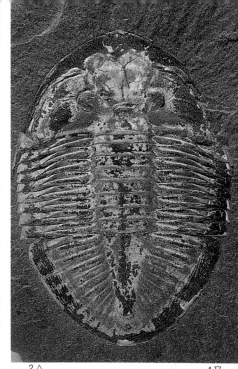

3 ▽   2 △   4 ▽

TRILOBITES
Phylum Arthropoda Class Trilobita

Harpes [1] Order Ptychopariida Family Harpidae
CHARACTERISTICS: high cephalon U-shaped in plan, broad marginal band and pronounced marginal ridge; length of cheek extensions equal to central length of head-shield; glabella has front lobe at edge, which is broader than rear lobe, hollow on inner edge of marginal band broader than that between inner edge and marginal ridge or between inner edge and glabella; eyes on mound, never more than 2 lenses. PROVENANCE: Silurian to Devonian. DISTRIBUTION: Asia, Europe, North Africa, Australia. North Wales.

Encrinurus [2] Order Phacopida Family Encrinuridae
CHARACTERISTICS: three-part cephalon includes glabella and two side areas, which are set with pimples; glabella widens towards front and carries 3 pairs of short side furrows; eyes present, no eye-ridges; thorax of 11 or 12 segments, pleura without furrows, pygidium somewhat elongated triangle with less than 10 pairs of ribs. PROVENANCE: Middle Ordovician to Silurian. DISTRIBUTION: world-wide. Shropshire, Worcestershire, Dudley, South Staffordshire/England.

Onnia [3] Order Ptychopariida Family Trinucleidae
CHARACTERISTICS: three-part cephalon includes glabella and two side areas, also broad marginal band with 4 concentric rows of small hollows; cheek spines reach backwards over pygidium; glabella broadens towards front with 1 pair of side furrows; no eyes or eye-ridges; thorax of 6 segments, ends of pleura curved to rear; pygidium triangular with rounded corners, with shallow pleural furrows. PROVENANCE: Middle to Upper Ordovician. DISTRIBUTION: England, Czechoslovakia, France, Portugal, North Africa, Venezuela. Middle Ordovician, Shropshire/England.

Flexicalymene [4] Order Phacopida Family Calymenidae
CHARACTERISTICS: cephalon semicircular, glabella divided into 3 pairs of lobes which decrease in size towards rear; deep, broad pre-glabellar furrow; eye-mounds level with or slightly in front of second pair of glabellar furrows; thorax of 12 or 13 segments; pygidium has deep pleural furrows. PROVENANCE: Middle to Upper Ordovician. DISTRIBUTION: Europe, North America; southern Scotland.

1 *Harpes macrocephalus*, Middle Devonian, Gerolstein/Germany. Length: 4.5cm.
2 *Encrinurus variolaris*, Upper Silurian, Dudley/England. Length: 4cm.
3 *Onnia ornata*, Ordovician, Tribun/Czechoslovakia. Length: 1.8cm.
4 *Flexicalymene meeki*, Upper Ordovician, Cincinnati/USA. Length: 3.5cm.

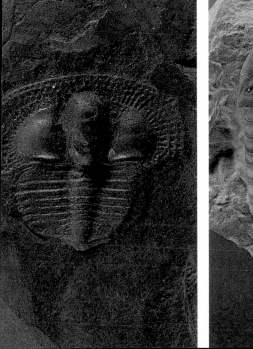

3 ▽　　2 △　　4 ▽

TRILOBITES
Phylum Arthropoda Class Trilobita

Phacops [1] Order Phacopida Family Phacopidae
CHARACTERISTICS: cephalon semicircular, cheek corners rounded, glabella divide
from eyes on sides by angled furrows, base of glabella separated into ring-shape
front section and smaller, roundish side sections by furrows; at front edge of
cephalon glabella sharply cut off or even overhanging edge, set with pimpling;
lower edge of cephalon has continuous furrow, into which pygidium and ends o
pleura engage when animal in rolled position; eyes with numerous lenses; thorax
of 11 segments, pleura furrowed and rounded at ends; pygidium short.
PROVENANCE: Silurian to Devonian. DISTRIBUTION: world-wide.
Torbay/Devon/England; New York/USA.

Dalmanitina [2] Order Phacopida Family Dalmanitidae
CHARACTERISTICS: cephalon with clear marginal band and parallel marginal
furrows running only as far as glabella, cheek spines no more than half length of
cephalon at centre; glabella broadens towards front, with 3 side furrows, of whic
first and second pairs converge towards edge; pygidium pointed at end or
provided with spine, glabella axis has 8-14 rings and 7 or 8 pairs of segmental
ribs. PROVENANCE: Middle to Upper Ordovician. DISTRIBUTION: Europe. Upper
Ordovician, Lake District/England, North Wales, southern Scotland.

Radiaspis [3] Order Odontopleurida Family Odontopleuridae
CHARACTERISTICS: glabella runs to point at front, with 3 pairs of side lobes;
occipital ring with pairs of spines and side lobes; spines also on margin of front
edge of cephalon, also with cheek spines; thorax of 9 segments, pleura furrowed,
with short and long spines alternating; rear of pygidium axis has 2 lobes,
pygidium with 7 pairs of marginal spines. PROVENANCE: Middle Ordovician to
Middle Devonian. DISTRIBUTION: Europe, North America.

Selenopeltis [4] Order Odontopleurida Family Odontopleuridae
CHARACTERISTICS: cephalon broad, rectangular with rounded corners, long cheek
spines; glabella slightly convex, narrowing somewhat towards front, with 3 side
furrows, occipital ring with 1 knot; thorax of 9 segments, axial rings with convex
side lobes at front, pleura with 1 pair of spines, front one rather short and leanin
to side, rear one very much longer and directed backwards; pygidium axis has 3
rings and 1 pair of spines. PROVENANCE: Lower to Upper Ordovician.
DISTRIBUTION: Europe, North Africa.

1 *Phacops rana*, Middle Devonian, Ohio/USA. Length: 5.5cm.
2 *Dalmanitina socialis*, Middle Ordovician, Vesela/Czechoslovakia. Length: 6cm.
3 *Radiaspis barrandii*, Silurian, Dudley/England. Length: 3cm.
4 *Selenopeltis buchii*, Middle Ordovician, Zahorany/Czechoslovakia. Length of body: 5cm.

KING CRABS (HORSESHOE CRABS)
Phylum Arthropoda

A small marine group, as rare as fossils as they are as living creatures today; i.e. only common very locally.

Mesolimulus [1/2] Order Xiphosurida Family Limulidae

CHARACTERISTICS: sword-tails of small or moderate size; body divided into three parts: head-shield (cephalothorax), centre section (opisthosoma) and spike (telson). Head-shield, originated by coalescence of head and 6 body segments, is semicircular in shape, at sides ends somewhat extended to rear, and rear edge roughly parallel to sides of front edge of opisthosoma. Arched central section of cephalothorax is also divided into three with its edge clearly marked to distinguish this from rest of cephalothorax. There are 2 point-like eyes (ocelli) at front end of central ridge, 2 facetted eyes on sides of opisthosoma; opisthosoma has central ridge, with moveable spines on sides, the first pair of which is placed in front third of opisthosoma; tail spike also ridged, equal in length to both front sections of body together; below cephalothorax are the mouth and 6 pairs of legs, of which the first is formed as chelicerae for seizing food, the others used for locomotion; below the opisthosoma 5 pairs of gills. PROVENANCE: Jurassic, Cretaceous(?). DISTRIBUTION: Europe, Asia Minor(?).

All fossil forms of Xiphosurida (sword-tails), to which *Mesolimulus* belongs, were inhabitants of marine shallows, but were also occasional visitors to brackish or fresh waters. Recent types, and presumably also the fossil ones, are burrowers in sand and mud, whose food consists of worms, crustaceans and molluscs. If they need to move rapidly, they turn on to their backs and try to escape the danger by making swimming movements, jerking the body parts relative to one another.

SEA SCORPIONS
Phylum Arthropoda

Fossils very fragmentary for the most part. Most fossils marine, but some forms brackish water or fresh-water dwelling. Predatory.

Eurypterus Sub-class Eurypterida Family Eurypteridae

CHARACTERISTICS: chelicerata up to 40cm in length, of scorpion-like appearance. Body in four parts: 1. prosoma (head-shield) rounded or square, on centre line across prosoma two ocelli, beside these number of larger, unfacetted, kidney-shaped eyes; underside of prosoma has at front pair of tripartite chelicerae (for feeding), to the side of these are 3 pairs of walking legs, whose length increases from front to rear, finally a pair of swimming legs protruding a long way from the prosoma and ending in enlarged terminal sections; 2. pre-abdomen with 7 moveable segments; 3. post-abdomen with 5 moveable segments, of which the last has broad extensions at sides; 4. telson (spike). PROVENANCE: Ordovician to Carboniferous. DISTRIBUTION: Europe, North America, Asia. Upper Silurian, Welsh Borderland, southern Scotland.

Originally marine forms, but later found in brackish and fresh water. Devonian form *Pterygotus*, 1.80m in size, is the largest known arthropod.

1/2 *Mesolimulus walchi,* juvenile form, Upper Jurassic of Solnhofen limestone plates, showing form in two interfacing plates. Length: 10cm.
3 *Eurypterus lacustris,* Silurian, Buffalo/USA. Length from edge of prosoma to fifth segment of post-abdomen 14 cm.

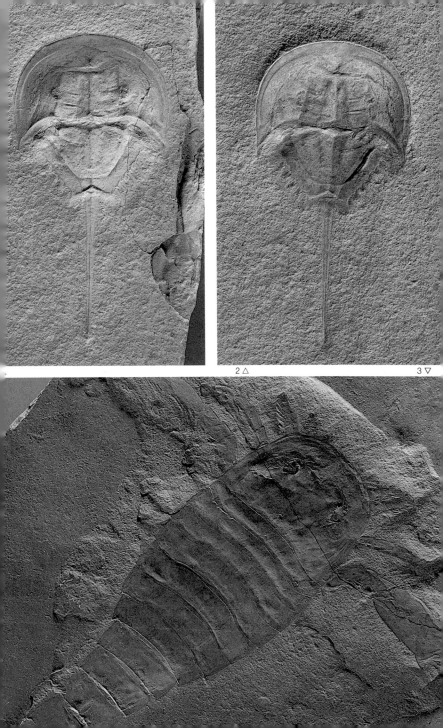

CRUSTACEANS

Phylum Arthropoda   Sub-phylum Crustacea

A widely varying group known from all systems. The ostracodes are useful in local stratigraphy.

Leperditia [1] Class Ostracoda

CHARACTERISTICS: palaeozoic ostracod, bean-like in shape, no sculpturing on either valve; on inner side V-shaped muscle impressions below eye-mounds. DISTRIBUTION: Europe, North America. Upper Silurian, Welsh Borderland.

Cypris [2] Class Ostracoda

For comparison in size, a small, smooth-shelled ostracod.

Balanus [3] Class Cirripedia

CHARACTERISTICS: fossil cirripedes with conical shells consisting of 6 plates and also provided with a two-part lid, which is seldom preserved. PROVENANCE: Eocene to Recent. DISTRIBUTION: world-wide. Sessile, marine forms.

Aeger [4] Class Decapoda

CHARACTERISTICS: fossil shrimp; first 3 pairs of legs transformed into chelicerae, third pair has long appendages; to the rear, on the thorax, 5 pairs of walking legs, the first three pairs of which are developed as pincers; antennae also long-stemmed. PROVENANCE: Triassic to Upper Jurassic. DISTRIBUTION: world-wide.

Lobocarcinus [5] Class Decapoda   Sub-order Brachyura

CHARACTERISTICS: fossil crab; front edge of cephalothorax has jagged extensions not found at rear; surface has bilaterally symmetrical swellings; first pair of walking legs has smoothed, flattened pincers set with thorny growths.

INSECTS

Phylum Arthropoda   Class Insecta

Uncommon as fossils, but of spectacular size in some rocks. Preservation often due to very unusual circumstances.

Hydrophilus [6] Order Coleoptera

CHARACTERISTICS: fossil water-beetle with club-shaped antennae and no swimming legs.

Cymatophlebia [7] Order Odonata

CHARACTERISTICS: fossil dragonfly; shape of wings and wave-like configuration of wing veining, as well as hemispherical shape of head indicate relationship to large modern libellids, Aeshnidae (Mosaic Libellida) or Gomphida (damselflies); the excellent preservation of the most delicate veining of wings is only possible under extremely favourable conditions, as in the limestone ooze of a lagoon.

1 *Leperditia hisingeri,* Upper Silurian, Gotland/Sweden. Length: 2cm.
2 *Cypris* sp., Miocene, Ries/Germany. Length: 2mm.
3 *Balanus ornatus,* Miocene, Ortenburg bei Passau/Germany. Length of single individual: 1cm.
4 *Aeger bronni,* Upper Jurassic, Solnhofen/Germany. Size of rock slab: 20×18cm.
5 *Lobocarcinus paulinowúurttembergensis,* Eocene, Mokattam/Egypt. Width: 9cm.
6 *Hydrophilus* sp., Pleistocene, California/USA. Length: 4cm.
7 *Cymatophlebia longiolata,* Plattenkalke, Upper Jurassic, Eichstätt/Germany. Wingspan: 14cm.

2 △ 4 ▽   3 △   5 ▽

6 ▽   7 ▽

BRYOZOANS
Phylum Bryozoa
Common to abundant in many shallow water limestones. Increasing importance in biostratigraphy.

Bryozoa [1-6]
Bryozoans (moss animals) owe their name to the delicate interlacing tracery of their calcified skeletons. They are sea- or fresh-water colonising animals, equipped with tentacles, used to propel their food towards them. Their chitinous or calcareous tubes of only a few millimetres in diameter are called zooecia, and in these is located the creature's body or polyp. The upper part of the polyp, consisting of the mouth opening surrounded by its wreath of tentacles and the anus located outside, can be withdrawn into the zooecium by muscular action. The sub-phylum of the Ectoprocta is of particular interest to the palaeontologist; here the zooecia are calcified. Within one colony of many of these groups of creatures can be found variously formed individuals, living in the zooecia, which possess different specialised functions. There are the avicularia, armed with pincers for defence, the vibracularia with feelers to sweep in food, and the ovicella which take in the fertilised eggs; there is true division of labour within the colony. Most of the marine bryozoans are encrusting forms, known from the Cambrian onwards. Their classification is based on the structure and shape of the zooecia, the circular or horse-shoe shape of the ridge bearing the tentacles, the presence or absence of a lid for the mouth, the opening of the zooecium and the presence of various polyp-forms. A few representative examples follow.

Class Stenolaemata: marine forms, tentacles round, zooecia tube-like, with opening at end.
Order Cyclostomata [1/2]: with ovicella and vibracularia, zooecium without lid.
Order Trepostomata [4]: type forming layers, solid clumps or fine branches, long zooecia with sub-central opening, walls thickened, transverse partitions in tubes.

Class Gymnolaemata: marine forms, zooecia cylindrical or box-shaped.
Order Cryptostomata [5/6]: zooecia short, square or six-sided.
Order Cheilostomata [3]: zooecia short, usually box-like, arranged in series or in apposition, openings on side, lid present, has specialised polyps, most highly developed group.

1 *Meandropora aurantium,* Pliocene, Sussex/England. Solid structure of zooecia gathered into irregularly ramified bundles, arranged on surface as meandering ridges. Thickness of clump: 3cm.
2 *Terebellaria ramosissima,* Middle Jurassic, Calvados/France. Colony ramifies into branches; zooecia carry, according to zone, either normal or perforated calcareous lids.
3 *Hagenowinella odontophora,* Cretaceous, Maastricht/Holland. Zooecia with horseshoe-shaped ridge on upper part of opening. Magnification × 8.
4 *Subretepora furcata,* Lower Silurian, Estonia. Finely branched fan form, frontal side with zooecia arranged in several rows, rear side without openings, finely striated. Width of largest fan 11cm.
5 *Archimedes reversus,* Carboniferous, Illinois/USA. Screw-like axis, from which fan forms radiate, zooecia have 2 rows of openings. Length: 17cm.
6 *Fenestella* sp., Lower Devonian, Oklahoma/USA. Fan form, zooecia in two rows divided by central ridge. Height of fan: 7cm.

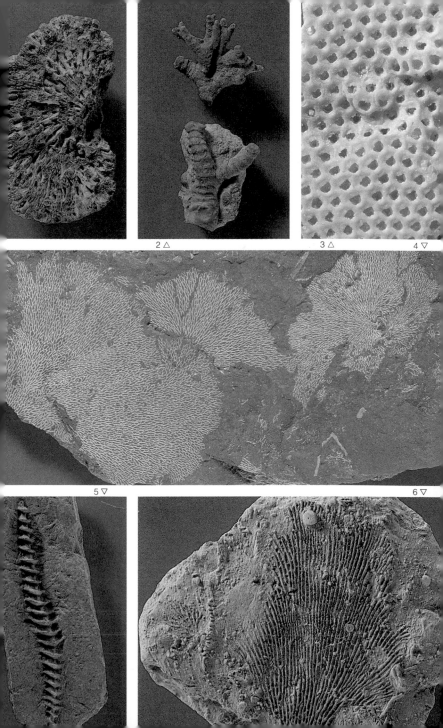

2 △   3 △   4 ▽

5 ▽   6 ▽

BRACHIOPODS (LAMP SHELLS)
Phylum Brachiopoda

Small, robust, exclusively marine bottom-dwelling animals abundant at many levels; immensely varied and stratigraphically of world use in correlation.

Discinisca [1] Class Inarticulata Order Neotremata

CHARACTERISTICS: shell horny, phosphatic, outer surface striped or with fine radial ribs; pedicle valve concave, with a roundish, marginally banded opening for the pedicle; in interior central, triangular septum; both valves have apex at centre. PROVENANCE: Lower Jurassic to Recent. DISTRIBUTION: world-wide.

Lingula [2] Class Inarticulata Order Atremata

CHARACTERISTICS: thin shell, elongated oval in shape, marked only with growth lines; pedicle valve without septum, in brachial valve sometimes a ridge between muscle-scars; shell horny-phosphatic. PROVENANCE: Silurian to Recent. DISTRIBUTION: world-wide.

Enteletes [3] Class Articulata Order Orthida

CHARACTERISTICS: clearly bi-convex form, shell with fine radial striping; deep, zig-zag folds in valve edges; on exterior at centre, a furrow on pedicle-valve and mound on brachial valve; pedicle valve has tooth supports and thick central septum; brachiophore tooth-like. PROVENANCE: Upper Carboniferous to Upper Permian. DISTRIBUTION: world-wide.

Plaesiomys [4/5] Class Articulata Order Orthida

CHARACTERISTICS: brachial-valve more arched than pedicle-valve, ribbing on both radial; pedicle-valve has bipartite muscle scar (diductor), surrounding oval muscle impression (adductor); teeth at hinge-line have short tooth supports, teeth show crooked pits. PROVENANCE: Upper Ordovician. DISTRIBUTION: USA.

Leptagonia [6] Class Articulata Order Strophomenida

CHARACTERISTICS: pedicle valve convex, brachial valve concave with edge turned back, teeth at closure slightly jagged; brachial valve has short central septum with lateral extensions, valve has concentric folds with radial ribbing. PROVENANCE: Lower Carboniferous. DISTRIBUTION: Europe, Asia.

Geyerella [7/8] Class Articulata Order Strophomenida

CHARACTERISTICS: pedicle valve slightly curved, beaker-shaped, attached to substrate; brachial valve convex, both valves with radial ribbing; tooth supports of pedicle valve coalesce with central septum in middle of shell cavity. PROVENANCE: Lower Carboniferous to Permian. DISTRIBUTION: world-wide.

1 *Discinisca papyracea,* Lias, Holzmaden/Germany. Diam. 1cm.
2 *Lingula tenuissima,* Alpine Triassic, Berchtesgaden/Germany. Length: 2cm.
3 *Enteletes lamarcki,* Upper Carboniferous, Russia. Width: 4cm. Top: brachial valve; bottom: pedicle valve.
4/5 *Plaesiomys subquadrata,* Ordovician, Louisville/USA. Width: 3cm.
  4 Exterior of brachial (top) and pedicle valve (bottom)
  5 Interior of brachial (top) and pedicle valve (bottom).
6 *Leptagonia analoga,* Lower Carboniferous, Tournai/Belgium. Width: 5cm. Top: brachial-valve; bottom: pedicle-valve.
7/8 *Geyerella gemmelaroi,* Lower Permian, Sicily. Length/Height: 7cm.
  7 Brachial valve
  8 Pedicle valve, side view.

4 ▽   2 △   5 ▽   3 △   6 ▽

7 ▽   8 ▽

BRACHIOPODS
Phylum Brachiopoda

Buxtonia [1/2] Class Articulata Order Strophomenida
CHARACTERISTICS: moderate to large size, pedicle valve convex with slight central indentation, concave brachial valve with umbo, greatest width at hinge; both valves have rather coarse concentric ribbing and finer radial striping; largish spines developed at ears; bipartite cardinal extension of brachial valve, inclined to rear. PROVENANCE: Upper Devonian to Upper Carboniferous. DISTRIBUTION: world-wide. Yorkshire, Derbyshire, Avon/England.

Pustula [3] Class Articulata Order Strophomenida
CHARACTERISTICS: small to moderately large in size, pedicle valve clearly convex, with shallow central furrow, pronounced whorl, shallow, concentric ribs, usually with 2 rows of spines arranged alternately; brachial valve clearly concave, also with rows of spines; inner side shows tripartite, rod-like cardinal extension, 2 low brachia in form of open loop. PROVENANCE: Lower Carboniferous. DISTRIBUTION: Europe, North Africa. North Staffordshire, Yorkshire/England.

Halorella [4] Class Articulata Order Rhynchonellida
CHARACTERISTICS: rounded, oval form, with radial ribbing, whorl of pedicle valve protrudes, hinge edge straight, aperture for pedicle somewhat elongated, furrows on each valve placed opposite one another, brachial has long extensions as supports for brachia. PROVENANCE: Triassic. DISTRIBUTION: southern Europe, Turkey.

Uncinulus [5] Class Articulata Order Rhynchonellida
CHARACTERISTICS: roundish, bulbous form, pedicle valve with furrow, brachial valve with fold, towards edges radial corrugations end in thin, overlapping spines, at edge of shell right-angled kink made by coincidence of furrow and fold; brachial valve with thick central septum, hinge extension with parallel ridges. PROVENANCE: Lower Devonian to Upper Devonian. DISTRIBUTION: world-wide.

1/2 *Buxtonia scabriculus,* Lower Carboniferous, Lancashire/England. Width: 6cm.
  1 Pedicle valve
  2 Brachial valve.
3 *Pustula pustulosa,* Lower Carboniferous, Tournai/Belgium. Pedicle valve on left, brachial valve on right.
4 *Halorella pedata,* Alpine Triassic, Berchtesgaden/Germany. Width: 3cm.
5 *Uncinulus signatus,* Middle Devonian, Eifel/Germany. Width: 1.8cm.

3 ▽   2 △   4 ▽

5 ▽   6 ▽

BRACHIOPODS
Phylum Brachiopoda

Stenocisma [1] Class Articulata Order Rhynchonellida
CHARACTERISTICS: valves biconvex, pedicle valve with clear central furrow, brachial valve with weak fold, whorl of pedicle valve overlaps that of brachial valve; whorl smooth, ribbing only clearly marked at valve edges, pedicle valve has tooth-supports combined to form platform and a median septum, brachial valve has spoon-shaped platform for attachment of adductor muscles, buttressed by central septum, brachidia in form of two curved extensions. PROVENANCE: Lower Carboniferous in Europe. DISTRIBUTION: world-wide in Permian; Upper Permian, Durham.

Rhynchonella [2] (acid-etched specimen)
In many cases fossils cannot be removed from the rock by mechanical means, but must be washed out by careful treatment with dilute acids. In the specimen shown silicified examples of *Rhynchonella genifer* have been washed out of a rock with low silica content, using dilute hydrochloric acid. Lower Jurassic, Bavarian Alps/Germany.

Torquirhynchia [3/4] Class Articulata Order Rhynchonellida
CHARACTERISTICS: large rhynchonellida, asymmetric in shape, valves convex, radial ribbing, central indentation of pedicle valve divides the valves into 2 unequal halves, displaced relative to one another; beak of pedicle valve slightly protuberant; brachial valve has extensions combined into platform to support arms and long, low central septum; closure teeth of pedicle valve notched. PROVENANCE: Upper Jurassic. DISTRIBUTION: Europe, Russia.

Atrypa [5] Class Articulata Order Spiriferida
CHARACTERISTICS: both valves convex, brachial valve more bulbous, pedicle valve with central indentation pronounced only at edge and small, peaked whorl; pedicle aperture triangular, bordered on both sides by triangular deltidial plates; shell with fine radial ribbing, crossed by concentric growth lines, attachments of arm supports strengthened by simple cross-member, the apices of the hollow brachidia point towards centre but are inclined towards rear. PROVENANCE: Lower Silurian to Upper Devonian. DISTRIBUTION: world-wide. Silurian, Shropshire; Devonian, South Devon/England.

Homoeospira [6] Class Articulata Order Spiriferida
CHARACTERISTICS: small, biconvex valves, elongated oval in outline, sometimes pedicle valve with furrow; radial ribbing, ribs thicker towards edges; beak of pedicle valve bent into plane of brachial valve, closure of brachial valve joined to central septum, which extends to half length of valve, attachments of brachidia have cross-member. PROVENANCE: Upper Silurian. DISTRIBUTION: Europe; North America, Ohio, Ontario, Newfoundland.

1 *Stenocisma pourdoni,* Permian, Timor. Width: 3cm. Top: brachial valve; bottom: pedicle valve.
2 Acid-etched specimen of *Rhynchonella genifer.*
3/4 *Torquirhynchia asteriana,* Upper Jurassic, Kelheim/Germany. Width: 6cm.
  3 Pedicle valve
  4 Brachial valve.
5 *Atrypa reticularis,* Middle Devonian, Eifel/Germany. Width: 2.5cm. Top: pedicle valve, bottom: two brachial valves.
6 *Homoeospira nux,* Upper Silurian, Indiana/USA. Width: 1.5cm. Top: two brachial valves; bottom: pedicle valves.

3 ▽   2 △   4 ▽

5 ▽   6 ▽

BRACHIOPODS
Phylum Brachiopoda

Spirifer [1/2] Class Articulata Order Spiriferida
CHARACTERISTICS: valves biconvex, greatest width at level of hinge line, actual hinge line only marginally less in width; shell with radial folds of simple or forked form or in clusters, these extended to the central indentation of the pedicle valve and the bulge of the brachial valve, this radial folding intersected by concentric growth-lines; pedicle valve has angular interarea and short tooth-supports; no central septum or triangular closure plate for pedicle aperture. PROVENANCE: Carboniferous. DISTRIBUTION: world-wide. Yorkshire, Derbyshire, Somerset/England.

Choristites [3] Class Articulata Order Spiriferida
CHARACTERISTICS: valves biconvex, hinge line almost as long as greatest width, whorl of pedicle valve more clearly folded inwards than that of brachial valve and extending over interarea; trapezoidal, toothed interarea extends below beak; stem aperture triangular, central furrow of pedicle valve and bulge of brachial valve not clearly developed; simple radial surface ribs at bulge and furrow themselves furrowed, radial ribbing intersected by growth-lines; interior of pedicle valve has parallel, closely spaced tooth supports, brachial valve lacks inner part of closure plate between crura; semi-circular in outline from front edge to hinge line. PROVENANCE: Lower Carboniferous to Lower Permian. DISTRIBUTION: world-wide.

Spiriferides Arm Support [4]
Acid treated specimen of brachidium of spiriferid brachiopod, double hollow cone in shape, consisting of spirally wound bands.

Neospirifer [5/6] Class Articulata Order Spiriferida
CHARACTERISTICS: wing-like extensions of corners of hinge line, greatest width at this point, hinge line toothed, interarea of pedicle-valve greater than that of brachial valve, pedicle valve has central furrow, brachial valve bulge; radial fine folds in shell, with concentric growth-lines, pedicle-valve has short tooth-supports, brachial valve lacks centre part of closure plate between crura. PROVENANCE: Upper Carboniferous to Permian. DISTRIBUTION: world-wide.

1/2 *Spirifer striatus,* Lower Carboniferous, Kildare/Ireland. Width: 10cm.
  1 Pedicle valve:
  2 Brachial valve.
3 *Choristites mosquensis,* Lower Carboniferous, Moscow/Russia. Width: 4cm. Top: brachial valve, bottom: pedicle valve.
4 spiriferides arm support – see above
5/6 *Neospirifer condor,* Lower Permian, Bolivia. Width: 8cm.
  5 Brachial valve
  6 Pedicle valve.

3 ▽   2 △   4 ▽

5 ▽   6 ▽

BRACHIOPODS
Phylum Brachiopoda

Terebratula [1-3] Class Articulata Order Terebratulida
It is not only their outer form which is important in identifying brachiopods, but also their hinge characteristics and the form of the brachidia. For this purpose a series of sections through the fossil body is prepared, to give a three-dimensional picture of the essential characteristics. A further difficulty is that in many types fossils represent different stages of maturity, which not only vary in outward form, but also demonstrate changes in interior characteristics such as the brachidia. Outwardly similar forms may possess completely different features in the interior, which would then justify a generic distinction. In some genera (Mesozoic terebratulids) the form of the brachidia has not yet been investigated. Jurassic, East Midlands, Gloucestershire, Dorset/England.

Stringocephalus [4] Class Articulata Order Terebratulida
CHARACTERISTICS: valves biconvex, large beak of pedicle valve extended forwards, pedicle aperture a raised triangle, limited on both sides by deltoidal plates, pedicle valve with large interarea and distinct tooth supports; brachial valve has looped arm support without depression, but with spines inclined to rear; both valves have strong central septum. PROVENANCE: Middle Devonian. DISTRIBUTION: Europe, North America, Asia. Newton Abbot/Devon/England.

Tropeothyris [5/6] Class Articulata Order Terebratulida
CHARACTERISTICS: medium to large form, valves biconvex, as if distended, extended oval in outline, concentric growth-lines; beak of pedicle valve clearly inclined forwards, front closure surface has central indentation, terebratulid brachidium. PROVENANCE: Upper Jurassic. DISTRIBUTION: Europe.

1-3 Terebratulids from the Upper Jurassic of Saal bei Kelheim/Germany, showing preserved brachidia.
  1 Clearly shows the brachidium with its loop and depression
  2 Calcite crystals have subsequently been deposited on the brachidium.
4 *Stringocephalus burtini,* index fossil of Middle Devonian, Paffrath/Germany. Length of largest specimen: 9cm. Left: exterior of brachial valve, centre: interior of pedicle valve, right: side view.
5/6 *Tropeothyris isomorpha,* Upper Jurassic, Koniakau/Czechoslovakia.
  5 Exterior of brachial valve
  6 Side view.

BRACHIOPODS
Phylum Brachiopoda

Ornithella [1] Class Articulata Order Terebratulida
CHARACTERISTICS: shell smooth except for growth-lines, in outline extended oval or pentagonal with rounded corners, closure surface of valves planar, beak of pedicle valve slightly bent to front or vertical to closure surface, buttresses on both sides of beak run to lower edge of stem aperture, deltoidal plates fused together; brachial-valve septum up to half length of valve, on both sides longish oval muscle scars set slightly obliquely, brachidium long loop shape bending to rear, brachial valve tooth supports short and curved. PROVENANCE: Middle to Upper Jurassic. DISTRIBUTION: Europe.

Cererithyris [2] Class Articulata Order Terebratulida
CHARACTERISTICS: shell smooth except for growth-lines, valves biconvex, in outline broadened oval or pentagonal with rounded corners, front commissure straight or with 1 or 2 waves; beak of pedicle valve short, pedicle aperture with clearly defined edge, buttresses of beak fuse below aperture, brachidium half as long as valve. PROVENANCE: Middle to Upper Jurassic. DISTRIBUTION: Europe.

Rhaetina [3] Class Articulata Order Terebratulida
CHARACTERISTICS: shell smooth except for growth-lines, valves biconvex, front commissure has 2 folds, pedicle valve beak almost upright, buttresses fuse below stem aperture; brachial valve septum minimal or lacking, brachidium forms simple loop in younger specimens, but has depression in older ones; no tooth supports in pedicle valve. PROVENANCE: Upper Triassic. DISTRIBUTION: Europe.

Flabellothyris [4] Class Articulata Order Terebratulida
CHARACTERISTICS: a small form with biconvex valves, indistinct central depression of brachial valve surface, bulge on pedicle valve; up to 16 radial ribs with fine folds, whorl buttresses on pedicle valve fuse above pedicle aperture, triangular deltoidal plates separate or fused, large pedicle aperture with collar; short tooth supports. PROVENANCE: Middle to Upper Jurassic. DISTRIBUTION: Europe.

Pygope [5] Class Articulata Order Terebratulida
CHARACTERISTICS: smooth shell, pedicle valve has central bulge, brachial valve with furrow, in younger forms central furrow gives 2 almost distinct halves, older specimens show sides almost or completely joined, leaving central opening; commissure at sides has S-shaped curves, brachidium short, no tooth supports. PROVENANCE: Upper Jurassic to Lower Cretaceous. DISTRIBUTION: Europe.

1 *Ornithella ornithocephala,* Upper Jurassic, Wiltshire/England. Length up to 3.5cm.
2 *Cererithyris intermedia,* Upper Jurassic, Wiltshire/England. Length 4cm, width 3.5cm.
3 *Rhaetina gregaria,* Upper Triassic, Wössen/Germany. Length: 3.5cm.
4 *Flabellothyris petersi,* Upper Jurassic, Stramberg/Czechoslovakia. Width: 2cm.
5 *Pygope janitor,* Upper Jurassic, Stramberg/Czechoslovakia. Forms at different stages of maturity up to 5cm broad.

3 ▽

2 △

4 ▽

5 ▽

ECHINODERMS
Phylum Echinodermata
Marine calcareous fossils, commonly found in brachiopod/coral assemblages.

Cystoidea [1-3] Class Cystoidea
Cystoidea are primitive, stemmed echinoderms found mainly in the Palaeozoic. The body wall or theca consists of a number of four- to six-cornered or polygonal plates, usually bearing fine sculpturing. At the top of the spherical body is located the mouth aperture, also covered by small platelets, as well as the ambulacral furrows, the anus, the genital aperture and a pore-bearing "sieve plate". The thecal plates originally consisted of 3 layers, but after fossilization usually only the middle layer, penetrated by its pores, is preserved. Classification is based on the number and form of the thecal plates and the arrangement of the types of pore. In Plate 1, *Caryocrinites ornatus*, the dimple at the top marks the attachment of the stem. In this species ribs also extend from the centre of the plates and the pores, which to the naked eye appear simply as ornamentation, are arranged parallel to these.

The genera *Caryocrinites* and *Orocystites* (Plate 2) belong to the order Rhombifera, in which the pores are arranged in rows in romboid formation. In *Orocystites helmhackeri* (Plate 2) the ribs originate at the centres of the plates and extend to the edges; the intervening areas are filled by the symmetrically arranged pores.

In Plate 3, *Sphaeronites pomum*, the roundish theca consists of over 100 plates, which are covered by pores arranged in pairs and often surrounded by a low circular barrier. The mouth and anus are close together, divided by a low wall; there are short ambulacral furrows, but no stem; the theca are directly attached to the substrate.

Deltoblastus [4] Class Blastoidea
CHARACTERISTICS: lower side of bud-like cup or calix always concave, form symmetrically divided into five parts, consists of 14 plates, 3 basal plates on under-side, 5 forked radials and 5 deltoid plates extending to tip of calix, this bears 10 small openings around the mouth aperture, and the anus; ambulacrals depressed with occasional pores at edge. PROVENANCE: Permian. DISTRIBUTION: Indonesia.

SEA LILIES
Phylum Echinodermata Class Crinoidea
Columnals abundant, rock-forming in many parts of the Palaeozoic. Complete calices rare.

Woodocrinus [5] Sub-class Inadunata Order Diplobathrida
CHARACTERISTICS: low calix with broadly extended crown, 5 wedge-shaped infrabasals, 5 large, six-sided basals, 5 five-sided radials with straight, short cropped jointed surface; first brachial five-sided, edges chamfered at top for attachment of branching arms, these branch further at the 6th to 8th brachials, brachials usually very broad and short, 20 arms.

1 *Caryocrinites ornatus,* Silurian, New York/USA.
2 *Orocystites helmhackeri,* Lower Silurian, Czechoslavakia. Steinkern.
3 *Sphaeronites pomum,* Lower Ordovician, Kinnekulla/Sweden.
4 *Deltoblastus* sp., Permian, Timor/Indonesia.
5 *Woodocrinus macrodactylus,* Lower Carboniferous, Yorkshire/England. Height: 5cm.

3 ▽   2 △   4 ▽

5 ▽

SEA LILIES
Phylum Echinodermata   Class Crinoidea

Eretmocrinus [1] Sub-class Camerata Order Monobathrida
CHARACTERISTICS: calix (lower part of cup) low and broad, 3 basals forming distinct brim, above this 5 radials and the anal plate broad, hexagonal; above primary anal plates 4-7 further anal plates, not in contact with upper cover of cup; between 2 neighbouring arm-rays 4 interbrachials, also between the attached arms 1-3 additional plates; cover of calix asymmetrical, peaked at front, flattened at rear; 12-20 free arms, 2 arm-rays with more than 4 arms; upper parts of arms broadened, no pinnules attached. PROVENANCE: Lower Mississippian (Lower Carboniferous). DISTRIBUTION: Ohio, Illinois, Indiana, Pennsylvania/USA.

Marsupiocrinus [2] Sub-class Camerata Order Monobathrida
CHARACTERISTICS: lower part of cup low, bowl-like, 3 unequal basal plates, 5 large, broad radial plates; at centre above each radial a solid triangular plate from which branching begins, these flanked on each side by 2 further similar plates also in contact with radial; large, long interbrachials between arm-rays; cup cover with numerous plates, flat or low cone in shape, 4 twin-row arms per ray (20 arms); stem has both broad and narrow elements. PROVENANCE: Middle Silurian to Lower Devonian. DISTRIBUTION: Europe, North America; Ontario, Wisconsin.

Aesiocrinus [3] Sub-class Inadunata
CHARACTERISTICS: low, bowl-shaped cup with slightly hollow underside, which is formed by the 5 infrabasals, 5 basals; broad anal plate between radials; anal tube large and long, covered in hexagonal, pimpled plates with slit-like pores. Anus at end of tube; 10 long arms set with pinnules. PROVENANCE: Lower Carboniferous, Middle Carboniferous. DISTRIBUTION: Indiana, Illinois/USA.

1 *Eretmocrinus magnificus*, Lower Mississippian (Lower Carboniferous), Crawfordsville/USA. Top: cup with arms attached; height: 8cm; bottom: upper and lower parts of cup without arms, showing erect anal tube.
2 *Marsupiocrinus coelatus*, Middle Silurian, Trividale/England. Height: 8cm.
3 *Aesiocrinus magnificus*, Lower Carboniferous, Kansas City/USA. The long tube inclined towards the top left is the anal tube. Length: 6cm.

2 △   3 ▽

SEA LILIES
Phylum Echinodermata Class Crinoidea

Encrinus [1] Sub-class Inadunata Order Cladida
CHARACTERISTICS: low, bowl-shaped theca formed of 15 plates altogether; 5 submerged infrabasals hidden below stalk, above these 5 basals and 5 trapezoid radials, these last based in the extensions above the infrabasals, with jointed surface chopped short at top; either 2 or 4 arms per ray, total of 10 or 20 arms; stalk elements in upper part have thick intermediate discs, the end of the stalk has thickened disc for attachment to substrate. PROVENANCE: Middle Triassic. DISTRIBUTION: Europe.

Pellecrinus [2] Sub-class Inadunata Order Cladida
CHARACTERISTICS: low, bowl-shaped cup, 5 small infrabasals, 5 broad, pentagonal basals, pointed towards top, also 2 anal plates, smaller of which rectangular, 5 radials broadening at top with semicircular joint face for arm attachment; arms divide into 2 equal parts at third joint and have extensions set alternately after every second joint and these also branch in similar fashion; cup cover in panel-like plates, with short anal tube. PROVENANCE: Lower Pennsylvanian (Upper Carboniferous). DISTRIBUTION: Indiana, Iowa/USA.

Crinoid Limestones
Rocks of which the bulk is made up of the remains of fossil sea lilies are called crinoidal limestones. Examples of these are known from the Muschelkalk in Germany (also called trochitic limestones), from the Silurian in Sweden and from the Devonian in Morocco. In North America these limestones occur in the Mississippi basin and the Front Ranges of the Canadian Rockies in vast quantities.

1 *Encrinus carnalli,* Lower Middle Triassic, Freyburg/Germany. Height of cup: 7cm.
2 *Pellecrinus lyoni,* Lower Pennsylvanian (Upper Carboniferous), Crawfordsville/USA. Height of cup: 10cm.
3 Crinoid Limestone, Devonian, Morocco. The surface exposed by weathering shows the stalks and one cup of *Scyphocrinus.*

2 △

3 ▽

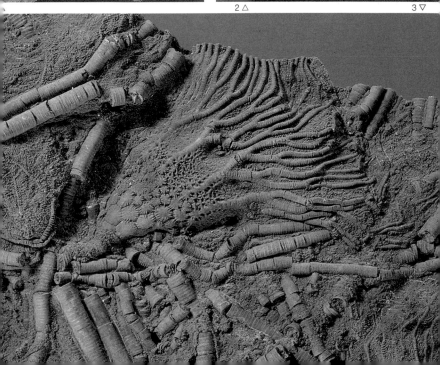

SEA LILIES
Phylum Echinodermata   Class Crinoidea

Dadocrinus [1] Sub-class Articulata   Order Millericrinida
CHARACTERISTICS: delicate cup of conical shape, infrabasals covered by union of stalk; tall, pentagonal basals, broad radials; arms branch at second joint, have extensions; stalk has thick attachment disc, stalk elements pentagonal close to cup base, elsewhere round. PROVENANCE: Middle Triassic. DISTRIBUTION: central and southern Europe.

Potamocrinus [2] Sub-class Articulata   Order Millericrinida
CHARACTERISTICS: cup with thick walls, flattened sphere in shape, no infrabasals, 5 broad basals, 5 radials with strong joints for arm attachment, arms branch at second joint, 10 arms. PROVENANCE: Jurassic. DISTRIBUTION: Europe.

Pterocoma [3] Sub-class Articulata   Order Comatulida
CHARACTERISTICS: fossil featherstar with 10 arms, lower side set with cirri for seizing and holding. PROVENANCE: Upper Jurassic to Upper Cretaceous. DISTRIBUTION: Europe, Lebanon.

Saccocoma [4] Sub-class Articulata   Order Roveacrinida
CHARACTERISTICS: free-swimming, stalkless sea lily; small body with 5 arms branching close to radials. Most frequent fossil of Solnhofen Limestone. PROVENANCE: Upper Jurassic to Lower Cretaceous. DISTRIBUTION: Europe, North Africa.

Solanocrinites [5] Sub-class Articulata   Order Comatulida
CHARACTERISTICS: free-swimming, stalkless sea lily; theca consists of centrodorsal (under-plate), 5 basals and 5 radials; 5 arms originating close to base. PROVENANCE: Middle to Upper Jurassic. DISTRIBUTION: Europe.

BRITTLE STARS
Phylum Echinodermata   Class Stelleroidea
Very rare in most systems but certain formations have yielded many complete specimens.

Ophiura [6] Order Ophiurida
CHARACTERISTICS: fossil brittle stars, classified by detailed structure of disc-like body and arms. Representatives of this still extant family of Ophiuridae are found from Lower Carboniferous on.

1 *Dadocrinus gracilis,* Middle Triassic, Gogolin/Poland. Cup diameter: 1cm.
2 *Potamocrinus mespiliformis,* Upper Jurassic, Sontheim/Germany. Width of cup capsule: 4cm.
3 *Pterocoma pinnata,* Upper Jurassic, Zandt/Germany. Length of arm: 15cm.
4 *Saccocoma pectinata,* Upper Jurassic, Solnhofen/Germany. Diam. 6cm.
5 *Solanocrinites imperialis,* Upper Jurassic, Kelheim/Germany. Diam. 10cm.
6 *Opiura egertoni,* Upper Lias, Lower Jurassic, Dorset/England. Diam. 8cm.

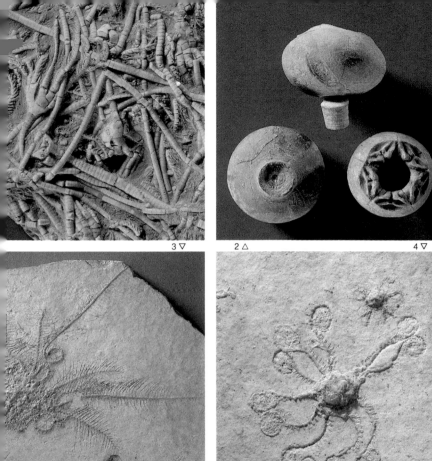

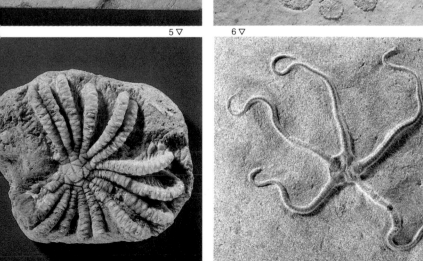

3 ▽   2 △   4 ▽

5 ▽   6 ▽

SEA URCHINS
Phylum Echinodermata Class Echinoidea
Compact bottom-dwelling types common in certain Mesozoic marine shallow water limestones and sandstones. Some species useful in biostratigraphy.

Archaeocidaris [1] Order Cidaroidea
CHARACTERISTICS: test is flattened sphere in shape, inter-ambulacral areas in more than 4 rows, with large tubercles, which extend beyond sides of ambulacral plates; main spiky tubercles perforated, base of spiked tubercles crenellated; ambulacral plates arranged in 2 rows, each plate with pair of pores, every third plate enlarged; spines smooth or finely ribbed or with lateral broadening. PROVENANCE: Lower Carboniferous. DISTRIBUTION: Europe, North America.

Melonechinus [2] Order Palechinoida
CHARACTERISTICS: test roughly spherical, ambulacral areas depressed, but raised in centre; ambulacral areas with up to 12 rows of plates, of which outer ones formed of small half-plates, middle ones short, broad complete plates, between two rows sometimes further rows, pores on plates arranged in pairs in at least 2 rows; inter-ambulacral areas have up to 11 plate rows, outer ones five-sided, inner ones six; spines small, spiny tubercles not perforated. PROVENANCE: Lower Carboniferous. DISTRIBUTION: Europe, Russia, North America, China.

Pedina [3] Order Pedinoida
Fossilisation complete with attached spines. More usually the spines, which are attached to the body by muscles, fall away after the animal's death, and the rather fragile shell, whose plate arrangement and ambulacral pores aid its disintegration, is broken up by wave action. Parts of the shell and the spines are thus usually deposited in different areas. Only under special conditions such as rapid embedding is the shell preserved together with its attached spines. The specimen illustrated is a sea urchin of the genus *Pedina*, which was washed into the Upper Jurassic lagoon of Solnhofen and covered in fine limy ooze.

1 *Archaeocidaris rossica,* Lower Carboniferous, Myachkovo/Russia. Diam. 4.5cm.
2 *Melonechinus multiporus,* Lower Carboniferous, St Louis/USA. Height of shell 8cm.
3 *Pedina lithographica,* Upper Jurassic, Solnhofen/Germany. Diam. 8cm.

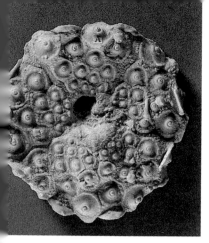

2 △   3 ▽

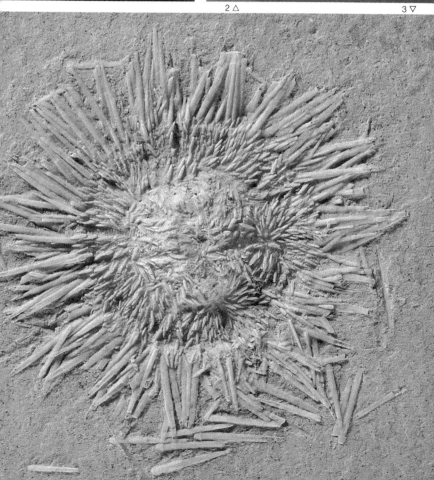

SEA URCHINS
Phylum Echinodermata   Class Echinoidea

Diplocidaris [1] Order Cidaroida
CHARACTERISTICS: test turban-shaped, inter-ambulacral plates always in 2 rows, one large, perforated, one spined tubercle per plate, base of tubercle notched; ambulacral plates in pairs, marginal warts next to pore zones only in alternate plates, pore zones in double rows with a pair of pores at bottom of each dimple; main spines short, cylindrical, with granulated surface. PROVENANCE: Lower Jurassic to Lower Cretaceous. DISTRIBUTION: Europe.

Hemicidaris [2] Order Hemicidaroidea
CHARACTERISTICS: inter-ambulacral plates in double rows, with large, perforated spine tubercles; ambulacral areas at level of greatest diameter broad with large tubercles; towards top narrowing and with noticeably smaller tubercles; ambulacral plates on upper side in groups of 3, but single on lower side; main spines long, cylindrical. PROVENANCE: Middle Jurassic to Upper Cretaceous. DISTRIBUTION: Europe, North Africa. Upper Jurassic, Calne/Wiltshire/England.

Phymosoma [3] Order Phymosomatoidea
CHARACTERISTICS: squat, turban-shaped test, ambulacral plates in groups of 3, several pairs of pores arranged in double rows towards top; main spine tubercles of both ambulacral and inter-ambulacral areas roughly of same size, large opening on underside. PROVENANCE: Upper Jurassic to Eocene. DISTRIBUTION: Europe, North Africa.

Conoclypus [4] Order Holectypoidea
CHARACTERISTICS: tall test shaped like cupola, at summit pentagonal sieve-plate with 4 genital pores; on upper side ambulacral areas leaf-shaped, ambulacral pores linked in furrows, outer pores elongated; mouth at centre of underside, star-shaped as ambulacral areas depressed and interambulacral areas arched; inter-ambulacral plates very broad, anus large and elongated, located towards rear edge. PROVENANCE: Eocene, in region of former Tethys Sea (South Europe).

Clypeaster [5] Order Holectypoidea
CHARACTERISTICS: in outline pentagon with rounded corners; ambulacral areas with pores leaf-shaped, may be closed or open at bottom, pores linked by furrows, ambulacral areas arched upwards, 5 genital pores distributed around peak of upper side, mouth with 5 furrows in depression on underside, anal aperture at rear edge; within test calcareous supports. PROVENANCE: Eocene to Recent. DISTRIBUTION: world-wide.

1 *Diplocidaris etalloni,* Upper Jurassic, Nattheim/Germany. Diam. 8cm.
2 *Hemicidaris agassizi,* Upper Jurassic, Tonnere/France. Diam. 5cm.
3 *Phymosoma granulosum,* Cretaceous (Chalk), Rügen/Germany. Diam. 5cm.
4 *Conoclypus conoideus,* Eocene, Kressenberg/Germany. Height: 8cm.
5 *Clypeaster aegyptiacus,* Pliocene, Gizeh/Egypt. Diam. 15cm.

3 ▽

2 △

4 ▽

5 ▽

SEA URCHINS
Phylum Echinodermata   Class Echinoidea

Amphiope [1] Order Clypeasteroida
CHARACTERISTICS: flat, disc-like test, summit slightly displaced to front, front ambulacral area longer than others, 4 genital pores; mouth at centre of underside, anus close to rear edge, roundish or obliquely oval openings in region of rear ambulacral areas. PROVENANCE: Oligocene to Miocene. DISTRIBUTION: Europe, North Africa, Angola, India.

Heliophora [2] Order Clypeasteroida
CHARACTERISTICS: extremely flat test, rear edge with number of deep indentations, no isolated openings, inner pair of pores on ambulacral areas located in dimple, outer pores single; anal aperture on underside close to rear edge, mouth aperture central; inter-ambulacral areas unsymmetrical, 4 genital pores, food supply furrows on underside branch close to mouth. PROVENANCE: Miocene to Recent. DISTRIBUTION: West Africa.

Hemipneustes [3/4] Order Holasteroida
CHARACTERISTICS: tall, arched, egg-shaped test; front ambulacral area has small pores sunk in a furrow, which extends from the vertex to the mouth on the underside, which itself is slightly displaced towards front edge; petal-shaped ambulacral plates arranged in pairs, front and rear pore rays have small pores, mouth half-moon shaped with "lower lip"; anal aperture on gently flattened rear side, no fasciole. PROVENANCE: Upper Cretaceous. DISTRIBUTION: Europe, North Africa. A form which buries itself in the sea-bed.

Micraster [5/6] Order Spatangoida
CHARACTERISTICS: test heart-shaped or oval, shield at apex with 4 genital pores, front ambulacral area sunk into furrow, which extends over front edge to mouth on underside; ambulacral pores round slightly elongated, located in depression; mouth surrounded by "lips", anus high on flattened rear side. PROVENANCE: Upper Cretaceous. DISTRIBUTION: Europe, Mediterranean area, Madagascar. North and South Downs/Kent, Yorkshire/England.

Recent forms of this group with very dense and highly varied spines churn up the sandy bottom to a depth of 20cm in search of food. At rest they use their spines and long, mobile, "cleaning feet" to keep open their breathing and drainage tubes, and to maintain good water circulation.

1 *Amphiope bioculata,* Miocene, Libya. Length: 6.5cm, height: 0.8cm.
2 *Heliophora orbiculus,* Pleistocene, Gambia. Diam. 3.5cm.
3/4 *Hemipneustes radiatus,* Cretaceous, Maastricht/Holland. Height: 7cm.
  3 Side view.
  4 Underside.
5 *Micraster* sp., Upper Cretaceous, northern Germany. Diam. 6cm.
6 *Micraster cortestudinarum,* Upper Cretaceous, Meudon/France. Diam. 5cm.

3 ▽   2 △   4 ▽

5 ▽   6 ▽

GRAPHOLITES

Phylum Hemichordata Class Graptolithida

Restricted to fine-grained sediments; may occur in prodigious numbers as carbonised or pyritised films.

Graptolites [1-5]

The extinct marine animal group Graptolithida is now classified among the Hemichordates. Their structure, with its gilled intestinal tract, dorsal intestinal opening and neural tube, has some features in common with the Chordates, which are characterized by their flexible dorsal axial stem, the chorda. This may give rise to the interpretation of the Hemichordates as very early forms leading to the Vertebrates.

The extant marine forms of these animals, the enteropneusta and pterobranchia, play a comparatively modest role among the marine fauna, but the graptolites represent important index fossils for the Ordovician and Silurian. Similarly to the pterobranchia they built external skeletons consisting of scleroproteins. The single individuals lived in variously shaped thecae, arranged in a row as a rhabdosome and joined by a common tube. The thecae could be grouped in single, double or quadruple rows, the rhabdosomes united into a central capsule, which was attached to a swim-bladder. In addition to these planktonic forms (Graptoloidea), there were also sedentary types (Dendroidea). This latter group, with growth patterns like small trees, probably attached to sea grasses, appeared in the Middle Cambrian and outlived the planktonic varieties (from Ordovician to Devonian), surviving into the Upper Carboniferous.

Most graptolite remains are preserved as prints in shales, but entire, three-dimensional preservation in limestones is known. Under particularly favourable conditions it was even possible for the rhabdosomes with the attached swim-bladder to be preserved.

Order Dendroidea [1]: rhabdosomes branching like small trees, joined together by lateral supports, thecae of various sizes (sexual dimorphism), sessile or semi-planktonic.

Order Graptoloidea [2-5]: planktonic forms, number of rhabdosomes between 1 and 4, classified by theca structure.

1 *Dictyonema flabelliforme,* Middle Devonian, Leicester/USA. Height: 5cm. Also in Upper Cambrian, North Wales; East Midlands, England; eastern Canada.

2 *Spirograptus spiralis,* Silurian, Reporye/Czechoslovakia. Diam. 2cm. Rhabdosome turned inwards, thecae at largish intervals (see centre of plate, other forms also present).

3 *Monograptus* sp., Silurian, Senorbi/Sardinia. Length: 5cm.

4 *Monograptus colonus,* Silurian, Krotoszyn/Poland. Length: 2.5cm. Rhabdosomes form only 1 branch (stipe), thecae located only on one side.

5 *Didymograptus bifidus,* Lower Ordovician, South Wales. Length: 4cm. Rhabdosome forms 2 branches (stipes); simple, tube-like thecae located only on one side.

3 ▽   2 △   4 ▽

                                                                              5 ▽

AGNATHA (JAWLESS FISHES)
Phylum Vertebrata Class Agnatha
Bony fragments and scales occur in many Lower Old Red Sandstone rocks. Identification is often difficult.

Hemicyclaspis [1] Order Cephalaspidiformes Family Cephalaspidae
CHARACTERISTICS: head-shield triangular in outline; total of 3 sensory fields present, one on each edge of side of head and a smaller one behind eyes. Main nerve canals of side fields join marginally in front of eye apertures. Mouth aperture on lower side much elongated. Cross-section of body triangular, except for flattened, oval tail region. 2 well developed pectoral fins, front fins on back developed only as comb of larger scales, rear fins on back have spine at leading edge. Tail fin forked, upper part bigger, but with a ventral axis supporting the membranes of the end of the tail. PROVENANCE: Upper Silurian. DISTRIBUTION: England, Norway, Canada.

With the exception of the Petromyzontida (lampreys) and Myxinoida (Hag-fish), the agnatha died out in the early part of the Middle Devonian. They were bottom-living fish-like, aquatic jawless vertebrates, with strong external armour but only a minimal internal skeleton. The Osteostraci group, to which the genus *Hemicyclaspis* belongs, possessed strong armour which covered not only the head, but even parts of the front of the body. The rest of the body was covered in bony scales. On the upper side of the head-shield were apertures for the nostrils, the pineal opening and the closely spaced eyes. In the centre and at the sides were areas covered with small bony plates, in which were special sensory organs.

PRIMITIVE FISHES
Phylum Vertebrata Class Aphetohyoidea (Placodermi)
Isolated bones, scales and plates, more rarely complete fossils: may be common in many Old Red Sandstone formations. Identification is dependent on the preservation of complete parts or whole bodies.

Bothriolepis [2] Order Asterolepiformes Family Bothriolepidae
CHARACTERISTICS: head and front part of body covered by large bony plates, moveable in relation to each other, rear part of body without thick scales. Paddle-like front extremities also armoured, but separately moveable and joined to body by ball-joint. Bony plates externally patterned with net of ridges, which in mature specimens is resolved into small knots and ribs. Front central dorsal plate narrows at its two rear ends, while rear central dorsal plate narrows towards front; the front central dorsal plate overlaps the front lateral dorsal plates; rear lateral dorsal plates overlap front central dorsal plate; 2 dorsal fins, tail fin unevenly bilobed. PROVENANCE: Upper Devonian. DISTRIBUTION: North America, Greenland, Europe, Russia, China, Australia, Antarctica.

Various groups of primitive, Palaeozoic fishes are assembled in the class Aphetohyoidea or Placodermi (jaw-gilled, primitive fishes). Their common feature is a true gill opening between the lateral and extralateral head plates and curved jaws with teeth-like cusps. The sac-like attachments of the gullet observed in *Bothriolepis* are interpreted as a kind of lung. On the basis of the settings in which finds have been made and of the excellent preservation (fossil spiral intestine) *Bothriolepis* is regarded as a sediment-eater adapted to life at the bottom of Devonian waters.

1 *Hemicyclaspis murchisoni,* Upper Silurian, England. Length: 18cm.
2 *Bothriolepis canadensis,* Upper Devonian, Quebec/Canada. Length: 9cm.

CARTILAGINOUS FISHES

Phylum Vertebrata Class Chondrichthyes

Complete bodies or skeletons are rare but teeth and fin spines are common in some late Palaeozoic, Mesozoic and Cainozoic formations.

Hybodus [1] Order Selachii Family Hybodontidae

CHARACTERISTICS: fossil shark; teeth with longitudinal folds and central main cusp, straight or hook-shaped, and several smaller cusps; conical, radially ribbed placoid scales. Fin spines of triangular cross-section inclined to rear, grooved longitudinally on front side, at rear set with 2 rows of hooked points. PROVENANCE: Lower Triassic to Lower Cretaceous. DISTRIBUTION: Europe, USA, Spitsbergen. Lyme Regis/Dorset, Westbury-on-Severn/Gloucestershire/England.

Odontaspis [2 top] Order Selachii Family Odontaspidae

CHARACTERISTICS: fossil shark; teeth with slender, sharp-sided main cusps, front side arched, rear side flat, on each side 1 or 2 sub-cusps, root forked. PROVENANCE: Lower Cretaceous to Recent. DISTRIBUTION: world-wide.

Notorynchus [2 bottom] Order Selachii Family Hexanchidae

CHARACTERISTICS: fossil shark; teeth in upper and lower jaws very different, at side of lower have unsymmetrical tooth-crowns; main point set at angle has at mid-point row of very small cusps decreasing in size; distal sub-cusps very much bigger, increasing in size similarly. PROVENANCE: Cretaceous to Recent. DISTRIBUTION: world-wide.

Procarcharodon [3] Order Selachii Family Lamnidae

CHARACTERISTICS: fossil shark; large, triangular tooth, front side arched, rear side flat, edges of cusp finely toothed, each side of tooth swells out at base. PROVENANCE: Miocene to Recent. DISTRIBUTION: world-wide.

Ptychodus [4] Order Rajiformes Family Ptychodontidae

CHARACTERISTICS: fossil ray; "cobble-stone" palatal teeth of front part of jaw, large and powerful, thick enamel layer of convex crown divided by cross furrows in middle part; these end in irregular wrinkles at edge of crown; rear side tooth crown has distinct indentation; tooth root is longish rectangle with rounded corners, shield-shaped; teeth arranged in transverse rows in original formation. PROVENANCE: Upper Cretaceous. DISTRIBUTION: Europe, Asia, North Africa, North America, East India.

1 *Hybodus aschersoni,* Lower Cretaceous, Egypt. Length of fin spike: 29cm.
2 Top *Odontaspis cuspidata,* Oligocene, Weinheim/Germany. Length: 3cm.
2 Bottom *Notorynchus primigenius,* Oligocene, Weinheim/Germany. Length 2.4cm.
3 *Procarcharodon megalodon,* Miocene, Lower Bavaria/Germany. Length: 12cm.
4 *Ptychodus decurrens,* Upper Cretaceous, Regensburg/Germany. Width of teeth: 3-5cm.

BONY FISHES
Phylum Vertebrata Class Osteichthyes Super-order Teleostei

Most bony fishes have very fragile skeletons so fossils are rare; under certain conditions, however, they occur in an almost perfect state of preservation. Spectacular instances involve fish in lacustrine or lagunal sediments, as at Monte Bolca/Italy, Solnhofen/Germany and SW Wyoming/USA.

Dapedium [1] Order Semionotoidea Family Semionotidae
CHARACTERISTICS: powerful body with short head and flattened sides; ventral and pectoral fins small, dorsal and anal fins long with feathered edge, tail fin with almost straight edge. Scales on sides taller than broad, rhomboid in shape; keel-scales present. Operculum arch-shaped, eyes surrounded by ring of (sclerotic) small bony plates. Mouth short, jaw with outer teeth of pointed cudgel-shape, inner teeth smaller, brush-like. Protective bony plates of head granulated on surface and covered with ganoid layer, back-bone cartilaginous; neural arches with spiny extensions, ribs and fin bases ossified. PROVENANCE: Lower Jurassic. DISTRIBUTION: Europe, South Asia. Lower Jurassic, Lyme Regis/Dorset/England.

In representatives of the Holostei, the ossification of the skeleton has progressed further than in Chondrostei, but has still not reached the final stage found in Teleostei (bony fishes in the narrower sense). Holostians are known from the Permian onwards, but the only recent form is the genus *Amia*, a mud-fish found in fresh-water lakes in the USA.
Dapedium is one of the fishes most frequently found in the famous Lias of Holzmaden,Germany, also on the Dorset coast, England. Its dentition is the basis for believing that these fish fed on both soft and hard-shelled prey.

Palaeoniscus [2] Order Palaeonisciformes Family Palaeoniscidae
CHARACTERISTICS: elongated, spindle-shaped body covered in moderately large scales. Fins relatively small; paired pectoral fins with separate rays, a single dorsal fin located above the space between belly and anal fin, upper and lower parts of caudal fin of different length (heterocercal); at front edge of dorsal and anal fins and also in front of dorsal part of tail 3 or more V-shaped scales, which pass over into keel-scales; the glazed fin rays also covered in keel-scales; other scales rhombic, covered in shiny ganoid glaze. Interoperculum and operculum broad, lower edge of latter angled. Lower jaw prognathous. PROVENANCE: Permian. DISTRIBUTION: Germany, England, Czechoslovakia, Greenland, USA, eastern Canada, South Africa, Australia.

The common feature of *Actinopterygia* (ray-finned fishes) is the reduction of cartilaginous or bony supporting skeleton of the paired fins. The outer parts of these are carried only by thin rays. *Palaeonisciformes* are called primitive bony fishes because of the ossification of the endocranium. According to the finds made of the skeletons they developed from a primitive group of Acanthodians (spiny-finned fishes). One of the most familiar species is *P. freieslebeni* from the Permian of the Mansfeld Küpferschiefer (copper-bearing shales).

1 *Dapedium pholidotum*, Lower Jurassic, Holzmaden/Germany. Length: 21cm, height: 8cm.
2 *Palaeoniscus freiselebeni*, Permian copper-bearing shales, Riechelsdorf bei Eisleben/Germany. Length: 22cm.

BONY FISHES
Phylum Vertebrata Class Osteichthyes Super-order Teleostei

Leptolepis [1] Order Clupeiformes Family Leptolepidae
CHARACTERISTICS: small to medium sized fishes with roundish head; body covered with thin, shiny cycloid scales, pectoral and pelvic fins in pairs, small, short anal fin, forked tail fin; dorsal fin directly above pelvic; numerous powerful ribs and bones, neural arch (= part of vertebrae above spinal cord) not unified with rest of column, spinal element smooth surfaced, as are bones of head; jaws set with very small teeth, dental with high processus coronoideus (= rising part of jawbone to which large muscles attach), upper jaw with maxillary and pre-maxillary, lower jaw with dental and articular bones; 2 supramaxillar, 2 supraorbital bones present. PROVENANCE: Lower Jurassic to Lower Cretaceous. DISTRIBUTION: Europe, Spitsbergen, USA, South America, North Africa.

Leuciscus [2] Order Cypriniformes Family Cyprinidae
CHARACTERISTICS: small to medium sized fishes with body flattened at sides; scales relatively large, fins very small, dorsal and anal fins very similar, tail fin forked; jaws and bones of mouth cavity without teeth, crushing teeth arranged in triple rows on bone of lower gullet, no barbels at mouth; anal fin with 9-11 rays. PROVENANCE: Oligocene to Recent. DISTRIBUTION: Europe; North America and Asia in Miocene; Africa Recent.

Sphenocephalus [3] Order Beryciformes Family Sphenocephalidae
CHARACTERISTICS: large, pointed head, body relatively short and deep, flattened at sides, covered in ctenoid scales; paired ventral fins towards thorax, dorsal fins undivided, front 3 spine rays shorter than following unified rays, anal fin has 4 short spines and 7 unified rays; gullet bone divided, jaws with small teeth. PROVENANCE: Upper Cretaceous. DISTRIBUTION: Europe.

All 3 genera illustrated represent different orders of Teleostei (bony fishes in the strict sense), the most highly developed group of the fishes. Fossil forms are found from the Lower Triassic onwards; they reach their first peak in the Upper Cretaceous, their second in the Miocene. Today, these fishes, with more than 25,000 species, form the largest group of vertebrates.

1 *Leptolepis sprattiformis*, Upper Jurassic, Solnhofen/Germany. Length: 6cm.
2 *Leuciscus* sp., Miocene, Oningen/Germany. Length: 10cm.
3 *Sphenocephalus* sp., Upper Cretaceous, Westfalia/Germany. Length: 11cm.

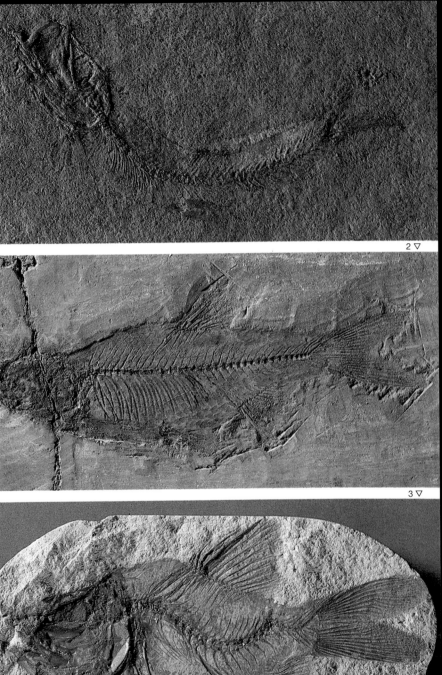

2 ▽

3 ▽

BONY FISHES
Phylum Vertebrata Class Osteichthyes Super-order Teleostei

Mene Order Perciformes Family Menidae
CHARACTERISTICS: body extremely flattened at sides, usually no scales or at least not visible to naked eye; head with comb, which may vary in development. Small mouth tilted upwards, teeth very small, worn away in older specimens; pre-operculum and operculum fully developed, also 7 gill rows, 23 vertebrae present. Only one ventral and one dorsal fin, both of which extend to tail, ventral fin bears prominent leading spine; tail fin triangular or deeply indented.
PROVENANCE: Eocene to Recent. DISTRIBUTION: as fossil: Europe, North Africa, West Indies; recent forms from Indian Ocean, China Sea and Japanese Sea of single species, *M. maculata*.

Four species of the genus *Mene* are known as fossils, 2 of them from the Eocene of Monte Bolca. The species illustrated is one of the types of fish most frequently found at this locality and drawings of it were made, although under another name, as early as 1755. The genus and species names indicate its exceptionally flattened, round body shape.
Mene in Ancient Greek means moon, and the Latin term *rhombea* refers to a flat fish (*Rhombus*), the flounder. A further characteristic of the species is the backwards curving appendage on the lower side. This is not an elongated fin ray, but an extension of the pelvic girdle.
The exceptionally good state of preservation of the fish points to special conditions of fossilisation at this locality. In fact, in some layers of the rock series at Monte Bolca the majority of fossils are preserved as entire bodies. These were rapidly buried in fine limestone ooze, which cut off the oxygen supply and so prevented decay of the corpses. At Monte Bolca the now famous marine fishes together with the other fossils, including submerged land plants, point to a predominantly tropical character. The palaeontological discoveries indicate this prehistoric habitat as an off-shore lagoon of calm, tropically warm water, protected by small islands. From time to time the lagoon water was enriched with carbon dioxide by eruptions of volcanic gases. This led to a depletion of oxygen and so to more rapid deposition of limestone, which destroyed the lagoon as a habitat. Only after a considerable time, when the living conditions had again stabilised, was this area re-settled. The geological evidence points to the repeated occurrence of these catastrophic events.

180 *Mene rhombea*, Eocene, Monte Bolca/Italy. Length: 22cm.

BONY FISHES
Phylum Vertebrata Class Osteichthyes

Ceradotus [1] Sub-class Dipnoi Order Ceratodiformes Family Ceratodidae
CHARACTERISTICS: fossil lungfish; classification of genus primarily based on teeth
features (organogeneric); rounded triangular outline of enamelled teeth with
ridges inclined forwards and to sides, decreasing in height and size towards sides.
Four to six ridges in both upper and lower jaw. Within one species teeth of upper
jaw usually broader; surface structure of tooth-plates porous and scarred, also
shows largish wrinkles. Clear growth-lines at median edge of tooth plate and in
profile of ridges. PROVENANCE and DISTRIBUTION: Lower Triassic to Upper
Jurassic, Europe; Lower Triassic to Upper Cretaceous, North Asia; Upper
Cretaceous, South America. Westbury/Bedfordshire/England; Upper Triassic,
Gloucestershire, Somerset, Dorset/England.

It was only in 1870, when the Australian lungfish *Neoceratodus forsteri* was
discovered in the rivers of Queensland, that the classification of *Ceratodus* was
clarified. The tooth-plates of the recent genus have a very similar structure,
although they are only half the size of those of the fossil genus and have only 6
ridges in both upper and lower jaws. Whilst other recent species of lungfish can
survive without water for up to 4 years, wrapped in their capsule of mucus, the
Australian form has to swim to the surface in order to take air into its lungs.

Libys [2] Sub-class Crossopterygia Order Coelacanthiformes
Family Coelacanthidae
CHARACTERISTICS: fossil fish with tassel-like fins; body of compressed shape, little
longer than 4 times head length, max. height 1½ times head length; with
exception of head region, body covered by large, four-layered cycloid scales with
sparse markings. Malar (cheek) bone with indistinct grooves; large mucal canal
pores in head bones, forming denticles on roof of skull, short teeth, either blunt or
pointed; rays of dorsal and ventral fins sparsely set with denticles, tripartite tail fin
with relatively small median tassel. PROVENANCE: Upper Jurassic. DISTRIBUTION:
Germany.

Whilst the Coelacanthiformes (hollow-spined fishes), an order of Crossopterygia
(tassel-finned fishes), are found in deposits clearly of fresh water origin in the
Devonian, in the Mesozoic period they have been discovered only in marine beds
and were considered to have died out by the end of the Cretaceous. Only in
1938, when the now famous tassel-finned fish *Latimeria* was caught off the coast
of South Africa, was it proved that this is a living fossil. There was great scientific
interest in the investigation of this creature not least because the ancestors of land
vertebrates descended from a still more primitive group of Crossopterygia,
(Devonian), the Rhipidistia. It is possible to trace the bone structure of the
earliest forelimbs in land vertebrates from the pectoral fin skeleton of the
Devonian rhipidistian genus *Eusthenopteron.*

1 Tooth-plates of upper and lower jaw, *Ceradotus runcinatus,* Upper Triassic,
Ludwigsburg/Germany. Max. length: 4cm., max. width: 6cm.
182 2 *Libys superbus,* Upper Jurassic, Solnhofen/Germany. Length: 44cm.

2 ▽

AMPHIBIANS
Phylum Vertebrata Class Amphibia
Recognisable remains are virtually confined to Carboniferous and later non-marine rocks. The majority are isolated teeth, bones and skull parts. Identification is very difficult.

Sclerocephalus Sub-class Labyrinthodontia Order Temnospondyli
Family Eryopidae
CHARACTERISTICS: This genus is introduced here simply to represent the huge number of fossil amphibians, and in particular the sub-class of Labyrinthodontia. This name refers to the internal enamel structure of the teeth, which in cross-section reveal an extreme form of fine folding of the dentine resembling a labyrinth. A further feature of these amphibians is a continuous roof to the skull, formed of epidermal plates and pierced only by the apertures for the eyes, nose and foramen parietal (pineal opening). They lack the temple apertures found in primitive reptiles. In addition to the dentary which bears the teeth, there are several more bones which form important parts of the lower jaw. One of the main classification features is the development of the vertebrae. Among the Labyrinthodontia, the vertebrae consist primarily of the front pleurocentrum and the rear intercentrum which is the dominant element (rhachitomous vertebral structure). The limbs were usually small in relation to the body and projected sideways, the body was plump and salamander-like.

One of the best known genera is *Ichthyostega* from the Upper Devonian of eastern Greenland. Its body structure shows features which on the one hand resemble fishes, on the other amphibians. The genus *Eryops*, over 3 metres long, was the largest of the labyrinthodonts. With its powerful fore and hind limbs, an armoured skin of bony elements, and planting each foot firmly as it crawled, it could certainly have left the shallow water of the marshes and passed some time on land. Its original habitat was, however, the shallow marsh, in which it also went through its larval stage, when its gills were formed. New finds of some genera with gills preserved are simply the larval stages of adult individuals (as in *Branchiosaurus*). Larval forms were also discovered in the fossil stems of Sigillaria and Lepidodendra, which supports the assumption that these animals passed the daytime hidden in protected places. The labyrinthodonts are a fossil group of amphibians found from the Upper Devonian until they died out at the end of the Triassic. It is generally assumed that they are descended from the Devonian tassel-finned fishes (*Crossopterygia*). The orders of amphibians existing today, the Anura, Urodela and Gymnophiona, derive from the Triassic (Jurassic) amphibians.

REPTILES
Phylum Vertebrata Class Reptilia

Fragmentary bones, armour and teeth occur in many late Palaeozoic and later rocks.
Complete skeletons occur in marine formations and where sudden burial took place.
Identification of isolated skeleton parts is very difficult.

Bradysaurus [1] Sub-class Anapsida Order Cotylosauria Family Pareiasauridae
CHARACTERISTICS: reptiles up to 3m in length; broad, relatively flat skull with
rounded snout and cheek wings, which cover the ear depression; no temple
apertures, up to 4 pairs of symmetrically arranged thickenings of the skull. 19-20
teeth in each half of jaw, tooth crowns flat, leaf-shaped, with 11-15 jagged points;
palate also set with teeth, at front 2 longitudinal rows of small teeth, at rear 3
diverging double rows. PROVENANCE: Middle Permian. DISTRIBUTION: South
Africa.

Bradysaurus belongs to the Cotylosauria, the basic group of reptiles with
continuous skulls, a parietal foramen and separate outer nostrils. Their
forerunners were amphibians of the group of Anthracosauria from the Lower
Carboniferous. *Bradysaurus* was a herbivore incapable of rapid locomotion
because its limbs extended sideways from the body.

Trionyx [2] Sub-class Anapsida Order Testudinata Family Trionychidae
CHARACTERISTICS: fossil turtle; dorsal and ventral armour not firmly linked by
bone (roof-like); dorsal armour broad, flat outer side of bony plates
characteristically with net-like or honeycomb structure; large, wing-like plate at
front edge (nuchal); 7-11 hexagonal central plates lying along body (neuralia), of
which first 4 have shorter lateral edges and point to rear, fifth is rectangular,
remainder also with short lateral edges point forwards. Ventral armour reduced to
8 bony plates with areas left uncovered. PROVENANCE: Cretaceous to Recent.
DISTRIBUTION: North America, Africa, Asia, Europe (only as fossil).

Clemmydopsis [3] Sub-class Anapsida Order Testudinata Family Emydidae
CHARACTERISTICS: fossil turtle; bony plates of ventral and dorsal armour joined by
lateral bridge. Horny carapace: first 3 central plates fused with lateral plates,
which are in direct contact with plates at actual edge. Bony plates: centrally
located plates (neuralia), first 3 hexagonal, with short lateral edges to rear;
fifth and sixth point forwards; in other specimens all plates of this latter type.
Ventral plates continuous. PROVENANCE: Lower Upper Miocene to Pliocene.
DISTRIBUTION: Germany, Austria, Hungary, France.

Considered as inhabitant of shallow waters along shores of lakes. On basis of
anapsidal skull structure (without lateral temple aperture) the turtles are derived
from the Cotylosauria. The first forms, such as *Procanochelys* from the Triassic of
Württemberg, have a completely developed carapace, but also small teeth on the
palate and edges of the jaws. Giant marine forms over 4m long are known from
the Upper Cretaceous in North America.

1 *Bradysaurus seleyi*, Middle Permian, South Africa. Skull length: 44cm.
2 *Trionyx brunnhuberi*, Miocene, Dechbetten bei Regensburg/Germany. Length of dorsal armour:
26cm. Soft-shelled turtle; habitat ponds, lakes, rivers.
3 *Clemmydopsis sopronensis*, Miocene, Sandelzhausen bei Mainburg/Germany. Length of
carapace: 10cm.

2 ▽

3 ▽

REPTILES
Phylum Vertebrata Class Reptilia

Stenopterygius [1] Sub-class Ichthyopterygia Order Ichthyosauria
Family Stenopterygiidae
CHARACTERISTICS: marine reptiles, which are called fish-saurians or fish-lizards
because of their physical features which are reminiscent of various animal types
(snout like a dolphin, crocodile teeth, fins like a whale, head like a lizard,
backbone like a fish). Skull elongated, with pointed conical teeth, bony eye-socket
roof of skull with upper temporal aperture, which on lower side is limited by
postfrontal and supratemporal bones; head directly joined to body without neck;
tail fin stands vertical, the backbone with its sudden curve continues into the
lower lobe of the tail fin and acts as stiffener; nostrils placed close to eye
apertures; front limbs larger than rear, development of tall dorsal fin; species
distinguished by form of shoulder girdle, structure of front fins and body size of
adult specimens. PROVENANCE: Lower Jurassic. DISTRIBUTION: western, central
Europe, Spitsbergen, North America.

The Ichthyopterygia derive from palaeozoic terrestrial lizards but their body form
is excellently adapted to an aquatic life. Their food consisted of dibranchiate
squid (cephalopods). The earliest forms are found in the Triassic, the last in the
Upper Cretaceous.

Pachypleurosaurus [2] Sub-class Synaptosauria Order Sauropterygia
Family Pachypleurosauridae
CHARACTERISTICS: small reptiles probably of amphibious habit; complete skeletons
of this genus between 0.3 and 1.2m long, large variation in body features and
length; small upper skull temporal aperture bounded on lower side by postorbital
and squamosal bones, greatest skull breadth behind large eye apertures; number
of vertebrae very variable: neck 13-21, torso 17-24, sacrum 3-4, tail 40-58; teeth
conical with longitudinal grooves at point, located in single rows in depressions on
jaw edges; relatively long, thin limbs. PROVENANCE: Middle Triassic.
DISTRIBUTION: Switzerland, Italy.

Macroplacus [3] Sub-class Synaptosauria Order Placodontia
Family Placodontidae
CHARACTERISTICS: marine reptiles of somewhat rounded shape; armoured skin
developed, skull of flattened heart shape; teeth developed as powerful plates, 2
small teeth on upper jaw, 1 small and 1 very large, broad tooth on top of palatal
bone; probably fed on molluscs or brachiopods, cracking shells with strong teeth.
PROVENANCE: to date only skull from Upper Triassic, Sonthofen, Allgäu,
Germany.

Placodus [4] Sub-class Synaptosauria Order Placodontia Family Placodontidae
As comparison, lower jaw of genus *Placodus*.

1 *Stenopterygius quadriscissus*, specimen with skin preserved. Length: 1.05m.
2 *Pachypleurosaurus edwardsii*, Middle Triassic, Mt San Giorgio/Switzerland. Length: 22cm.
3 *Macroplacus raeticus*, Length of upper jaw: 20cm.
4 *Placodus gigas*, Middle Triassic, Kulmbach/Germany. Right lower jaw with teeth and replacement
teeth below; length 16cm.

3 ▽   4 ▽

REPTILES
Phylum Vertebrata Class Reptilia

Kallimodon [1] Sub-class Lepidosauria Order Rhynchocephalia
Family Sphenodontidae
CHARACTERISTICS: small reptile up to 20cm long; skull outline rounded triangle,
with upper and lower temporal aperture, top of skull narrows to form ridge, outer
nostril at tip of snout, bases of teeth combined with bone surface of jaw; teeth of
blunt, conical shape either rounded or elongated; 14 teeth in lower jaw, 13 in
upper, at rear taller than long, at front longer than tall, palate also with 3 teeth; 2
pre-sacral vertebrae, 7 neck, 50 tail; belly ribbed, limbs with 5 claws, scaly skin.
PROVENANCE: Upper Jurassic. DISTRIBUTION: Germany, France.

Eichstaettisaurus [2] Sub-class Lepidosaurus Order Squamata
Family Ardeosauridae
CHARACTERISTICS: skull rounded triangle; short, broad snout, large eye apertures,
frontal bones fused in towards front, narrowest in width above eyes, small parietal
cavity, mandible shorter than head, postorbitally skull touches squamosal and
jugal, numerous small teeth, shoulder and collar bone with apertures; 31
pre-sacral vertebrae, limbs short, body covered in horny plates. PROVENANCE:
Upper Jurassic. DISTRIBUTION: Germany.

Steneosaurus [3] Sub-class Archosauria Order Crocodilia
Family Teleosauridae
CHARACTERISTICS: marine crocodiles up to 4.8m long; snout like cayman's,
varying in length; 4-5 teeth in front part of jaw adapted to seize prey, eye sockets
directed upwards, upper temporal apertures large, trapezoidal, lower flattened;
small, pointed, conical teeth with sharp edge along length at front and rear; body
covered in armour-plated skin, c. 40 tail vertebrae. PROVENANCE: Jurassic.
DISTRIBUTION: Europe, South America, Morocco, Madagascar.

Ctenochasma [4] Sub-class Archosauria Order Pterosauria
Family Ctenochasmatidae
CHARACTERISTICS: elongated snout with rounded end; teeth only in front half of
jaw, long, curved and pointed, arranged along lateral edges of jaws, decreasing in
length towards skull, up to 360 in number; skull length up to 24cm, wing span up
to 120cm. PROVENANCE: Upper Jurassic. DISTRIBUTION: Germany, France.

C. gracile, Plate 4, was a specialised flying saurian, which could sieve minute
living creatures from the water with its fishtrap-like jaws.

1 *Kallimodon pulchellus*, Upper Jurassic, Solnhofen beds (at Solnhofen)/Germany. Length: 25cm.
2 *Eichstaettisaurus schroederi*, Upper Jurassic, Solnhofen beds/Germany. Length: 12cm.
  Considered related to geckos.
3 *Steneosaurus bollensis*, Lower Jurassic, Holzmaden/Germany. Length of skull: 50cm.
4 *Ctenochasma gracile,* Upper Jurassic, Solnhofen beds/Germany. Skull length: 11cm.

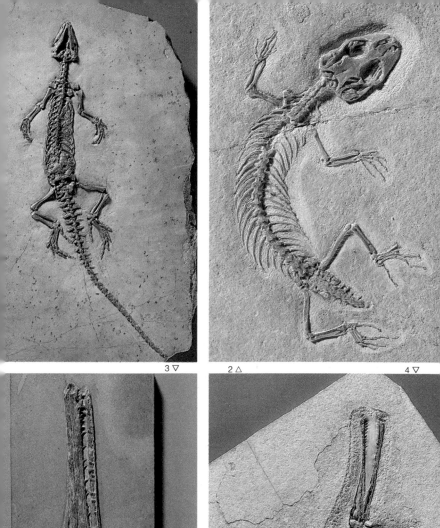

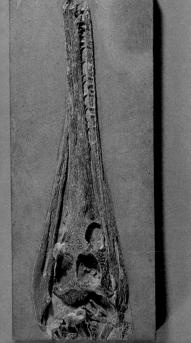

3 ▽   2 △   4 ▽

REPTILES
Phylum Vertebrata Class Reptilia

Tyrannosaurus [1] Sub-class Archosauria Sub-order Theropoda
Order Saurischia Super-family Carnosauroidea Family Tyrannosauridae
CHARACTERISTICS: skull length up to 1.4m; between nostrils and relatively small eye apertures 2 further pre-orbital apertures; rear temporal apertures narrowed squamosal and quadratojugal; max. length of teeth 20cm, but vary in length wit jagged edges; pelvis (hip girdle) tri-radiate, shoulder girdle much reduced; powerful tail, strongly developed rear legs, three-toed feet, small arms ending in fingers, fingers and toes with claws. PROVENANCE: Upper Cretaceous. DISTRIBUTION: western North America, China.

With its head-to-tail length of 15m, a height of 6m when erect and a weight of ˙ tons, *Tyrannosaurus* belonged to the larger representatives of the dinosaurs. It moved in the upright position, using its massive tail as a support when sitting ar for balance when running. The small hands could at best be of some help in eating, but were important props for support when the animal wished to stand up. Its prey, mostly unarmoured herbivores, were overpowered and held fast by its feet. Using its sharp teeth it was able to tear great pieces of flesh from the body of its victim.

Triceratops [2] Sub-class Archosauria Sub-order Ceratopsia
Order Ornithischia Family Ceratopsidae
CHARACTERISTICS: 1 horn above large nostril apertures, 2 further horns above ey sockets; large neck shield from specialised head bones; point of snout forms bon beak, teeth of upper and lower jaws twin-rooted, arranged in superimposed 'batteries', so that root ends of each tooth worn down by mastication enclose crown of next as it grows on. PROVENANCE: Upper Cretaceous. DISTRIBUTION: North America.

The group of Ceratopsia originated from bipedal animals from the eastern Asiar area. The first four-footed forms, like *Protoceratops* from Mongolia, already show signs of the thickening of the bones of the head, which in later forms, now havir migrated to North America, like *Triceratops*, formed powerful horns. According the latest research the neck-shield of the Ceratopsia was integrated into the body as the attachment point for the powerful muscles of the mouth and head and di(not serve, as was earlier assumed, as an external shield to protect the otherwise exposed neck. Since the horns appear in both male and female, they are thought to have been defensive weapons. In spite of its rounded shape, its weight of 6-8 tons and length of 11m, *Triceratops* is regarded as an agile and relatively quick-moving herbivore, which could consume even the harder plants with its parrot-like beak and scissor-like teeth.

1 *Tyrannosaurus rex*, Upper Cretaceous, North America. Skull length: 1.3m.
2 *Triceratops horridus*, Upper Cretaceous, North America. Skull length: 1.8m.

2 ▽

REPTILES
Phylum Vertebrata   Class Reptilia

Mesosaurus [1] Sub-class Synapsida   Order Mesosauria   Family Mesosaridae
CHARACTERISTICS: slender body up to 60cm long; snout more than
$2/3$ of skull length, closely set, curved teeth forming fishtrap-like sieve; nostril
apertures set towards rear; close to eye apertures, one lateral temporal aperture;
shoulder girdle reptilian with short, broad scapula and large coracoid bones; front
feet short, rear long, fifth toe has 1-2 phalanges more than others, tail flattened
laterally. PROVENANCE: Lower Permian. DISTRIBUTION: South America, western
South Africa.

All the palaeontological finds indicate that *Mesosaurus* was an excellent swimmer
and used its sieve-trap snout to feed on fresh-water crustacea. This is one of the
fossils whose present distribution in distant localities establishes the earlier land
connection between Africa and South America (the theory of Continental Drift).

Cynognathus [2/3] Sub-class Synapsida   Sub-order Cynodontia
Family Cynognathidae
CHARACTERISTICS: large upper temporal apertures, surrounded by yoke-bone
consisting of squamosal and jugal; short secondary palate, snout-like front section
of skull with nostril apertures at very front; dentition varies in upper jaw: 4 front
teeth with single point, 1 canine tooth, 10 post-canines, rear ones of which have
several points; in lower jaw correspondingly 3, 1 and 11 teeth; dentary forms
main bone of lower jaw. PROVENANCE: Middle Triassic. DISTRIBUTION: South
Africa.

Cynognathus is one of the reptiles with a number of skull and skeleton features
similar to mammals. The location of the feet below the body enabled this predator
to move rapidly. The form and surface sculpturing of the bone at the snout
suggest the existence of a mobile nose with sensitive hairs.

BIRDS
Phylum Vertebrata   Class Aves

Archaeopteryx [4] Sub-class Sauriurae   Family Archaeopterygidae
CHARACTERISTICS: In *Archaeopteryx* characteristics of both reptiles and birds are
present. Reptilian features: teeth in upper and lower jaws, raised ring around eye,
small skull to contain brain, lizard-like tail, 3 fingers with claws, breastbone not of
hard bone, ventral ribs, metatarsal bones not fused. Avian features: feathers,
furcula (wishbone) part of shoulder girdle. PROVENANCE: Upper Jurassic.
DISTRIBUTION: Bavaria, Germany.

It is considered on the basis of its well developed claws that *Archaeopteryx* was a
tree-climbing animal capable only of brief gliding or fluttering flights. This view is
made the more likely since no breast-bone has yet been found in any specimen,
which in recent birds serves as the anchorage for the flight muscles.

---

1 *Mesosaurus brasiliensis,* Permian, Brazil. Length of juvenile specimen: 14cm.
2/3 *Cynognathus platiceps,* Middle Triassic, South Africa.
  2 Lower jaw, length 30cm
  3 Skull, length 32cm.
4 *Archaeopteryx lithographica,* Upper Jurassic, Solnhofen/Germany. Length of feather: 6cm.

3 ▽

4 ▽

MAMMALS
Phylum Vertebrata Class Mammalia

Teeth are the commonest remains, but bones may be found in many Cainozoic rocks and in cave deposits. Some are tiny and some are very large. Identification is for the specialist. The dentition formula gives the numbers of different kinds of teeth (incisors, canines, premolars, molars) in each side of the jaws, upper and lower.

Halmaturus [1] Order Marsupialia Family Macropodidae

CHARACTERISTICS: fossil kangaroo; dentition formula $^{3014}/_{1014}$; tooth crowns of upper and lower 4 molars consist of 2 ridges (concave and convex respectively), which are connected by further ridges lying in the longitudinal direction, P_4 has one cutting edge, P^4 a cutting outer edge and on the inner side 2 humps lengthways bordering longitudinal valley, $M^{1-3}/_{1-3}$ increase in size, $M^4/_4$ smaller than $M^3/_3$; herbivore. PROVENANCE and DISTRIBUTION: Pliocene to Pleistocene, New Guinea; Pleistocene, Australia.

Galerix [2] Order Insectivora Family Erinaceidae

CHARACTERISTICS: extinct hedgehog of rat size; dentition formula $^{3143}/_{3143}$; pre-molars: P^3 with 1-2 cusps inner side, P_3 larger than P_2, P_4 with high cusp at front; molars: M^{1-2} with 2 outer and inner cusps opposite each other, in rear half further smaller cusp; M_{1-2} with 3 inner cusps and 2 outer, front 2 inner cusps joined via front outer cusp, similar joining of rear cusps, from which a ridge extends at front to border tooth crown on both sides. In contrast to genuine hedgehogs, no spines, but with long tail. PROVENANCE and DISTRIBUTION: fossil genera are found in the Miocene of North America, south and west Europe, Turkey, North Africa; the four Recent genera are limited to the east Asian region. They are thought to be inhabitants of damp forests.

Archaeonycteris [3] Order Chiroptera Family Palaeochiropterygidae

CHARACTERISTICS: fossil bat; dentition formula $^{3133}/_{3133}$; P_2 single-rooted, smaller than P_3 and P_4; tooth crowns of M_{1-3} six-pointed, 3rd inner point and 2nd outer point equal size, 4th inner point slightly smaller and lower than 3rd; in M^{1-2} no central outer cusp, in place of rear inner cusp a broad rounded surface. PROVENANCE: Middle Eocene. DISTRIBUTION: Messel, Germany.

It is assumed that the bats derive from insectivorous mammals of the Mesozoic. They are the only mammals which, as a result of the extension of the 2nd to 4th fingers and development of a skin flap between the fingers, are capable of genuine fluttering flight. Even the oldest known bats from the lower Eocene of North America possessed these physical features. Except for a few more rare forms, members of the most important recent groups of bats have been known from the Oligocene on.

1 *Halmaturus vinceus*; top: upper jaw fragment showing P^3, M^{1-3} (right to left); bottom: lower jaw fragment showing P_3, M_{1-3} (right to left); Pleistocene cave debris from Wellington Caves/Australᵗ
2 *Galerix exilis*, view of skull interior from below showing dentition C, P^{1-4}, M^{1-3}; Middle Miocene, Goldberg im Ries/Germany. Skull length: 3.5cm.
3 *Archaeonycteris* sp., complete individual, one side sealed in plastic; Middle Eocene, Messel/Germany. Length head to tail: 7.5cm.

2 △

3 ▽

MAMMALS
Phylum Vertebrata   Class Mammalia

Mesopithecus   Order Primates   Sub-order Anthropoidea
Family Cercopithecidae   Sub-family Colobinae
CHARACTERISTICS: primitive member of Colobinae; length head to tail c. 1.6m,
reconstructions give appearance of guenon monkey, rear limbs longer than front,
upper arm shorter than lower, fingers shorter than toes, in contrast to modern
Colobinae no degeneration of thumb; tail long, more than $\frac{1}{3}$ of total length; snou
extended, large eye sockets; dentition formula $\frac{2123}{2123}$; 2 incisors, 1 canine, 2
pre-molars, 3 molars per half of jaw both upper and lower, as found in more
highly developed primates; canines curved like daggers, much more prominent in
male; pre-molars and molars with 4 cusps, each pair of front and rear cusps
joined by ridge running at right angles to jaw axis and becoming gradually lower,
only rearmost tooth of lower jaw has 5th cusp outside other 4. PROVENANCE:
Uppermost Miocene. DISTRIBUTION: Greece, Persia, Czechoslovakia. A further
small form from the Pliocene or Pleistocene in Europe can be allocated to this
genus, but only with reservations.

The history of *Mesopithecus* finds began in 1838, when a Bavarian soldier posted
to archaeological digs in Greece brought some souvenir pieces home. The then
director of the Zoological collection in Munich (Wagner) identified one of the
various bone fragments as a piece of the snout of a prehistoric ape. The use of
the name *Mesopithecus* was meant, as Wagner saw it, to indicate an intermediate
position between the gibbons and the guenon monkeys. The species name
pentelicus refers to a range of mountains called Pentelicon, east of Athens, at the
foot of which the find was located. More than 100 individuals were disinterred
from these beds alone. On the basis of the conditions of the find locality, the
skeletal findings and the dental morphology it is assumed today that at the time
Mesopithecus wandered through the landscape in troupes as a ground-living
animal feeding mainly on plants. Present research counts *Mesopithecus* among the
Colobinae, even though the endocranium and tooth pattern are similar to those of
modern Cercopithecidae. It is assumed that both groups developed in Africa and
migrated into Eurasia in the Miocene.

Mesopithecus pentelicus, Pikermi/Greece.
1 Front view of female skull with eye and nostril apertures; breadth of skull across eye apertures
6.3cm:
2 Lateral view of palate of male with complete dentition of left half of jaw; length and width of las
tooth on left 0.7cm.

2 ▽

MAMMALS
Phylum Vertebrata   Class Mammalia

Potamotherium [1] Order Carnivora Family Mustelidae
CHARACTERISTICS: slender, fish-eating otter (Lutrinae) up to 1.4m long, adapted to aquatic existence; differs from recent otters (*Lutra*) in dentition: 1st upper pre-molar larger; 4th upper pre-molar shorter, as also 1st upper molar with its angled, rear outer edge; 2nd upper molar present; in lower jaw 1st pre-molar present. PROVENANCE: Upper Oligocene to Middle Miocene. DISTRIBUTION: Germany, France.

From the more than 10,000 remains recovered at the St Gerand site in France it was possible at a rough estimate to reconstruct about 200 single individuals of this species. Considered as a gregarious fish-eater found in lakes.

Adcrocuta [2] Order Carnivora Family Hyaenidae
CHARACTERISTICS: smaller than recent spotted hyena (*Crocuta*). The 4th upper pre-molars extended to rear and the 1st molars extended to front are developed as cutting teeth; tendency to enlargement of rear pre-molars upper and lower; 4th upper pre-molar with front inside cusp. Bones of prey broken by use of conical main points of upper and lower pre-molars. PROVENANCE: Upper Miocene to Lower Pliocene. DISTRIBUTION: Greece, Turkey, China.

Machairodus [3] Order Carnivora Family Felidae
CHARACTERISTICS: cats reaching size of lion; very large, sabre-like canine teeth in upper jaw, front and rear edges of which finely jagged (sabre-toothed tiger). Canine teeth of lower jaw smaller but also jagged on edges, as are incisors. Upper jaw with P^{2-4}, M^1; lower jaw with P_{3-4}, M_4; cutting function performed by long P^4 and shorter M_1. PROVENANCE and DISTRIBUTION: Upper Miocene to Lower Pliocene, Europe; Lower Pliocene, North America.

The formation of the musculature of head and jaws indicates that the lower jaw could be lowered considerably, so allowing free use of the sabre-like canines as a weapon to strike with.

1 *Potamotherium valletoni* Miocene, St Gerand/France. Skull length: 12cm.
2 *Adcrocuta eximia,* Upper Miocene/Garkin, Turkey. Top: upper jaw with I^{1-3}, C, P^{1-4}; length: 12cm. Bottom: lower jaw with C, P_{1-4}, M_1.
3 *Machairodus* sp.; front part of skull with lower jaw, Lower Pliocene, Pikermi/Greece. Length of canine tooth: 12cm.

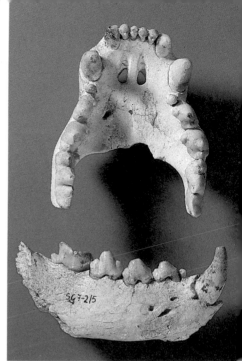

2 △   ▽ 3

M A M M A L S
Phylum Vertebrata   Class Mammalia

Squalodon [1] Order Cetacea   Family Squalodontidae
CHARACTERISTICS: extinct predatory toothed whale up to 5m long; skull $\frac{1}{5}$ of body length; up to 62 teeth, triangular at rear, double or triple roots; incisors and canines single roots, teeth at front form rake-like sieve.

Hyotherium [2] Order Artiodactyla   Family Suidae
CHARACTERISTICS: fossil pig; dentition formula $\frac{3143}{3133}$; upper and lower molars made up of cusped bony forms to aid squashing of food, front pre-molars used for cutting; sexual dimorphism in skull structure and in canines; powerful upper canines in male, in female poorly developed. Thought to inhabit damp lowlands and marshy forests, omnivore. PROVENANCE: Lower Miocene to Lower Pliocene. DISTRIBUTION: Europe.

Caenomeryx [3/4] Order Artiodactyla   Super-family Cainotherioidea
CHARACTERISTICS: small artiodactyl of size of hare; dentition formula $\frac{3143}{3133}$; gap between canine and 1st very small pre-molar, inner cusp of P^{4-2} decreasing in mass and height towards front; tooth crowns of upper molars consist in front area of 2, in rear area of 3 parallel, interlocking cusps; sometimes gap between lower canine and P_2; lower molars with V-shaped cusps directed inwards and located one behind the other, these completed by tall points towards inner side. Herbivore. PROVENANCE: Middle to Upper Oligocene. DISTRIBUTION: Europe.

Dicroceros [5/6] Order Artiodactyla   Family Cervidae   Sub-family Muntiacinae
CHARACTERISTICS: fossil muntjac stag of fallow deer size; juvenile forms with single-spike horns, adults have relatively long antler stem with tines branching above, of which rear one more powerfully developed; full antlers as in modern stags not present, shedding of antlers leads only to thickening of tines, but not to larger number; tooth enamel of teeth typical of deer has scarred surface; upper canines have sabre-like curve and are longer in male than female. PROVENANCE and DISTRIBUTION: Lower Miocene to Upper Pliocene, Europe; Upper Miocene to Lower Pliocene, Asia.

1 *Squalodon* sp., Miocene, Simbach am Inn/Germany. Length of incisor: 7.5cm.
2 *Hyotherium soemmeringi,* upper jaw with teeth (boar), Miocene, Mainburg/Germany. Length: 15cm.
3 *Caenomeryx filholi,* complete skull with lower jaw, crevices filled, Upper Oligocene, Ingolstadt/Germany. Silicified specimen. Length of skull: 7.5cm.
4 *Caenomeryx filholi,* view of upper jaw with teeth.
5 *Dicroceros* sp., series of upper jaw teeth showing P^{2-4}, M^{1-3}; Miocene, Sansan/France.
6 As above, lower jaw showing P_{3-4}, M_{1-3}.

3 ▽   2 △   4 ▽

5 ▽   6 ▽

MAMMALS
Phylum Vertebrata Class Mammalia

Gomphotherium [1] Sub-order Mastodontoidea Family Trilophodontidae
CHARACTERISTICS: generalised group of widely differing forms of mastodon
(related to elephants). Tooth crowns of upper and lower molars consist of several
succeeding rows of cusps (at least 3), which each form a transverse ridge,
depressions in these ridges may themselves be closed by further cusps; last upper
and lower molars with more than 3 rows; 1 pair of tusks in each jaw. Principal
PROVENANCE and DISTRIBUTION: Miocene, Eurasia, Africa, North America.

Dinotherium [2] Sub-order Deinotherioidea Family Deinotheriidae
CHARACTERISTICS: animals with powerful trunks, resembling elephants; in each of
upper and lower jaw 2 pre-molars and 3 molars; tooth crowns of molars formed
by succeeding transverse ridges; no tusks in upper jaw, those of lower jaw bent
downwards and backwards. PROVENANCE and DISTRIBUTION: Miocene, Europe
and Asia; Miocene to Pleistocene, Africa.

Palaeoloxodon [3] Sub-order Elefantoidea Family Elfantidae
CHARACTERISTICS: steppe-living elephant up to 4.5m tall; tusks only in upper jaw;
molars with high crowns, consisting of laminated enamel filled with dentine and
joined by tooth cement; of 3 permanent molars only 1 in use at any one time,
replacement sequence runs from front to back, as does movement of jaws;
adapted to harder types of plant food on steppes. PROVENANCE and DISTRIBUTION:
Pleistocene, Europe (steppe period of the Mindel (Elster) glaciation).

The circular aperature in front of the left molar in Plate 3 is the result of
periostitis and the formation of pus in the tooth cavity. The unsymmetrical
position of the right tooth and its more pronounced wear may be traced to the
change of chewing movements to ease the load on the diseased tooth.

1 *Gomphotherium agustidens.* Top: lower 2nd molar, Miocene, Mallersdorf/Germany. Length:
11cm, breadth: 6cm; Bottom: last upper molar, Miocene, Pöttmes bei Augsburg/Germany.
Length: 16cm, breadth: 8cm.
2 Top: 1st upper molar, Miocene, Aichach/Germany. Length: 7.5cm, breadth: 5.5cm; Bottom: 2nd
lower molar, Miocene, Moosburg/Germany. Length: 7cm, Breadth: 5.5cm.

3 *Palaeoloxodon trogontherii,* Rhine gravels from Mannheim/Germany. Length of molar: 25cm.

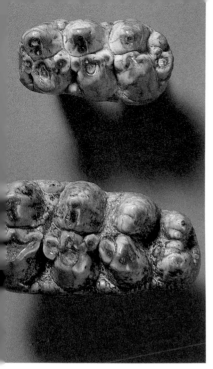

2 △

3 ▽

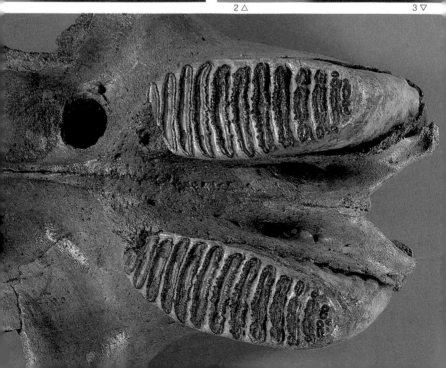

MAMMALS
Phylum Vertebrata Class Mammalia

Desmostylus [1] Order Desmostylia Family Desmostylidae
CHARACTERISTICS: four-footed mammal, resembling hippopotamus; upper and lower front teeth with chopping action; upper molars formed of 8 columns in 4 transverse rows, lower of 7 in 3 rows; wear in mastication progressively removes original covering layer of enamel of individual columns.
PROVENANCE and DISTRIBUTION: Oligocene to Miocene, former coasts of northern Pacific. Amphibious herbivore.

Tapirus [2] Order Perissodactyla Family Tapiridae
CHARACTERISTICS: fossil tapir; dentition formula $^{3143}\!/_{3133}$; teeth consist of combination of transverse ridges and humps; herbivorous inhabitant of marshy forests, known since Lower Oligocene. PROVENANCE and DISTRIBUTION: Lower Oligocene to Pleistocene, Europe.

Chilotherium [3] Order Perissodactyla Family Rhinocerotidae
CHARACTERISTICS: short-footed fossil rhinoceros of the steppe, with high-crowned teeth. PROVENANCE and DISTRIBUTION: Lower Miocene to Lower Pleistocene, Asia; Upper Miocene to Upper Pliocene, Europe.

Chalicotherium [4] Order Perissodactyla Family Chalicotheriidae
CHARACTERISTICS: extinct herbivore; front legs longer than rear, 3-toed feet, with retractable claws; high-crowned teeth, in upper jaw reminiscent of rhinoceros. PROVENANCE: Middle Miocene to Lower Pliocene. DISTRIBUTION: Europe.

Hipparion [5] Order Perissodactyla Family Equidae
CHARACTERISTICS: fossil grazing (as distinct from browsing) horse; migrated from North America to Europe during Pliocene; front and rear feet with 3 elements but considerable reduced side toes and powerful hoof; high-crowned molars with dense folding in enamel and deposition of dental cement, P^2 longer than other molars, with triangular outline. PROVENANCE: Upper Miocene to Lower Pleistocene. DISTRIBUTION: Europe.

Anchitherium [6] Order Perissodactyla Family Equidae
CHARACTERISTICS: fossil browsing horse, migrated from North America to Europe during Miocene; front and rear feet with 3 elements, but side toes not as reduced as in *Hipparion*, molars with low crowns. PROVENANCE and DISTRIBUTION: Miocene, North America; Middle Miocene to Lower Pliocene, Europe and Asia.

1 *Desmostylus* sp., lower left molar, Miocene, Fresno/California/USA. Tooth length: 8cm.
2 *Tapirus* sp., Top: upper jaw with P^{1-4}, M^{1-3}; Bottom: lower jaw with I_{1-3}, C, P_{2-4}, M_{1-3}; Upper Oligocene with Tertiary crevice filling, Ingolstadt/Germany. Lower jaw length: 22cm.
3 *Chilotherium intermedium,* Lower Pliocene, Pakistan. Length of tooth row: 11cm.
4 *Chalicotherium goldfussi,* teeth of upper jaw, Lower Pliocene, Czechoslovakia. Length of tooth row: 16cm.
5 *Hipparion minus,* Pliocene, Samos/Greece. Left upper jaw with tooth row showing P^{2-4}, M^{1-3}; length: 12cm.
6 *Anchitherium aurelianense,* Miocene, Steinheim/Germany. Upper left tooth row with P^{2-4}, M^{1-3}; length: 12cm.

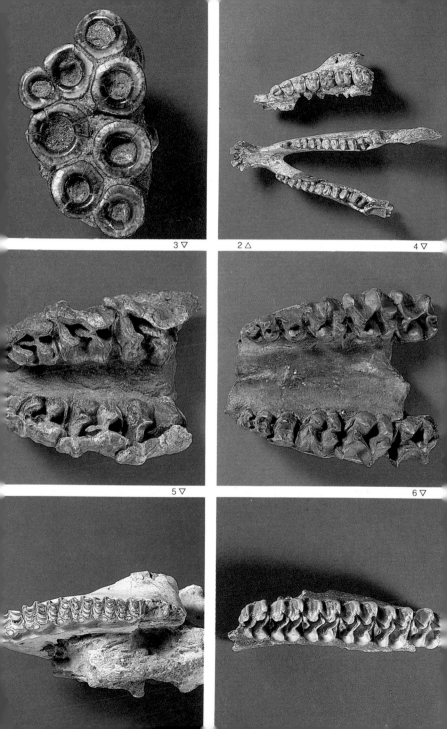

3 ▽   2 △   4 ▽

5 ▽   6 ▽

M A M M A L S
Phylum Vertebrata   Class Mammalia

Prolagus [1] Order Lagomorpha Family Ochotonidae
CHARACTERISTICS: fossil whistling hare of size of rat, limbs of equal length; 2 pair of gnawing teeth in upper jaw as in hares and rabbits, also gaps between these and pre-molars; dentition formula $^{2032}/_{1022}$; teeth without roots grow continuously throughout life, with high crowns; in contrast to hares and rabbits usually only 2 upper molars; transverse oval depression at joint of lower jaw indicates mainly sideways jaw movement in chewing; considered as a burrowing herbivore.
PROVENANCE: Miocene to Holocene. DISTRIBUTION: Europe.

Pseudosciurus [2] Order Simplicidentata Family Pseudosciuridae
CHARACTERISTICS: extinct rodent genus of size of rat; dentition formula $^{1013}/_{1013}$, tooth crowns of upper and lower jaw consist of cusps tending to point, opposite cusps joined by ridges which in middle of tooth may develop into secondary humps; division of surface of crown so becomes deeply wrinkled or honeycomb-like. Habitat dry terrain. PROVENANCE: Upper Eocene to Middle Oligocene. DISTRIBUTION: Europe.

Steneofiber [3] Order Simplicidentata Family Castoridae
CHARACTERISTICS: extinct beaver; small to medium-sized form; dentition formula $^{1013}/_{1013}$; well-preserved tooth crowns consist of 5 parallel succeeding loop-shapes of enamel, teeth high-crowned, adapted for much wear, powerful, chisel-shaped, pointed gnawing teeth. PROVENANCE: Upper Oligocene to Upper Miocene. DISTRIBUTION: Europe.

Melissiodon [4] Order Simplicidentata Family Melissiodontidae
CHARACTERISTICS: extinct rodent of size of rat; dentition formula $^{1003}/_{1003}$; surface of tooth crowns marked by number of small ridges running in both directions so divided into very small zones, teeth with low crowns, 1 pre-molar missing.
PROVENANCE: Upper Oligocene to Lower Miocene. DISTRIBUTION: Europe.

1 *Prolagus oeningensis*, Miocene, Öningen/Germany. Lower jaw length: 2.5cm.
2 *Pseudosciurus suevicus*, view of inner side of skull with dentition P^4, M$^{1-3}$; crevice filling from Lower Oligocene, Möhren/Germany. Skull length: 7cm.
3 *Steneofiber jaegeri*, front part of left lower jaw with I, P$_4$, M$_1$, Miocene, Günzburg/Germany. Length: 6cm.
4 *Melissiodon chatticum*, fragment of upper jaw with M$^{1-3}$ (from top), crevice filling from Upper Oligocene, Ingolstadt/Germany. Tooth row length: 8mm.

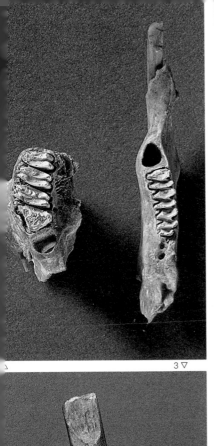

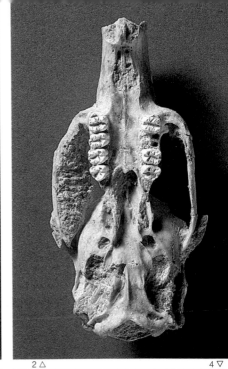

1

3 ▽

2 △

4 ▽

TRACE FOSSILS

Fossilised burrows, tracks, footprints etc ("fossil behaviour") are produced by almost every kind of vagrant animal living in or on top of sediments. Some are confined to selected parts of the sea, others occur only in rocks of a certain age. The oldest are Precambrian.

Chondrites [1]

CHARACTERISTICS: branching structures resulting from feeding process, of different colour from surrounding rock. PROVENANCE: Cambrian to Tertiary. DISTRIBUTION: world-wide.

Believed to be produced by sediment-eating worms. The change in colour is explained as the result of a chemical change in the originally soft sediment, when it was passed through the digestive tract of the worms and certain substances extracted from it.

Asteriacites [2]

This imprint was described as a five-armed ophiuroid as early as 1755 in a Latin description of genera. Starfish or ophiuroids burrow into the sediment using their ambulacral tube feet located on the underside of the body. When the animal moves on, a hollow relief is produced in the sand, which is later filled by sediment, producing a somewhat broadened outline marking the outward reach of the ambulacral feet. The trace-fossil genus *Asteriacites* is known from the Ordovician to the Tertiary (North America, Europe).

Roll Traces [3]

This bottom illustration is meant to serve as a representative example of how impressions in the sediment, made by hard body parts, can be preserved without the layman being able to spot the creature which made them as a whole (see centre section of photo). If drifting ammonite shells are deposited in an area of finely grained sediments, as here in the fine limestone ooze of the Solnhofen lagoon, an impression may be made in the sediment, showing the shell's impact under the influence of its own buoyancy and slow rate of sinking to the bottom. In the case illustrated an ammonite from the Perisphinctoid group was rolled along on its edge by the current after its first impact and so left the ribbed pattern of its back in the sediment. Cases are also known where the ammonite shell has made contact several times and itself been preserved nearby.

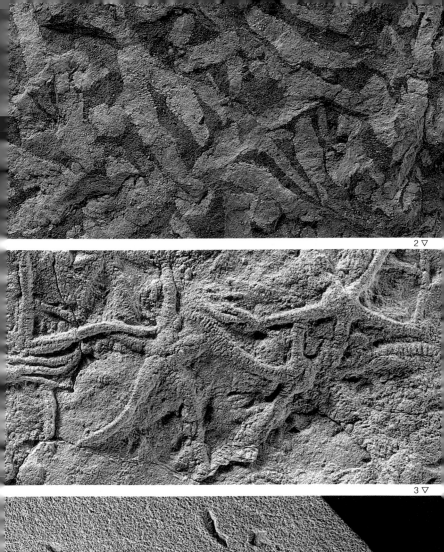

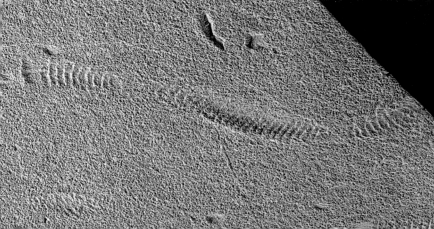

ALGAE

Diatoms [1-3] Sub-phylum Bacillariophyta

The common name of these forms, siliceous algae, indicates that these microscopic organisms (up to 2mm long) possess a cell-wall composed of silica, which is commonly covered on the outside by an organic substance. The wall is divided into two parts; the larger (epitheca) encloses the smaller (hypotheca) like the lid on a cheese box. With the exception of some forms which are only slightly silicified, the cell wall is seen under the electron microscope to be extremely complex. It consists of differently shaped chambers, the bases of which are perforated and which have further additional apertures. Diatoms are capable of locomotion and possess what is called a raphe. This is a split-like opening with thickened edges or a tube with apertures, which is in contact with the protoplasm of the cell; through it the diatom can extrude fibrous material and affix it to the surface below, so moving itself along. The structure of the raphe, or the lack of it, is, in addition to the fine structure of the silicified cell wall, an important feature in classification.

Two orders are differentiated on the basis of the general structure and symmetry of their valves. The Centrales possess a round or rounded triangular external cover, the wall-structure of which is arranged radially and concentrically. These are, with a few exceptions, marine forms which make up the major part of the plankton. The silicified walls of the Pennales have stick-, boat- or wedge-shaped structures; S-shaped and curved forms also exist. Their symmetrical axis runs along a centre line, from which the wall structures extend in a feather-like pattern. Genera of this order may be found in fresh, brackish or sea water and since they possess a raphe are mobile, in contrast to the Centrales (with the exception of one sub-order).

The oldest diatoms are found in the Lower Cretaceous; peaks of development were reached by the diatoms in the Tertiary period and at present. The immense deposits of kieselguhr (diatomite, diatomaceous earth) in Russia and the USA owe their existence to the enormous numbers of diatoms present in the seas. The beds in the Lüneburg Heath in northern Germany are interglacial accumulations arising in fresh water.

For the palaeontologist, fossil diatoms are of significance in the area of palaeoecology. When compared with first-hand knowledge of recent biotopes, they are indicators which allow the salinity and quality of the waters, their nutrient content and the depth to be estimated.

1 Longitudinal view of a large (200μ) *Pinnularia* and of smaller tube-like forms of the genus *Melosira* from the Miocene, Wackersdorf/Germany. Fresh- water.
2 Example from the marine Lower Eocene from Jutland, showing the circular valves of *Coscinodiscus* and triangular valves of *Triceratium* (200μ).
3 Example from Miocene fresh-water deposits from Castel de Piano/Italy: slender, stick-like forms of genus *Synedra*; 2 large, thick specimens of genus *Pinnularia* (200μ); very small boat-like specimens of the genus *Cymbella* and several other small types.

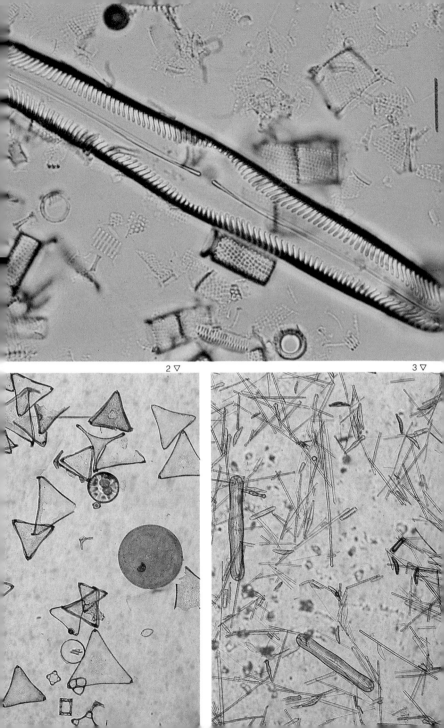

2 ▽   3 ▽

A L G A E

Stromatolite [1] Sub-phylum Cyanophyta (Blue-green algae)
CHARACTERISTICS: fossil mats of algae in limestones, layered in beds of millimetre thickness, showing alternate light and dark colouring: the light colour can be traced to a calcite component with magnesium content, deposited in the external mucal layer of the algae; the dark colour results from precipitated particles of sediment trapped in the interwoven algae. PROVENANCE: Precambrian to Recent. DISTRIBUTION: world-wide.

Archaeolithothamnium [2] Sub-phylum Rhodophyta (Red algae)
Family Corallinaceae
CHARACTERISTICS: calcified algae visible only in section; either forms encrustation or branching forms up to several centimetres in length, hypothallus multi-layered or arranged parallel to substrate: outer tissue usually thick, consisting of uniformly constructed rows of cells, in which conceptacles grouped in irregular rows. PROVENANCE: Upper Jurassic to Recent.

Recent representatives of the family Corallinaceae form encrustations on and solidify sediment particles, are capable of forming small reefs and cover up to 40% of the Hawaiian coastal reefs.

Stonewort Algae [3/4] Sub-phylum Charophyta (Stoneworts) Family Characeae
CHARACTERISTICS: inhabitants of fresh water of horsetail-like appearance: both the plant itself (its outer cuticular layer) and what are called the Charaoogonia (ovum buds) can precipitate lime. PROVENANCE: Devonian to Recent. DISTRIBUTION: world-wide.

Diplopora [5] Sub-phylum Chlorophyta (Green algae) Family Dasycladaceae
CHARACTERISTICS: calcified cylindrical basic cells of a green alga; diam. 0.9-8mm, inner side has roughly circular pores as attachment points for 3-4 branches (no further division), which extend to outer walls; these of cylindrical or cudgel-shaped form. PROVENANCE and DISTRIBUTION: Alpine Muschelkalk (Middle Triassic) in northern and southern Calcareous Alps.

M O S S E S

Neckera [6] Sub-phylum Bryophyta Class Bryatae
Fossil bryata (leafed gametophyte) from interglacial tufa, Laacher See, Germany c. 350,000 years old. Length of specimen: 2.5cm.

1 Stromatolite, Australia. Height: 7cm.
2 *Archaeolithothamnium* sp., Eocene, Neubeuern am Inn/Germany. Length of specimen: 5cm.
3 Charaoogonia of the genus *Nitellopsis* with their typical spiral shells, Miocene, Allgäu/Germany. Length: 2mm.
4 Calcified stalks of the *Chara* plant, whose external layer shows the contorted structure. Miocene fresh-water limestone, Ries/Germany. Width of stalks: 4mm.
5 Weathered-out remains of *Diplopora,* Triassic, Mittenwald/Germany.

6 *Neckera* - see above

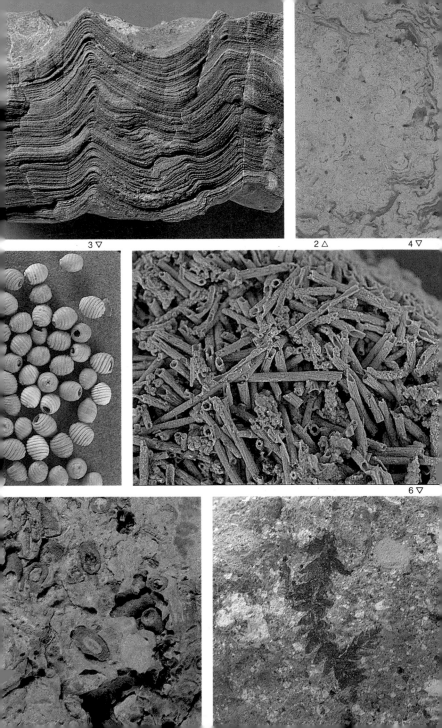

3 ▽

2 △   4 ▽

6 ▽

FUNGI

Mycelites [1] Sub-phylum Chytridiomycota (Flagellate Fungi) or Chlorophyta
CHARACTERISTICS: genus typical of tunnel-producing thread-like fungi or green algae (classification not yet clarified) which, after the death of some animal, invaded and occupied its bones, teeth or shell.

Polyporus [2] Sub-phylum Eumycota (Genuine Fungi) Class Basidiomycetes
CHARACTERISTICS: stemmed structures forming console-like projections, spore chambers consisting of pores and honeycombs on underside; this fossil tree fungus shows the multi-layered spore tissue arranged in vertical tube structures.

PRIMITIVE FERNS
Sub-phylum Pteridophyta   Class Psilophytatae

Taeniocrada [3] Family Rhyniaceae
CHARACTERISTICS: forking, bare, leafless, flat shoots; bundles of osmotic vascular tissue central, stemmed sporangia, shallow-water plant. PROVENANCE: Silurian to Upper Devonian. DISTRIBUTION: world-wide.

Thursophyton [4] Family Asteroxylaceae
CHARACTERISTICS: aerial shoots sprouting from rhizomes, up to 50cm high, main shoot bears small leaves decreasing in size with height and dichotomic branching on finest members; in this family cross-section of vascular tissue bundle star-shaped. PROVENANCE: Devonian. DISTRIBUTION: Europe.

CLUB MOSSES
Sub-phylum Pteridophyta (Ferns) Class Lycopodiatae
N.B. Practically all genera listed on pp. 216-230 as occurring in the Carboniferous of the Northern Hemisphere are present in the British and eastern North American coalfield areas.

Lepidodendron [5] Order Lepidodendrales Family Lepidodendraceae
CHARACTERISTICS: originally generic name only for the preserved outer cortex, later transferred to their forked, leaved branches (see 1, p.218); the rhombic cushioned leaves of *L. dichotomum*, 3cm in length, show the sideways extension of the sporangia at end of centre line of cushion. PROVENANCE: Devonian to Middle Permian. DISTRIBUTION: North America, Europe, Asia.

Lepidostrobus [6] Order Lepidodendrales Family Lepidodendraceae
CHARACTERISTICS: form-genus term for reproductive organ of this family; cone or cylinder in shape, sporangia-bearing leaves (sporophylls) arranged spirally along axis, sporangia carried on upper surface close to axis, in closed cone sporophylls overlap one another like roof-tiles, inclined upwards. PROVENANCE: Lower to Upper Carboniferous. DISTRIBUTION: Northern Hemisphere.

1 *Mycelites ossifragus,* tunnels in fossil rhinoceros tooth, Miocene, Sandelzhausen/Germany. Length of tooth: 4cm.
2 *Polyporus* sp., Tertiary, Libyan Desert. Breadth: 6cm.
3 *Taeniocrada decheniana,* Lower Devonian, Rheineck/Germany. This section: 15cm.
4 *Thursophyton elberfeldense,* Middle Devonian, Elberfeld/Germany. This section: 10cm.
5 *Lepidodendron dichotomum,* Upper Carboniferous, Neutischein/Czechoslovakia.
6 *Lepidostrobus* sp., Carboniferous, Nürschan/Czechoslovakia. Cone length: 5cm.

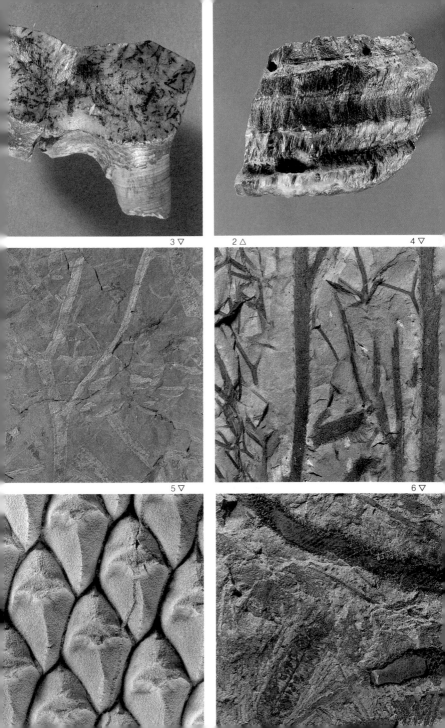

3 ▽

2 △   4 ▽

5 ▽   6 ▽

CLUB-MOSSES

Lepidodendron [1] Order Lepidodendrales Family Lepidodendraceae
CHARACTERISTICS: generic name for minute leaves (see 5, p.216) with central
vein, triangular in section: cortex consists of rhombic forms, the leaf cushions,
arranged in obliquely inclined rows: actual sporangium located in upper part of
leaf cushion. PROVENANCE: Lower to Upper Carboniferous. DISTRIBUTION:
Northern Hemisphere. Staffordshire, Yorkshire/England; South Wales; central
Scotland.

Lepidophloios [2] Order Lepidodendrales Family Lepidodendraceae
CHARACTERISTICS: generic name for preserved cortex in this family; in contrast to
Lepidendron lower part of leaf cushion folded back, sporangium broad rhombus in
shape. PROVENANCE: Carboniferous. DISTRIBUTION: Northern Hemisphere.

Sigillaria [3] Order Lepidodendrales Family Sigillariaceae
CHARACTERISTICS: generic name for preserved cortex in this family; leaf cushions
and sporangia six-sided or sometimes six-sided with rounded corners tending to
oval, often arranged in rows along longitudinal ribs. PROVENANCE: Lower to
Upper Carboniferous. DISTRIBUTION: Northern Hemisphere. Staffordshire,
Somerset, Yorkshire/England; South Wales.

Subsigillaria [4] Order Lepidodendrales Family Sigillariaceae
CHARACTERISTICS: generic name for preserved cortex in this family; leaf cushions
or usually large sporangia flat on cortex, never in longitudinal rows; sporangia
polygonal or extended sideways with sharp points at sides. PROVENANCE: Upper
Carboniferous to Lower Permian. DISTRIBUTION: Northern Hemisphere.

HORSETAILS
Sub-phylum Pteridophyta Class Equisetatae

Sphenophyllum [5/6] Order Sphenophyllales Family Sphenophyllaceae
CHARACTERISTICS: form-genus name for leaves of this family; small leaves
attached in threes at nodes on shoot, usually wedge-shaped with short stem,
several veins. PROVENANCE: Upper Devonian to Permian. DISTRIBUTION: Europe.
Considered as creeping or climbing plants, up to 1m long.

1 *Lepidodendron selaginoides,* leaved twig, leaves of triangular section; Carboniferous,
  Nürschan/Czechoslovakia. Height of section: 15cm.
2 *Lepidophloios laricinus,* Upper Carboniferous, St Ingbert/Germany. This section: 5cm.
3 *Sigillaria elongata,* pollen chambers along ribs; Upper Carboniferous, Bochum/Germany. Section:
  5cm.
4 *Subsigillaria ichthyolepsis,* sideways extension of sporangia; Upper Carboniferous, Reisbach
  mine/Saar/Germany. Section: 5cm.
5 *Sphenophyllum myriophyllum,* wedge-shaped leaf form divided into thin leaflets, forked at base,
  up to 3cm long; Upper Carboniferous, Radnice/Czechoslovakia. Section: 10cm.
6 *Sphenophyllum verticillatum,* Upper Carboniferous, Halle/Germany. Diam. of single leaf 2cm;
  index fossil for Upper Carboniferous.

$3 \triangledown$

$2 \triangle$ $4 \triangledown$

$5 \triangledown$ $6 \triangledown$

HORSETAILS
Sub-phylum Pteridophyta Class Equisetatae

Archaeocalamites [1] Order Equisetales Family Archaeocalamitaceae
CHARACTERISTICS: form-genus name for secretions of hollow interior of medulla
(sedimentary steinkern) of the family Archaeocalamitaceae: these steinkerns have
longitudinal furrows, interrupted by ring-shaped transverse depressions; these
correspond to the inwards pointing projections on the primary wood and run
without deviation over the nodes (attachment points for leaves): this implies that
the leaves were placed directly above one another, whereas in Calamitaceae they
are arranged in alternation. PROVENANCE: Upper Devonian to Lower
Carboniferous. DISTRIBUTION: Northern Hemisphere.

The allocation to a particular family is not only based on the structure of the
medullar steinkern, but also on the formation of forked leaves, which are
unknown in Calamitaceae, and the structure of the fructifications and other
anatomical details of the wood, which can be observed in sedimentary steinkerns
preserved in the original context. The Archaeocalamitaceae were tree-like
horsetails which, however, with a maximum height of 6m, never achieved the
dimensions of the Calamitaceae.

Calamodendron [2] Order Equisetales Family Calamitaceae
CHARACTERISTICS: form-genus term for trunk structure with its anatomical details
of family Calamitaceae: cross-section of trunk of this family may be divided into
central hollow space, the medulla, a thick section of secondary wood, particularly
well developed towards the exterior, and an equally well developed cortex, not
often preserved; in the specimen illustrated the medullar hollow can be seen,
surrounded by silicified secondary wood of variable striping without preserved
cortex; the whitish parts correspond to the radially thickened tracheids
(water-conducting cells), the apertures of which (gaps in cell-wall) are arranged
in one or two rows and somewhat elongated; the parts coloured black correspond
to the radiating members of the pith. PROVENANCE: Lower to Middle Permian.
DISTRIBUTION: Germany, France.

Representatives of this family of horsetails were tree-like plants reaching up to
30m in height and 1m in diameter. They grew in the marshy forests of the
Carboniferous. Although these trees possess a secondary growth of wood, no
annual rings are formed, which would suggest a uniform, tropical climate.

1 *Archaeocalamites radiatus,* sedimentary steinkern, Lower Carboniferous,
Peterswalde/Czechoslovakia. Length: 13cm.
2 *Calamodendron striatum,* silicified specimen, Lower Permian, Hilbersdorf bei Chemnitz/Germany.
17cm.

HORSETAILS
Sub-phylum Pteridophyta Class Equisetatae

Annularia Order Equisetales Family Calamitaceae

CHARACTERISTICS: form-genus name for leaves of family Calamitaceae. Leaves always single-veined, arranged in whorls, in single plane, always relatively small, spatulate, never forked, united as collar at base; number of leaves in each whorl from 4 to 40. PROVENANCE: Lower Carboniferous to Permian. DISTRIBUTION: Europe, North America. Radstock/Somerset/England.

In addition to this genus classified by its leaves there are a number of other Calamitaceae classified on a similar basis. The differences lie in the way that the leaves are joined at their base, the formation of the leaf whorl (with radial symmetry or circular) and the form of the small leaves (forked or simple in form), and also the number of leaves in each whorl. In the specimen illustrated, *A. stellata*, the unequal length of the leaves can be clearly seen; this gives the whorl its elliptical outline. Well preserved specimens show the hairy surface of the leaves and the central vein bordered by 2 furrows.

In the botanical system, the Calamitaceae are grouped with the Sphenophyllaceae and the Equisetaceae as Sphenophyta; these reached their peak in the Carboniferous and make up a considerable part of the coal seams. A number of writers consider the group Hyeniales to be the origin of these forms. They were weed-like plants of not more than 50cm in height, with creeping rhizomes. At their base, the aerial shoot (the actual plant) had a thickened secondary growth and forked leaves in whorls. The bearers of the sporangia were also arranged in whorls in the upper part of the shoot. It is this whorled arrangement of leaves and sporangia which lent them their common features with the Sphenophyta, although they lacked the intermediate subdivision of the shoots by nodes and internodes, which is widespread in the later group.

More recent examination, based above all on the structure of the sporangiophores, places the Hyeniceae among the primitive ferns (order Cladoxylales).

Annularia stellata, branch with foliage, Upper Carboniferous, Nassfeld/Austria. Length: 40cm.

HORSETAILS
Sub-phylum Pteridophyta Class Equisetatae

Equisetites [1/2] Order Equisetales Family Equisetaceae
CHARACTERISTICS: horsetail with distinctly subdivided stem; leaves in each whorl united to form cuff; points of leaves, inclined upwards, stand free; flowers (*Equisetostachys*) egg-shaped. PROVENANCE: Upper Carboniferous to Cretaceous DISTRIBUTION: Europe, Siberia.

Schizoneura [3] Order Equisetales Family Schizoneuraceae
CHARACTERISTICS: horsetail with relatively long internodia; leaves of lower whorl joined along whole edge, later divided into 2 or more lobes; conductive vessels c stem, not set alternately, run across nodes. PROVENANCE: Triassic. DISTRIBUTION Germany, Switzerland, Southern Hemisphere.

FERNS
Sub-phylum Pteridophyta Class Filicatae

Calamophyton [4] Order Cladoxylales Family Calamophytaceae
CHARACTERISTICS: shoot thickened at base, with multiple forking, up to 3m tall; leaves multiply-forked, arranged spirally; sporangiophores form bushy branches. PROVENANCE: Middle Devonian. DISTRIBUTION: western Europe.

Psaronius [5] Order Marattiales Family Marattiaceae
CHARACTERISTICS: generic name for fossil stems with anatomical details of tree-ferns; central element with conductive vessels of stem, seen in section as worm-like meandering forms, relating to the externally attached fronds or leaves arranged in 2 rows, alternatively in whorl or screw configuration; towards exteric follows inner part of root-mantle; roots embedded in basic tissue of plant. PROVENANCE: Upper Carboniferous to Middle Permian. DISTRIBUTION: North America, Europe, Asia.

Asterotheca [6] Order Marattiales Family Marattiaceae
CHARACTERISTICS: form-genus name for a particular sporangia-bearing frond of the fern genus *Pecopteris*; sporangia group composed of 4-5 adjoining sporangia arranged in circle, borne on lower side; fern featherlets of this species have parallel edges, depressed central vein, forked side veins. PROVENANCE: Upper Carboniferous to Middle Permian. DISTRIBUTION: North America, Europe.

1 *Equisetites arenaceus,* cuff with leaf points, Upper Triassic, Schweinfurt/Germany. Length: 7cm.
2 *Equisetites arenaceus,* steinkern of medullar hollow with furrows running vertically (imprint of conductive vessels) and, at right angles, the nodes (attachment points of leaf-cuff), Upper Triassic, Franconia/Germany. Breadth: 6cm.
3 *Schizoneura caricinoides,* Upper Triassic to Lower Jurassic, Bayreuth/Germany. Length: 6cm.
4 *Calamophyton primaevum,* Middle Devonian, Eifel/Germany. Length: 5cm.
5 *Psaronius tenuis,* silicified specimen showing stem conductive vessels, inner and outer root-mantles, Permian, Chemnitz/Germany. Diam. 21cm.
6 *Asterotheca cyathea,* underside of frond, Upper Carboniferous, St Etienne/France. Section: 10cm.

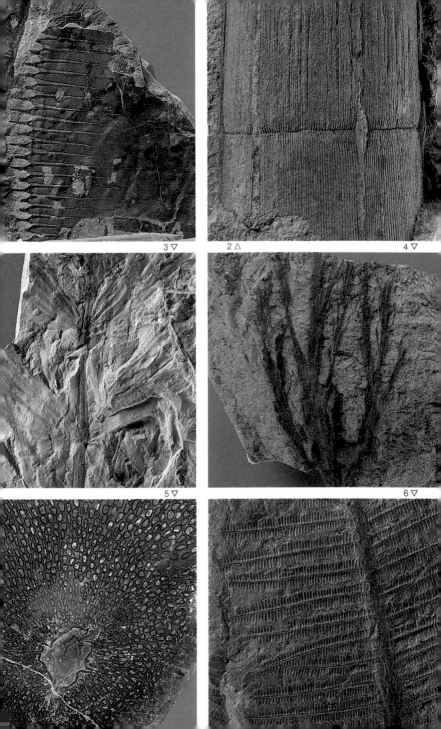

3 ▽   2 △   4 ▽

5 ▽   6 ▽

FERNS
Sub-phylum Pteridophyta Class Filicatae

Dactylotheca [1] Family Schizaeaceae (Split-branch ferns)
CHARACTERISTICS (species *D. plumosa*): large multiply-forked fronds, leaflets
rounded triangular, inclined obliquely upwards, edges notched or smooth, with
narrow joint at base, point of sporangium has cap-shaped ring. PROVENANCE:
Upper Carboniferous. DISTRIBUTION: Europe, North America.

Palaeosmunda [2] Family Osmundaceae (Royal Ferns)
CHARACTERISTICS: form-genus name for sections of stem showing anatomical
details of Osmundaceae: cross-section (see photo) shows at centre, thin, ring-like
double layer of inner and outer xylem (tracheida); this succeeded by white ring o
star-shaped figuration of parenchymatic inner cortex, then by dark layer of
sclerenchymatic outer cortex; the subsequent external rhombic forms mark the
fan attachments with inner leaf trace fibres (compressed at margin). PROVENANCE
Upper Permian. DISTRIBUTION: Queensland, Australia.

Phlebopteris [3] Family Matoniaceae
CHARACTERISTICS: form-genus name for fronds of Matoniaceae: fronds located at
ends of main stems, branching sympodially; leaflets alternating, elongated with
narrow joint at base, veining of feather or stitch-like pattern; sporangia separated,
arranged in circles on both sides of centre vein. PROVENANCE: Upper Triassic to
Cretaceous. DISTRIBUTION: Europe, North America, Asia.

Todites [4] Family Osmundaceae
CHARACTERISTICS: form-genus name for remains of leaves with fructifications of
Osmundaceae: fronds with double leaflets, leaflets attached by whole base of leaf;
classified in this family on basis of sporangia (separate, with cap-shaped ring).
PROVENANCE: Upper Triassic to Jurassic. DISTRIBUTION: Europe, South Africa.

Dictophyllum [5] Family Dipteridaceae (Split Fern Plants)
CHARACTERISTICS: form-genus name for remains of leaves with fructifications of
Dipteridaceae: fronds fork into 2 main arms, to which are attached on outside the
individual frond sections, themselves turned outwards; frond sections long, leaflets
with stitch pattern veining and pronounced central vein; sporangia not joined
though closely spaced, forming rings. PROVENANCE: Upper Triassic to Jurassic.
DISTRIBUTION: Europe, Siberia, China.

1 *Dactylotheca plumosa,* Upper Carboniferous, Kohlwald mine/Saarland/Germany. Section: 10cm.
2 *Palaeosmunda playfordi,* cross-section of stem, Upper Permian, Queensland/Australia. Diam.
9cm.
3 *Phlebopteris münsteri,* frond at stem end, Triassic to Lower Jurassic, Bayreuth/Germany. Section
20cm.
4 *Todites rösserti,* Upper Triassic to Lower Jurassic, Bayreuth/Germany. Section length: 20cm.
5 *Dictophyllum nathorsti,* Upper Triassic, Vietnam. Section: 30cm.

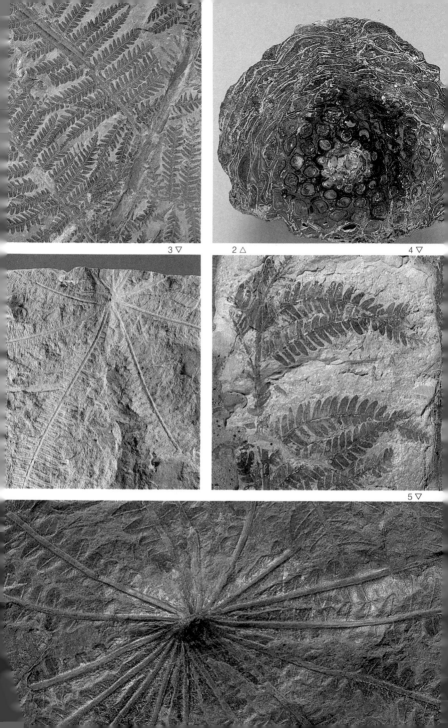

3 ▽　　2 △　　4 ▽

5 ▽

FERNS
Sub-phylum Pteridophyta   Class Filicatae

Salvinia [1] Order Salviniales Family Salviniaceae (Floating Ferns)
CHARACTERISTICS: plant consists of 2 rows of hairy floating leaves and 1 row of downwards-pointing submersible leaves divided into root-like forms, no genuine roots, underwater leaves bear micro- and macrosporangia. PROVENANCE: Upper Cretaceous to Recent. DISTRIBUTION: Europe, Central America, South America, South Africa.

Archaeopteris [2] Order Archaeopteridales Family Archaeopteridaceae
CHARACTERISTICS: generic name for fronds of this family: large frond thickly set with leaves; leaflets fan-shaped, with stem, inclined sharply upwards; veining branches dichotomously, intermediate feathering at frond axes. PROVENANCE: Upper Devonian (index fossil) to Lower Carboniferous. DISTRIBUTION: Europe, North America.

GYMNOSPERMS
Sub-phylum Spermatophyta

Trigonocarpus [3] Class Lyginopteridatae Order Pteridospermales
Family Medullosaceae
CHARACTERISTICS: generic classification based on form of seeds of Medullosaceae: several centimetres long, extended oval with 3-6 longitudinal ribs, cross-section triangular. PROVENANCE: Carboniferous to Middle Permian. DISTRIBUTION: Europe, North America.

Medullosa [4] Class Lyginopteridatae Order Pteridospermales
Family Medullosaceae
CHARACTERISTICS: form-genus name for sections of trunk with anatomical details of this family: in central part of cross-section of trunk many conductive vessels, round in cross-section, separated from one another, embedded in basic tissue; succeeded by double layer of secondary wood; the outermost layer consists of the periderm. PROVENANCE: Upper Carboniferous to Permian. DISTRIBUTION: Europe, North America.

Imparipteris [5] Class Lyginopteridatae Order Pteridospermales
Family Medullosaceae
CHARACTERISTICS: form-genus name for the fronds of this family: large fronds with as much as quadruple feathering; leaflets with heart-shaped base, veining branches dichotomously. PROVENANCE: Carboniferous to Middle Permian. DISTRIBUTION: Europe.

Dicksonites [6] Class Lyginopteridatae Order Pteridospermales
CHARACTERISTICS: form-genus name for fronds of Pteridospermae: fronds always doubly forked, leaflets attached to axis by whole width of leaf,   but joined at base, central vein begins at acute angle, side veins fork once or twice.
PROVENANCE: Upper Carboniferous. DISTRIBUTION: Carboniferous of Saarland.

---

1 *Salvinia mildeana,* Miocene, Dirnberg/Germany. Length of floating leaf: 1cm.
2 *Archaeopteris roemeriana,* Upper Devonian, Bear Island/Norway. Section: 10cm. Tree-like growth, considered forerunner of gymnosperms.
3 *Trigonocarpus noeggerathi,* steinkern; Carboniferous, Ostrau/Czechoslovakia. Length: 4cm.
4 *Medullosa stellata,* Middle Permian, Chemnitz/Germany. Diam. 10cm.
5 *Imparipteris ovata,* Upper Carboniferous, St Ingbert/Germany. Section: 8cm.
228 6 *Dicksonites pluckeneti,* Upper Carboniferous, Saarland/Germany. Section: 15cm.

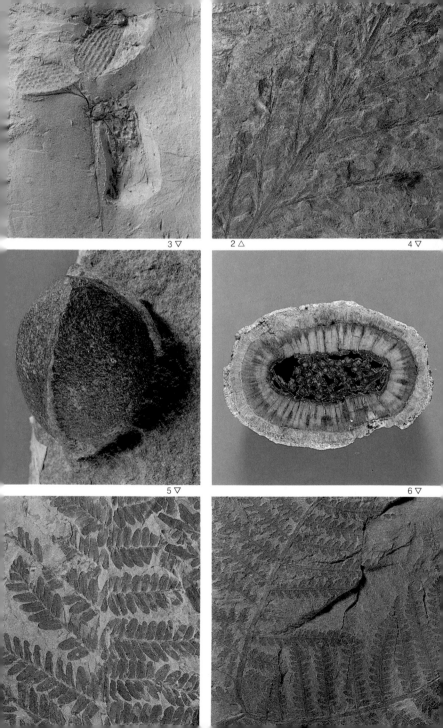

3 ▽ 2 △ 4 ▽

5 ▽ 6 ▽

GYMNOSPERMS
Sub-phylum Spermatophyta

Alethopteris [1] Class Lyginopteridatae Order Pteridospermales
CHARACTERISTICS: form-genus name for frond of Pteridospermae: frond bears
large number of feathers, but no intermediate leaflets; leaves at acute angle to
axis, attached by broad base extended towards main stem and growing into
neighbours; forked side veins close to base open into frond axis, as does central
vein. PROVENANCE: Upper Carboniferous. DISTRIBUTION: North America, Europe.
Staffordshire, Northumberland/England; South Wales.

Paripteris [2] Class Lyginopteridatae Order Pteridospermales
CHARACTERISTICS: form-genus name for frond of Pteridospermae: frond with
three or four sets of feathering, frond axis with longitudinal striping and
intermediate leaflets; these long, either gently curved upwards in sickle shape, or
elongated with edges parallel, or tongue-shaped; base of leaflets heart-shaped;
leaflets attached at base only at one point; frond and leaflets end in 2 final leaflet
forms: central vein variably pronounced, side veins multiply-forked. PROVENANCE:
middle Upper Carboniferous. DISTRIBUTION: Europe, North America.

Eusphenopteris [3] Class Lyginopteridatae Order Pteridospermales
CHARACTERISTICS: form-genus name for frond of Pteridospermae: frond forks
once, but multiply-feathered on these branches; leaflets various: roundish to
egg-shaped, with lobes or unbroken edges, attached to base by stalk, veining in
feather or fan pattern. PROVENANCE: lower-middle Upper Carboniferous.
DISTRIBUTION: Europe, North America

Glossopteris [4] Class Lyginopteridatae Order Glossopteridales
Family Glossopteridaceae
CHARACTERISTICS: form-genus name for leafage of tongue-ferns: tongue-shaped
leaves with unbroken edges, veining net-like with clear central vein. PROVENANCE:
Upper Carboniferous to Triassic, Jurassic (?). DISTRIBUTION: South Africa, South
America, North-east India, Australia, Antarctic.

Well preserved specimens of the organ genus *Vertebraria* (sections of stem of
forms classified as *Glossopteris*) show that these tongue-ferns reached a height of
up to 40cm and that the leaves were attached by a short stalk at the end of the
stem in the form of a tuft. This genus is a typical fossil of the province of
Gondwana fauna and flora restricted to the Southern Hemisphere during the
Carboniferous and Permian. Together with some mammal-like reptiles, its
distribution is taken to be a proof of the persistence of a united super-continent,
Gondwanaland (South America, Africa, India, Antarctica, Australia), into the
Triassic period.

1 *Alethopteris serli*, Upper Carboniferous, Saarland/Germany. Section: 11cm.
2 *Paripteris gigantea*, Upper Carboniferous, Mazon Creek/Illinois/USA. Length of individual feather:
10cm.
3 *Eusphenopteris sauveuri*, Upper Carboniferous, Saarland/Germany. Section: 10cm.
4 *Glossopteris browniana*, Permian, Talbraga/Australia. Leaf length: 9cm.

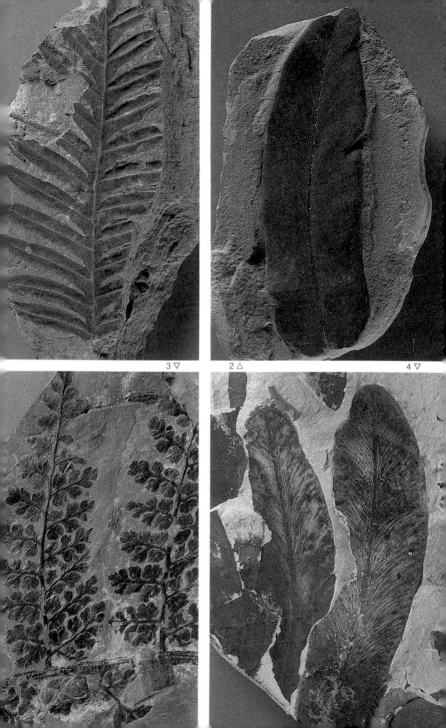

3 ▽   2 △   4 ▽

GYMNOSPERMS
Sub-phylum Spermatophyta

Callipteris [1] Class Lyginopteridatae Order Pteridospermales
CHARACTERISTICS: form-genus name for frond of seeding ferns; large feathered frond; frond axes have intermediate leaflets, whose structure corresponds to that of the particular feathering involved; leaflet structure either alethopteridic (attached by broad base extended downwards, side veins opening into axis) or sphenopteridic (featherlets wedge-shaped, roundish, attached to axis by narrow base). PROVENANCE: Permian. DISTRIBUTION: Europe, North America.

Dicroidium [2] Class Lyginopteridatae Order Caytoniales
Family Corystospermaceae
CHARACTERISTICS: form-genus name for type of foliage in family Corystospermaceae: forked fronds with single or double feathering, featherlets odontopteridic (featherlets with fan pattern veining without central vein). Classified among Caytoniales on basis of concealed macrosporangia and structure of leaf epidermis. Genus and species typical of Gondwana flora. PROVENANCE: Upper Triassic. DISTRIBUTION: Southern Hemisphere.

Zamites [3] Class Bennettitatae Order Bennettitales
CHARACTERISTICS: form-genus name for type of foliage in Order Bennettitales: leaflets placed alternately on each side of axis, rounded at base; attachment points of leaflets to one side, on upper side of axis; in outline longish triangle with pointed ends, forked veining seems to run parallel. PROVENANCE: Jurassic. DISTRIBUTION: Europe.

Cycadeoidea [4] Class Bennettitatae Order Bennettitales
Family Bennettitaceae
CHARACTERISTICS: form-genus name for sections of stem of Order Bennettitales showing typical structure: stem always gnarled; encircling the top of the stem were the leafy fronds (structurally like *Zamites*) with leaf bases triangular in cross-section (attachment points for fronds); hidden among them were the androgynous flowers, usually of circular cross-section, surrounded by the thick, scaly leaves. PROVENANCE: Cretaceous. DISTRIBUTION: Europe, North America.

1 *Callipteris conferta,* index fossil of Lower to Middle Permian, Rheinpfalz/Germany. Section: 15cm
2 *Dicroidium odontopteroides,* Upper Triassic, Bird River/South Africa. Section: 13cm.
3 *Zamites* sp., Upper Jurassic, Seysell/France. Section: 15cm.
4 *Cycadeoidea dakotensis,* Dakota/USA. Diam. of stem: 45cm; round aperture seen in upper part of

plate attachment point of flower, triangular apertures locations of fronds.

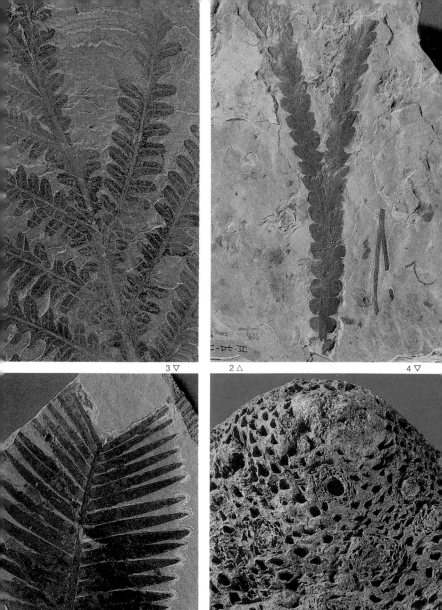

3 ▽   2 △   4 ▽

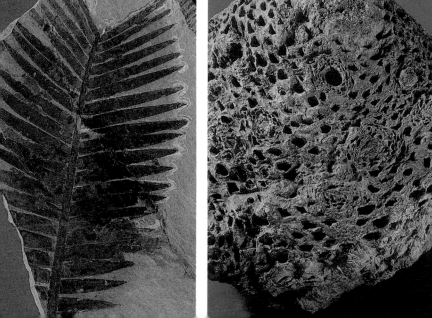

GYMNOSPERMS
Sub-phylum Spermatophyta

Ginkgo [1] Class Ginkgoatae Order Ginkgoales Family Ginkgoaceae
CHARACTERISTICS: form-genus name for foliage of ginkgo trees: leaves usually with central indentation, in outline fan-like, with unbroken edges divided into several lobes, veining fan pattern. PROVENANCE: Palaeocene to Recent. DISTRIBUTION: fossil forms Northern Hemisphere, Recent forms southeast China.

Baiera [2] Class Ginkgoatae Order Ginkgoales Family Ginkgoaceae
CHARACTERISTICS: form-genus name for deeply slit, long-stemmed leaves of family: leaves, fan-shaped in complete outline, have apparently parallel veining, separated by deep divisions; leaf stalk not included in fan. PROVENANCE: Permian to Lower Cretaceous. DISTRIBUTION: central Europe.

The unusual leaf form at first gave rise to classifications among algae or ferns. Only after finds had been made in the Jurassic of Spitsbergen, in which leaves, male flowers and seeds had been preserved in their natural context, was this leaf form assigned to the ginkgos. The peak of the development of the ginkgos was in the Jurassic; the only recent representative of the Order is the genus and species *Ginkgobiloba*. In this family the deep division of the leaves becomes more pronounced with the geological age.

Cordaites [3] Class Pinatae Order Cordaitales
CHARACTERISTICS: form genus name for foliage of Cordaitales: leaves arranged spirally, lancet-shaped or with rounded end, up to 1m long and 15cm broad; veining fine, apparently parallel but in fact running to a point. PROVENANCE: Carboniferous to Permian. DISTRIBUTION: Northern Hemisphere; British and eastern North American coalfields.

The *Cordaites* were tree-like plants up to 30m tall, and together with the *Lepidodendra* and *Sigillaria* were the main component of the Carboniferous forests. Form-genus name for typical structure of wood: *Dadoxylon*; for fructifications: *Cordaianthus*.

Lebachia [4] Class Pinatae Order Pinales Family Lebachiaceae
CHARACTERISTICS: form-genus name for leaved branches of this family: cross-section of stem up to 10cm, main branches arranged in whorl; main arms have forked leaves, other small leaves up to 4mm long, 1.5mm wide, either scale or needle-like in form, arranged spirally: smaller trees had appearance of araucarias as result of whorl arrangement of branches. PROVENANCE: Upper Carboniferous to Permian, main peak in Lower Permian. DISTRIBUTION: Northern Hemisphere.

1 *Ginkgo adiantoides,* Miocene, Freising/Germany. Width of 1 leaf: 9cm.
2 *Baiera münsteriana,* Upper Triassic-Lower Jurassic, Bayreuth/Germany. Section: 6cm.
3 *Cordaites palmaeformis,* Upper Carboniferous, Neunkirchen/Germany. Leaf length: 27cm.
4 *Lebachia piniformis,* Permian, Friedrichsroda/Germany. Width of section: 20cm.

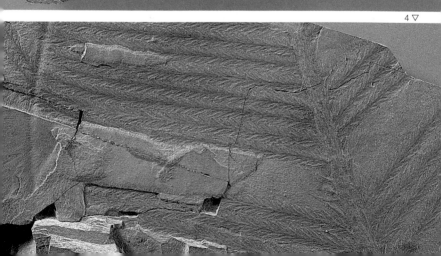

2 △   3 ▽

4 ▽

GYMNOSPERMS
Sub-phylum Spermatophyta

Ullmannia [1] Class Pinatae Order Coniferales Family Voltziaceae
CHARACTERISTICS: form-genus name for leaved twigs of family: leaves like scales
or needles, ends rounded or pointed, more than 1cm long, no central vein,
transpiration pores usually arranged in longitudinal rows. PROVENANCE: Upper
Permian. DISTRIBUTION: Northern Hemisphere.

Voltzia [2] Class Pinatae Order Coniferales Family Voltziaceae
CHARACTERISTICS: needles in screw-like arrangement on axis, upper side of
needles flat, underside arched, sharply pointed, with longitudinal striping
produced by transpiration pores in depressions; female cones with spirally
arranged outer scales and axial ovules, male cones with scales and stalk-like pollen
sacs. PROVENANCE: Upper Permian to Lower Triassic. DISTRIBUTION: Europe,
North America.

Hirmerella [3] Class Pinatae Order Coniferales Family Voltziaceae
CHARACTERISTICS: specialised generic name for cones and twigs of family:
complete female cone made up of spirally arranged double scales; outer scales
broad, undivided, with short point, seed-scales sub-divided into 6-10 lobes: twigs
leafed with short, spirally arranged, scaly leaves. PROVENANCE: Upper Triassic to
Lower Jurassic. DISTRIBUTION: Europe, Greenland.

Proaraucaria [4] Class Pinatae Order Coniferales Family Araucariaceae
CHARACTERISTICS: specialised generic name for form of cone of family: roundish
or egg-shaped; scale pattern arranged as screw around axis, each scale component
(outer scale, seed scale, seed) firmly joined together. PROVENANCE: Jurassic.
DISTRIBUTION: Southern Hemisphere.

Parauracaria [5] Class Pinatae Order Coniferales Family Paraucariaceae
CHARACTERISTICS: as *Proaraucaria*; outline more conical, woody axis more
slender, several cotyledons; details similar to *Pinus*. PROVENANCE and
DISTRIBUTION: as *Proaraucaria*.

Metasequoia [6] Class Pinatae Order Pinales Family Taxodiaceae
(Marsh Cypresses)
CHARACTERISTICS: twigs opposed, needles, in two rows, also opposed, needle
form linear, up to 2.5cm long. PROVENANCE: Upper Cretaceous to Recent.
DISTRIBUTION: in Tertiary, eastern Asia, North America, Arctic; Recent, China.

The Recent tree was discovered only in 1944 and was described in 1948 for the
first time.

1 *Ullmannia bronni,* Upper Permian, Frankenberg/Germany. Twig length: 8cm.
2 *Voltzia hungarica,* Upper Permian, Schlern/Italy. Cone length: 5cm.
3 *Hirmerella* sp., Upper Triassic-Lower Jurassic, Bayreuth/Germany. Twig length: 5cm.
4 *Proaraucaria mirabilis,* Jurassic, Cerro Cuadrado/Argentina. Diam. 6cm.
5 *Parauracaria patagonica,* longitudinal section, Jurassic, Cerro Cuadrado/Argentina. Diam. 2.5cm.
6 *Metasequoia occidentalis,* Palaeocene, Spitsbergen. Needle length: 1.5cm.

3 ▽   4 ▽   2 △

6 ▽

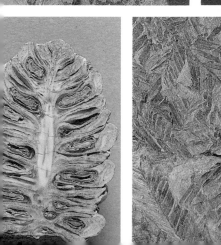

GYMNOSPERMS
Sub-phylum Spermatophyta

Glyptostrobus [1] Class Pinatae Order Pinales Family Taxodiaceae
CHARACTERISTICS: includes fossil and recent organs of genus; leaves scaly, or
pointed like short needles, as *Taxodium* overlapping one another like roof-tiles;
cones very small, up to 2.3cm tall, made up of 20 overlapping scales; scales
narrow towards attached base, semicircular and notched on front, seed scales with
2 winged seeds. PROVENANCE: Cretaceous, Tertiary, Recent. DISTRIBUTION: fossil,
Northern Hemisphere; Recent, one species, southern China.

Pinus [2] Class Pinatae Order Pinales Family Pinaceae (Pines)
CHARACTERISTICS: includes fossil and recent organs of genus: short shoots with
2-5 needles, cones consist of complex of scales arranged in whorl, grown
together, usually 2 seeds on upper side of seed scale, seed scales have broadened
front and hooked points. PROVENANCE: Cretaceous to Recent. DISTRIBUTION:
Northern Hemisphere.

Taxodioxylon [3-5] Class Pinatae Order Pinales Family Taxodiaceae
CHARACTERISTICS: specialised generic name for fossil remains of wood with
anatomical details typical of family: polished cross-section (Plate 3): 4 succeeding
growth zones from left to right; thin, radial bands of wood; rectangular or
polygonal tracheids in pattern of coarse stitches. Tangential section (Plate 4):
bands of wood running vertically; single-row, vertical parenchymatic strands with
dark-coloured substances inset in round points. Radial section (Plate 5): wood
bands as fine horizontal structures; the broad longitudinal elements represent the
tracheids of cross-section. Typical of genus tracheids with radial spots with hollow
centre and taxodioid solid spots at intersections. PROVENANCE: Cretaceous(?),
Tertiary. DISTRIBUTION: Northern Hemisphere.

ANGIOSPERMS
Sub-phylum Spermatophyta

Castanoxylon [6-8] Class Dicotyledoneae Family Fagaceae (Beeches)
CHARACTERISTICS: form-genus name for fossil wood remains with anatomical
details: comparable with *Castanea, Castanopsis:* cross-section (Plate 6): large,
isolated vessels of young wood succeeded by smaller vessels of summer and
autumn growth (from top); tangential section (Plate 7): vertically sectioned vessel
is sub-divided by thin-walled extrusions of cells: radial section (Plate 8):
horizontal bands of wood interesect with vertical structures: typical of this form
genus are pores in rings, single-row wood bands, simple apertures in vessels and
flame-shaped vessels. PROVENANCE: Tertiary. DISTRIBUTION: central Europe.

1 *Glyptostrobus europaeus,* Middle Miocene, Schwandorf/Germany. Height: 1.7cm.
2 *Pinus* sp., Lower Miocene, Bilin/Czechoslovakia. Height: 10cm.
3-5 *Taxodioxylon gypsaceum,* Middle Miocene, Vilsbiburg/Germany. Silicified remains of wood.
238 6-8 *Castanoxylon* sp., Middle Miocene, Prielhof/Germany. Silicified remains of wood.

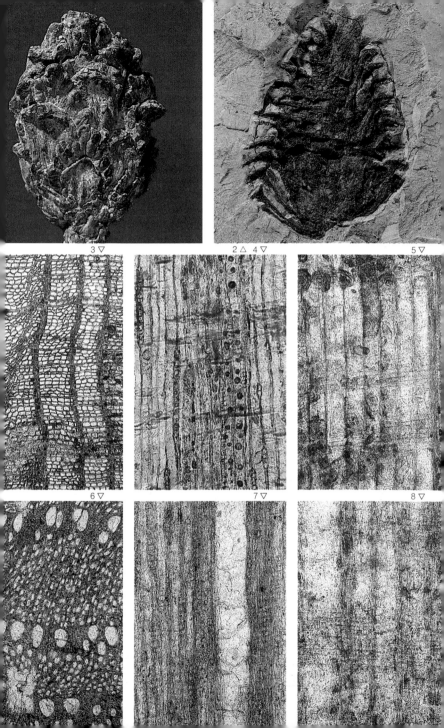

3 ▽　　　　　　　2 △　4 ▽　　　　　　　5 ▽

6 ▽　　　　　　　7 ▽　　　　　　　8 ▽

ANGIOSPERMS
Sub-phylum Spermatophyta

Daphnogene [1] Class Dicotyledoneae Family Lauraceae (Laurels)
CHARACTERISTICS: longish or broadish oval leaves with 3 main veins, veins curve away at base, leaf base sometimes restricted. PROVENANCE: Tertiary. DISTRIBUTION: world-wide.

Credneria [2] Class Dicotyledoneae Family Platanaceae (Planes)
CHARACTERISTICS: oldest leaf forms, assigned to forerunners of plane-trees; leaves with long stalks, form variable, base heart-shaped, with single or triple points, triple-lobed, indented or smooth-edged, veining in feather pattern. PROVENANCE: Upper Cretaceous. DISTRIBUTION: Europe, Greenland, Alaska.

Liquidambar [3] Class Dicotyledoneae Family Hamamelidaceae(Witch-Hazels)
CHARACTERISTICS: includes fossil and recent organs of genus: leaves usually five-lobed, main veins fork at base, saw-edged margin ends in elongated glands; arching secondary veins joined together, all veins form polygonal stitch-pattern network. PROVENANCE: Tertiary to Recent. DISTRIBUTION: Eurasia, North America.

Gleditsia [4] Class Dicotyledoneae Family Leguminosae (Pulses)
CHARACTERISTICS: includes fossil and recent organs of genus; seeds consist of two-part, triple-layered seed capsule with network of conductive vessels running at acute angle to axis, with stem, angle between stem and capsule from 0 to 45 degrees; seeds when swollen egg-shaped or elliptical; conductive vessels cover whole leaf, umbilicus at base. PROVENANCE: Tertiary to Recent. DISTRIBUTION: North America, China, Europe.

Acer [5] Class Dicotyledoneae Family Aceraceae (Maples)
CHARACTERISTICS: includes fossil and recent organs of genus; leaves attached opposite one another; leaf form simple or lobed or even feathered with up to 7 leaflets, reliably classified only by structure of epidermis. PROVENANCE: Cretaceous to Recent. DISTRIBUTION: fossil, Northern Hemisphere.

Palmoxylon [6] Class Monocotyledoneae Order Palmales Family Palmae (Palms)
CHARACTERISTICS: form-genus name for stems of palm-like structure: cylindrical conductive vessels running parallel to stem axis appear in cross-section of stem as roundish apertures, clearly distinguished from basic tissue of stem. PROVENANCE: Cretaceous to Recent. DISTRIBUTION: world-wide.

1 *Daphnogene scheuchzeri,* Oligocene, Littmitz/Czechoslovakia. Length: 10cm.
2 *Credneria triloba,* Blankenburg, Harz/Germany. Leaf length: 7cm.
3 *Liquidambar europaeum,* Miocene, Styria/Austria. Leaf height: 7cm.
4 *Gleditsia knorri,* Middle Miocene, Günzburg/Germany. Length with stalk: 4.5cm.
5 *Acer tricuspidatum,* Miocene, Aubenham/Lower Bavaria/Germany. Height: 6cm.
6 *Palmoxylon lacunosum,* silicified stem cross-section showing conductive vessels, Tertiary, USA. Height of section: 20cm.

3 ▽   2 △   4 ▽

5 ▽   6 ▽

ANGIOSPERMS
Sub-phylum Spermatophyta

Comptonia [1] Class Dicotyledoneae Family Myricaceae (Myrtles)
CHARACTERISTICS: includes fossil and recent form-genera: outline of whole leaf
elongated or linear, leaves and sub-leaves divided into deeply notched individual
lobes, whose main veins run at right angle to central leaf vein. PROVENANCE:
Tertiary to Recent. DISTRIBUTION: fossil, central Europe, North America; Recent,
North America only.

Engelhardtia [2] Class Dicotyledoneae Family Juglandaceae (Walnuts)
CHARACTERISTICS: includes fossil and recent form-genera: wind-borne seed
enclosed in three- or four-lobed capsule, central lobes always larger than lateral,
usually with 3 veins; seed in two halves with two chambers. PROVENANCE: Tertiary
to Recent. DISTRIBUTION: fossil, central Europe, North America; Recent,
Southeast Asia.

Salix [3] Class Dicotyledoneae Family Salicaceae (Willows)
CHARACTERISTICS: includes fossil and recent form-genera: leaves attached
alternately, leaf form variable, usually lancet-shaped, reliably classified only by
structure of leaf epidermis. PROVENANCE: Cretaceous to Recent. DISTRIBUTION:
fossil, Europe, America.

Populus [4] Class Dicotyledoneae Family Salicaceae (Willows)
CHARACTERISTICS: includes fossil and recent form-genera: leaves between egg and
lancet shape, unbroken or toothed edges, reliably classified only by structure of
leaf epidermis. PROVENANCE: Tertiary to Recent. DISTRIBUTION: Europe, North
America.

Carpinus [5] Class Dicotyledoneae Family Betulaceae (Birches)
CHARACTERISTICS: includes fossil and recent form-genera: leaf clearly in two
halves, simple toothed edge, reliably classified only by structure of leaf epidermis.
PROVENANCE: Tertiary to Recent. DISTRIBUTION: Europe, America, eastern Asia.

Castanea [6] Class Dicotyledoneae Family Fagaceae (Beeches)
CHARACTERISTICS: includes fossil and form-genera: leaf outline variable:
saw-edged, toothed, lobed, smooth-edged; reliably classified only by structure of
leaf epidermis. PROVENANCE: Tertiary to Recent. DISTRIBUTION: fossil, North
America, Europe, Malaysia, Australia.

Quercus [7] Class Dicotyledoneae Family Fagaceae (Beeches)
CHARACTERISTICS: includes fossil and recent form-genera: leaves saw-edged,
toothed, lobed, smooth-edged; reliably classified only by structure of leaf
epidermis. PROVENANCE: Cretaceous to Recent. DISTRIBUTION: fossil, Europe,
North America.

1 *Comptonia* sp., Lower Miocene, Bilin/Czechoslovakia. Length: 11cm.
2 *Engelhardtia* sp., Miocene, Randeck Maar/Germany. Length: 4cm.
3 *Salix* sp., Upper Miocene, Schneegattern/Austria. Length: 5cm.
4 *Populus* sp., Middle Miocene, Unterwohlbach/Germany. Length: 9cm.
5 *Carpinus* sp., Middle Miocene, Günzburg/Germany. Length: 7cm.
6 *Castanea* sp., Upper Miocene, Klettwitz/Poland. Length: 10cm.

7 *Quercus* sp., Upper Pliocene, Bergamo/Italy. Length: 9cm.

2 △ 4 ▽   3 △   5 ▽

6 ▽   7 ▽

ANGIOSPERMS
Sub-phylum Spermatophyta

Mastixicarpum [1] Class Dicotyledoneae Family Mastixiaceae
CHARACTERISTICS: includes fossil form-genus; single-chambered endocarps (steinkerns in botanical sense), up to 3.5cm long, ventral side rounded, dorsal flattened, surface with shallow longitudinal furrows, in cross-section U-shaped hollow chamber. PROVENANCE: Eocene-Pliocene. DISTRIBUTION: central Europe.

Mastixia [2] Class Dicotyledoneae Family Mastixiaceae
CHARACTERISTICS: includes all form genera: single-chambered endocarps of spindle or cylinder shape, ventral side arched, dorsal with longitudinal furrow, surface deeply furrowed along length, in cross-section U-shaped hollow chamber. PROVENANCE: Eocene to Recent. DISTRIBUTION: fossil, central Europe; Recent, Indo-Malaysia.

Retinomastixia [3] Class Dicotyledoneae Family Mastixiaceae
CHARACTERISTICS: includes fossil form-genera: endocarps up to 3cm long, cylindrical forms with conical or discus-shaped point, 10-12 longitudinal furrows on surface, in cross-section V-shaped hollow chamber. PROVENANCE: Eocene to Pliocene. DISTRIBUTION: central Europe.

Eomastixia [4] Class Dicotyledoneae Family Mastixiaceae
CHARACTERISTICS: includes fossil form-genera: endocarps up to 5cm long, usually two- or three-chambered, wing-like longitudinal ridges, in cross-section U-shaped hollow chambers. PROVENANCE: Oligocene to Pliocene. DISTRIBUTION: central Europe.

Carya [5] Class Dicotyledoneae Family Juglandaceae
CHARACTERISTICS: includes all organs of hickory-tree: seeds up to 4cm long, surface smooth or wrinkled, point only slightly developed or rounded off; cross-section shows 4 chambers in lower part. PROVENANCE and DISTRIBUTION: fossil, Oligocene to Pliocene, central Europe; Recent, southern North America, South-east Asia.

Rehderodendron [6] Class Dicotyledoneae Family Styracaceae (Storaxes)
CHARACTERISTICS: includes fossil and recent organs of genus: seeds woody, up to 7cm long, distinct longitudinal ribs, spindle-shaped, with 1-3 seeds. PROVENANCE and DISTRIBUTION: fossil, Tertiary, central Europe, North America; Recent, East Asia.

Spirematospermum [7] Class Monocotyledoneae Family Zingiberaceae
CHARACTERISTICS: specialised generic name for fructification of family: large fructifications up to 10cm long, longish rounded shape, in cross-section roundish, stalk long, point rounded off; seeds arranged in longitudinal rows. PROVENANCE: Cretaceous to Pliocene. DISTRIBUTION: Europe, western Siberia.

1 *Mastixicarpum limnophilum*, Middle Miocene, Schwandorf/Germany. Length to 6cm.
2 *Mastixia lusatica*, Middle Miocene, Schwandorf/Germany. Length up to 2.5cm.
3 *Retinomastixia oerteli*, Middle Miocene, Schwandorf/Germany. Length: 3cm.
4 *Eomastixia persicoides*, Middle Miocene, Schwandorf/Germany. Length: 4.5cm.
5 *Carya ventricosa*, Middle Miocene, Schwandorf/Germany. Length up to 4cm.
6 *Rehderodendron ehrenbergi*, Middle Miocene, Schwandorf/Germany. Length to 4cm.
7 *Spirematospermum wetzleri*, Middle Miocene, Schwandorf/Germany. Length: 8cm.

2 ▽   3 ▽   4 ▽

5 ▽   6 ▽   7 ▽

FORMS RESEMBLING FOSSILS

Pseudofossils [1]

This term describes objects which from their appearance may seem to be fossils, but whose development is in fact not organic. They owe their origin to mechanical, chemical or physical processes, whilst the events relating to the formation and weathering of the rock have principally determined the resulting appearance. In this way, for example, weathered elongated concretions have been interpreted as the eggs of birds or saurians, or limestones eroded into various forms by the action of water seen as bones. It is often the imagination of the observer which determines such interpretations, as he or she involuntarily compares these inorganic forms with those genuinely owing their origin and development to organisms.

The white limestone in Plate 1 has roughly the features of an animal's skull, but owes its form to weathering (variable hardness in individual zones) and abrasion during its transport in water.

Dendrites [2]

This term is used for moss-like branching markings of various colours, found on layering, shale, or split surfaces. Precisely because of their form which is so reminiscent of mosses or ferns, they were once interpreted as the remains of plants. They are not produced by organisms, however, but are the traces of iron or manganese solutions. After the formation of the rock, these solutions penetrated along fine hairline-cracks. The water evaporated and the iron or manganese compounds remained.

Forgeries [3]

Among the famous forgeries in the history of palaeontology are the Beringer "Lying Stones" (Lügensteine). In 1725 a member of the Medical Faculty of the University of Würzburg, Adam Beringer, was tricked by unfavourably disposed colleagues into accepting forged fossils. The uniqueness of these specimens led him to publish his *Lithographia Wirceburgensis*, in which 200 of these 'fossils" were illustrated and described. Since there were some copies of real fossils (e.g. ammonites) among the forgeries made from limestone taken from the Muschelkalk, Beringer first accepted the stones as genuine. As the cause of their development he cited the creative power of light, which under certain conditions could imprint a form on the rock. During the writing of his work, however, he began to doubt the genuineness of the stones, suspected the deception, but produced new arguments for the natural origin of the specimens. Of about 2,000 forgeries, 330 are still to be found in museums.

1 "Animal Head", length: 24cm. Detrital stone from the Inn/Lower Bavaria/Germany.
2 Dendrites, natural size, Upper Jurassic, Solnhofen/Germany.
3 Beringer "Lying Stone", Spider in Web, size 12cm. Bavarian State Collection for Palaeontology and Historical Geology/Munich.

FURTHER READING

BABIN, C. *Elements of Palaeontology.* John Wiley & Sons. Chichester, New York, Brisbane, Toronto, 1980.
BLACK, R. *The Elements of Palaeontology.* 2nd ed. Cambridge University Press, 1989.
BRASIER, M.D. *Microfossils.* Allen & Unwin, London, 1980.
BRITISH MUSEUM OF NATURAL HISTORY, London. *British Caenozoic Fossils*, 1971.
BRITISH MUSEUM OF NATURAL HISTORY, London. *British Mesozoic Fossils*, 1972.
BRITISH MUSEUM OF NATURAL HISTORY, London. *British Palaeozoic Fossils* ,1969.
CARROLL, R.L. *Vertebrate Palaeontology and Evolution.* Freeman & Co., New York, 1988.
CLARKSON, E.N.K. *Invertebrate Palaeontology and Evolution.* 2nd edn, Allen & Unwin. London, 1987.
DINELEY, D.L. *Fossils.* Collins Countryside Series, Collins, London, 1979.
GOLDRING, R. *Fossils in the Field.* Longman Scientific & Technical, 1990.
HAMILTON, R. *Fossils and Fossil Collecting.* Hamlyn, London, 1975.
KIRKALDY, J.F. *Fossils in Colour.* Blandford Colour Series. Blandford Press, Poole, 1980.
LEHMANN, V. & HILLMER, G. *Fossil Invertebrates.* Cambridge University Press, 1983.
McKERROW, W.S. (ed.) *The ecology of fossils.* Duckworth, London, 1978.
MOORE, R.C. (ed.) *Treatise on Invertebrate Paleontology.* University of Kansas Press, Lawrence, Kansas, 1953. Several volumes, some with more than one part.
MURRAY, J.W. (ed.) *Atlas of Invertebrate Macrofossils.* Longman, Harlow, 1985.
PROKOP, R. Hamlyn Colour Guide: *Fossils.* Hamlyn, London, 1981.
RAUP, D. & STANLEY, S.M. *Principles of Palaeontology.* 2nd edition, W.H. Freeman & Co., New York, San Francisco, 1978.
SCHULTZE, H.P. (ed.) *Handbook of Palaeoichthyology.* Gustav Fischer Verlag, Stuttgart, New York. 10 vols., 1978.
SIMPSON, G.G. *Fossils and the History of Life.* Scientific American Books. W.H. Freeman & Co., New York, San Francisco, 1983.
STEWART, W.N. *Palaeobotany and the Evolution of Plants.* Cambridge University Press, 1983.
THOMPSON, I. *Audubon Society Field Guide to North American Fossils.* Alfred A. Knopf, New York, 1982.

Guides to the geology of much of the British Isles and North America are published by several national and local museums and by the Geological Surveys. In the UK the outlets of H.M. Stationery Office provide a wide range of geological literature. Similar sources of information in North America are the offices of the Geological Survey of Canada and the US Geological Survey. There are also excellent outlets operated by the several State Surveys and by the National Parks Service.

The Geologists' Association in Britain (Burlington House, Piccadilly, London, W1V 9AG), publishes a large series of excellent pocket guides to local geology, while in North America the National Audubon Society (950 Third Avenue, New York, NY 10022) is the premier natural history society. There are many state or provincial societies which publish useful guides, maps and books.

NATIONAL MUSEUMS OF NATURAL HISTORY

The Natural History Museum (now incorporates The Geological Museum), Cromwell Road, South Kensington, London SW7, England.
National Museum of Wales Cathays Park, Cardiff, Wales.
Royal Scottish Museum Chambers Street, Edinburgh, Scotland.
National Museum of Ireland Dublin, Eire.
Canadian Museum of Nature Ottawa, Ontario, Canada.

The Smithsonian Institution Constitution Avenue, Washington D.C., USA.

GLOSSARY

Words used in the systematic review and in the diagnoses of fossil genera in the text.

abiogenesis The generation of organic molecules from others by non-organic processes.

adductor Muscle that closes and/or holds together brachiopod valves.

ambulacral furrow Groove or furrow in thecal or arm plates along the course of the ambulacrum.

ambulacral system Water vascular system from which arise the tube feet of the echinodermata.

ambulacrum Segment of echinoderm test extending radially from mouth, with two columns of plates perforated by paired pores.

ammonitic suture The line of intersection of septum and inner surface of shell wall in cephalopods. It is flexed into lobes which curve away from the aperture and into saddles which curve towards the aperture.

area The field or surface area lying on each side of the beak and extending from it to the hinge line in brachiopod valves.

auricle The "ear" or "wing" of bivalve shells: the extension of the shell along the hinge line to produce a triangular flat surface.

beak The pointed extremity of the brachiopod valve adjacent to the hinge line and on the mid-line of the valve.

benthonic Bottom-dwelling mode of life.

brachidia Calcareous loop-shaped structures to support lophophore inside brachiopod shell.

brachiophore Short plates or processes in the interior hinge line region of the brachiopod brachial valve which serve to anchor the lophophore.

brackish water Water of intermediate salinity between fresh water and normal sea water.

byssus Threadlike process secreted from the anterior part of the bivalve foot and used to attach shell to substrate.

calice Upper end of corallite upon which the base of the polyp rests. Typically bowl-shaped.

cardinal area Surface of bivalve between hinge line and umbo on each side of the beak.

cardinal process Ridge or boss on the inner surface of brachial valve between the diductor muscle scars in articulate brachiopods.

cephalon The headshield in trilobites.

cephalothorax The fused headshield and part of the segmented body region in arthropods.

ceratitic suture Cephalopod suture line with small lobes and saddles developed on major lobes.

chelicerae "Pincers", appendages in front of arthropod's mouth.

cirri Appendages attached to the side of the crinoid stem and formed of small articulated plates.

coenosteum Calcareous skeletal tissue connecting corallites of a colonial coral.

columella Longitudinal rod in axis of corallite.

coracoid One of a pair of large flat bones (right and left) of the shoulder girdle on underside of body of lower vertebrates.

costae (a) Ridges on external surface of brachiopod valve extending radially from umbo. (b) Continuation of septa beyond or above corallite wall.

crura Basal portions of calcareous supports for the brachiopod lophophore.

crural teeth Tooth or look-alike projections on outer surface of bivalve shell (e.g. *Spondylus*).

ctenoid scales Teleost fish scales spinate at the posterior margin.

cycloid scale Fish scales round in outline.

deltidial plate Plate on either side of pedicle opening in pedicle valve which may constrict or (with its mate) close the opening.

deltoid plate One of a ring of plates at oral end of blastoid theca lying between the ambulacra.

dental formula List of numbers of different types of teeth in jaw, always given in the form

incisors, canines, premolars, molars
incisors, canines, premolars, molars
(Upper/Lower)

desma Sponge spicule of irregular and knobbly form.

dibranchiate Possessing two gills.

diductor Muscle to open valves of brachiopod.

dissepiment A small curved plate between septa and with upward convex surface.

dissepimentarium A zone of dissepiments forming vesicles near the periphery of a corallite.

distal Distant from the axis, centre or point of origin.

dorsal Referring to the upper side.

ear See auricle.

endocarp Inner layer of fruiting body.

endocranium Part of skull enclosing the brain.

epidermis Outermost layer of tissue in animals and plants.

epitheca Sheath of skeletal material forming corallite wall.

evolute Type of coiled shell in which outer whorls do not cover lateral walls of adjacent inner whorls.

facial suture Line on trilobite head along which exoskeleton split when trilobite moulted.

fasciole Tracts of small spines which maintain a current over the echinoid body surface.

form-genus name used to identify an isolated fossil part of an organism or a trace of its activity, rather than for the organism itself.

fructification Fruit or fruit-like body.

ganoid scale Rhombic, three-layered scale common in early ray-finned fishes.

genital plate One of a ring of five plates on the aboral surface adjacent to the central plate in echinodermata.

genital pore The outlet of the gonad (re

productive) organs in the echinoid test.

glabella Raised central part of trilobite headshield.

goniatitic suture Suture line with very simple lobes and saddles.

infrabasals Lowest ring of plates in the crinoid cup, below the basals.

interarea Surface between umbo and hinge line on either brachiopod valve; commonly lacks coarse growth lines and ornamentation.

intercentrum Solid block of bone placed between the centra of adjacent vertebrae.

involute Type of coiled shell in which part of outer whorl extends towards umbilicus and covers part of adjacent inner whorl.

ligament Elastic tissue attaching bivalve valves along hinge line and permitting opening and closing.

lunule Flat or curved area between umbo or hinge-line and in front of umbo; anterior part of the cardinal area.

mantle Fold of the bivalve and cephalopod mollusc body wall enclosing the viscera and forming a sac or cone about them.

median septum Calcareous ridge or wall built along mid-line of interior of brachiopod

medusa (medusoid) Free living coelenterate, e.g. jellyfish, with inverted bowl-like form with mouth and tentacles downward.

metatarsal Referring to the bones of the foot of the hind limb in vertebrates.

monaxon Sponge spicule with single axis of growth.

myophore In brachiopod brachial valve, it is the bulbous end of the cardinal process. In bivalvia, plate or rodlike structure on the inside of the shell for the attachment of muscle.

nekton Swimming or active members of the aquatic biota.

occipital ring The posterior segment of the trilobite glabella, separated from the anterior part by the occipital furrow.

operculum Large moveable outer wall of gill chamber on each side of fish head.

opisthoparian (suture) Facial suture of trilobite which crosses the cheek, passes along the medial border of the eye and intersects the posterior margin of the cephalon medial to the genal angle.

orbit The skull opening for the eyes in vertebrates.

osculum Main opening to exterior from body cavity of a sponge.

palatal A bone forming part of the lateral front roof of the mouth, paired right and left.

pallial line Line on interior surface of bivalve shell, joining muscle scars and marking periphery of the innermost calcareous layer of the shell.

parietal A bone forming part of the skull roof, paired right and left with the pineal aperture situated on the suture between them: posterior to the frontal.

pedicle Muscular and/or fibrous stalk fixed to inner surface of brachiopod pedicle valve, and which passes out posteriorly to attach to substrate.

pedicle valve Brachiopod valve to which pedicle is attached.

pelagic Free-floating.

periproct Area surrounding echinoid anus covered by skin in which small plates are set; usually lost in fossils.

phalange digit, or bones of digit, of vertebrate limbs.

phragmocone Portion of cephalopod shell consisting of camerae (chambers).

phytoplankton Planktonic plants.

pineal organ A small part of the brain of vertebrates, said to be light sensitive, situated in the mid-line of the cranial roof.

placoid scale A form of scale found in sharks and shark-like fish.

plankton Free swimming organisms in sea or freshwater.

planispiral Coiled in a single plane.

pleura Lateral parts of body segments.

pleurocentrum Block of bone between upper parts of adjacent vertebrae.

polyp Hydra-like form of coelenterate; columnar body with attached base and tentacles and mouth directed upward.

postorbital Bone lying to the rear of the orbit in a vertebrate skull.

proostracum Calcareous blade projecting forward from dorsal border of belemnite phrogmocone.

proparian (suture) Facial suture of

trilobite which crosses the dorsal surface of the cephalon, passes along the medial edge of the eye and intersects the lateral border of the cephalon in front of, or at, the genal angle.

prosopores Apertures which allow inflow of water into the body cavity of a sponge.

pygidium Tail plate made up of fused segments.

rostrum A thick conical or bullet-shaped calcareous deposit enclosing the belemnite phragmocone.

saddle Posteriorly directed curve of the ammonoid suture line.

scapula Shoulder-blade bone of vertebrates.

schizodont Bivalve hinge-line structure with teeth diverging sharply from beneath the umbo.

selenizone Longitudinal band on gastropod shell marking previous site of slit.

septum (a) One of several longitudinal plates arranged radially between corallite axis and wall. (b) Calcareous transverse partition in cephalopod shell dividing it into camerae.

sessile Fixed to substrate.

sieve plate (Madreporite) a porous plate through which water is drawn into the water vascular system of echinoids.

siphon A pair of tubes produced from the mantle for the inhalation and expulsion of water from the bivalve mantle cavity.

siphuncle Tube extending back from living chamber in cephalopods.

species (in palaeontology) A basic unit of classification: a group of individuals sharing all major morphological features and many minor features.

spicules Tiny skeletal units of silica, calcium carbonate or horny material which make up supporting fabric of sponges.

steinkern Sediment infilling within a cavity or hollow fossil.

substrate The material upon which an organism rests or to which it is attached.

suture (a) Line of intersection between septum and inner surface of shell wall in molluscs. (b) See facial suture (trilobites), (c) Line marking junction of bones of vertebrate skull.

sympodial Springing from a common point or base.

tabularium Axial portion of corallite in which tabulae occur.

taphonomy The study of the conditions of burial of fossils.

taxodont Bivalve hinge-line structure characterised by numerous subequal teeth along hinge-line.

terebratellid Brachiopods with long loop lophophores, cardinalia and median septum.

terebratulid Major informal grouping of brachiopods like *Terebratula*.

test The hard skeleton, case or vessel containing the soft organs or protoplasm in echinoderms and foraminifera respectively.

tetraxon Sponge spicule with four axes of development.

theca (a) Skeletal deposit enclosing corallite. (b) Individual tube in graptolite colony.

thorax (a) In trilobites and other arthropods, portion of body between head and tail. (b) In vertebrates, portion of body between head and tail.

triradiate With three rays.

tubercles In gastropods, thickened nodes on shoulder of shell.

umbilicus In gastropods, space at centre of coil where whorls do not meet (= navel).

umbo Elevated and relatively convex portion of bivalve shell adjacent to the beak.

vagile Mobile or vagrant.

valve (a) One of two chitino-phosphatic or calcareous plates that enclose the soft parts of the brachiopod anatomy. (b) One of the two calcareous curved convex plates that lie on either side of the soft anatomy and articulate along a dorsal hinge line of bivalves (Mollusca).

venter Part of coil farthest away from axis of coiling.

ventral Referring to the underside.

wing See auricle.

xylem Tissue through which water and nutrients are transmitted in plants.